D1283697

FROM FICTION TO THE NOVEL

FROM
Fiction
TO THE
Novel

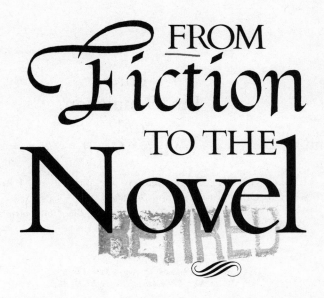

GEOFFREY
DAY

Routledge & Kegan Paul
London and New York

For
Ian Donaldson
and
Alan Ward

In the even Mr. Tipper read to me part of a – I know not
what to call it but *Tristram Shandy*.

(Thomas Turner, *Diary*, 14 September, 1762)

First published in 1987 by
Routledge & Kegan Paul Ltd
11 New Fetter Lane, London EC4P 4EE

Published in the USA by
Routledge & Kegan Paul Inc.
in association with Methuen Inc.
29 West 35th Street, New York, NY 10001

Set in 10/12 pt Baskerville
by Columns of Reading
and printed in Great Britain
by St Edmundsbury Press
Bury St Edmunds, Suffolk

Library of Congress Cataloging in Publication Data
Day, Geoffrey.
From fiction to the novel.
Includes index.
1. English fiction – 18th century – History and
criticism. 2. Books and reading – Great Britain – History
– 18th century. 3. Literary form. I. Title.
PR851.D34 1987 823'.5'09 86-20298

British Library CIP Data also available
ISBN 0-7102-0911-8

CONTENTS

———◆———

v

ACKNOWLEDGMENTS

———◆———

I have made extensive use of Ioan Williams (ed.), *Novel and Romance 1700-1800: A Documentary Record*, London, Routledge & Kegan Paul, 1970; and of two volumes in the same publisher's Critical Heritage series: *Henry Fielding*, edited by Ronald Paulson and Thomas Lockwood (1969), and *Sterne*, edited by Alan B. Howes (1970).

Figures 1, 2, 3 and 6, illustrating pages from *Clarissa* and *A Sentimental Journey*, are reproduced by permission of the Syndics of the Cambridge University Library.

I should like to thank Richard Luckett for suggesting that I take on this topic, and Gillian Beer, Paul-Gabriel Boucé, Kenneth Monkman, David McKitterick and Robert Wyke for making time to discuss points raised in this book and for offering details I might otherwise have missed.

There are three principal debts: to Ian Donaldson who first encouraged my interest in the period and who read the first draft of chapters 1 to 5 when on sabbatical; to Tony Tanner who has read several drafts and has been unfailingly good-humoured and stimulating in his comments; and to my wife Anna who found time to read and comment when engaged in a rather more major production of her own.

CHAPTER 1

———◆———

'A SMALL TALE, GENERALLY OF LOVE'

Johnson, *Dictionary* (1755), s.v. *Novel*

THE title page of Congreve's *Incognita* (1692) is almost aggressively insistent in its assertion of the work's nature: *Incognita: or, Love and Duty Reconciled. A Novel.* Justification for this appellation is provided in the preface in which Congreve carefully distinguished between the ideas of 'novel' and 'romance':

> Romances are generally composed of the constant Loves and invincible Courages of Hero's, Heroins, Kings and Queens, Mortals of the first Rank, and so forth; where lofty Language, miraculous Contingencies and impossible Performances, elevate and surprize the Reader into a giddy Delight, which leaves him flat upon the Ground whenever he gives of[f], and vexes him to think how he has suffer'd himself to be pleased and transported, concern'd and afflicted at the several Passages which he has Read, viz. these Knights Success to their Damosels Misfortunes, and such like, when he is forced to be very well convinced that 'tis all a lye. Novels are of a more familiar nature; Come near us, and represent to us Intrigues in practice, delight us with Accidents and odd Events, but not such as are wholly unusual or unpresidented, such which not being so distant from our Belief bring also the pleasure nearer us. Romances give more of Wonder, Novels more Delight. And with reverence be it spoken, and the Parallel kept at due distance, there is something of equality in the Proportion which they bear in reference to one another, with that between Comedy and Tragedy . . . .[1]

1

This neat distinction appears to have been accepted in certain areas throughout the subsequent century. Thus in the preface to the second edition of *The Castle of Otranto* (1765) Horace Walpole declared that he had been attempting to combine what he clearly saw as two essentially different types of literary production:

> It was an attempt to blend the two kinds of romance, the ancient and the modern. In the former all was imagination and improbability: in the latter, nature is always intended to be, and sometimes has been, copied with success. Invention has not been wanting; but the great resources of fancy have been dammed up, by a strict adherence to common life.[2]

That by 'the two kinds of romance' Walpole meant 'romance' and 'novel' may be deduced from the letter sent to Joseph Warton together with a presentation copy of the book:

> In fact, it is but partially an imitation of ancient romances; being rather intended for an attempt to blend the marvellous of old story with the natural of modern novels. This was in great measure the plan of a work, which, to say the truth, was begun without any plan at all.[3]

It is hardly surprising that Clara Reeve in her prefatory remarks to *The Old English Baron* (1778), while acknowledging her debt to Walpole's work, repeated his distinction:

> As this Story is of a species which, tho' not new, is out of the common track, it has been thought necessary to point out some circumstances to the reader, which will elucidate the design, and, it is hoped, will induce him to form a favourable, as well as a right judgment of the work before him.
> This Story is the literary offspring of the Castle of Otranto, written upon the same plan, with a design to unite the most attractive and interesting circumstances of the ancient Romance and modern Novel . . . to attain this end, there is required a sufficient degree of the marvellous,

to excite the attention; enough of the manners of real life,
to give an air of probability to the work; and enough of the
pathetic, to engage the heart in its behalf.[4]

What is rather more interesting about this opening is the
contention that in order to have a 'right judgment of the work
before him' the reader needs to be able to appreciate the
design. A work which combines the elements of novel and
romance must be judged and criticised in that light; and by
extension novels are to be judged as novels, and romances as
romances. This basic assumption is what makes Congreve's
distinction so vital.

But not all critics accepted that these two words denominated such clearly distinct ideas. In 1787 George Canning, at
that date still a seventeen-year-old at Eton, wrote an
entertaining piece for his own periodical, *The Microcosm*, in
which he explored with some perception both the distinguishing features and the similarities of the two forms:

> NOVEL-WRITING has by some late authors been aptly
> enough styled the young sister of ROMANCE. A family
> likeness is indeed very evident; and in their leading
> features, though in the one on a more enlarged, and in the
> other on a more contracted scale, a strong resemblance is
> easily discoverable between them.
>
> An eminent characteristic of each is Fiction; a quality
> which they possess, however, in very different degrees. The
> Fiction of ROMANCE is restricted by no fetters of reason, or
> of truth; but gives a loose to lawless imagination, and
> transgresses at will the bounds of time and place, of nature
> and possibility. The Fiction of the other, on the contrary, is
> shackled with a thousand restraints; is checked in her most
> rapid progress by the barriers of reason; and bounded in
> her most excursive flights by the limits of probability.
>
> To drop our metaphors: we shall not indeed find in
> NOVELS, as in ROMANCES, the hero sighing respectfully at
> the feet of his mistress, during a ten years' courtship in a
> wilderness; nor shall we be entertained with the history of
> such a tour, as that of *Saint George*; who mounts his horse

one morning in *Cappadocia*, takes his way through
Mesopotamia, then turns to the right into *Illyria*, and so by
way of *Grecia* and *Thracia*, arrives in the afternoon in
England. To such glorious violations as these of time and
place, ROMANCE writers have an exclusive claim.
NOVELISTS usually find it more convenient to change the
scene of courtship from a desert to a drawing-room; and far
from thinking it necessary to lay a ten years' siege to the
affections of their heroine, they contrive to carry their point
in an hour or two; as well for the sake of enhancing the
character of their hero, as for establishing their favourite
maxim of *love at first sight*; and their Hero, who seldom
extends his travels beyond the turnpike-road, is commonly
content to chuse the safer, though less expeditious,
conveyance of a post-chaise, in preference to such a horse
as that of *Saint George*.

But, these peculiarities of absurdity alone excepted, we
shall find that the NOVEL is but a more modern
modification of the same ingredients which constitute the
ROMANCE; and that a *recipe* for the one may be equally
serviceable for the composition of the other.

A ROMANCE (generally speaking) consists of a number
of strange events, with a Hero in the middle of them; who,
being an adventurous Knight, wades through them to one
grand design, namely, the emancipation of some captive
Princess, from the oppression of a merciless Giant; for the
accomplishment of which purpose he must set at nought
the incantations of the caitiff magician; must scale the
ramparts of his castle; and baffle the vigilance of the female
dragon, to whose custody his Heroine is committed.

Foreign as they may at first sight seem from the purposes
of a NOVEL, we shall find, upon a little examination, that
these are in fact the very circumstances upon which the
generality of them are built; modernized indeed in some
degree, by the transformations of merciless Giants into
austere Guardians, and of she-dragons into Maiden Aunts.
We must be contented also that the heroine, though
retaining her tenderness, be divested of her royalty; and in

the Hero we must give up the Knight-errant for the accomplished Fine Gentleman.

Still, however, though the performers are changed, the characters themselves remain nearly the same. In the Guardian we trace all the qualities which distinguish his ferocious predecessor; substituting only, in the room of magical incantations, a little plain cursing and swearing; and the Maiden Aunt retains all the prying vigilance, and suspicious malignity, in short, every endowment but the claws, which characterize her romantic counterpart. The Hero of a NOVEL has not indeed any opportunity of displaying his courage in the scaling of a rampart, or his generosity in the deliverance of enthralled multitudes; but as it is necessary that a Hero should signalize himself by both these qualifications, it is usual, to manifest the one by climbing the garden wall, or leaping the park-paling, in defiance of '*steel-traps and spring-guns*;' and the other, by flinging a crown to each of the post-boys, on alighting from his chaise and four.

In the article of *interviews*, the two species of composition are pretty much on an equality; provided only, that they are supplied with a '*quantum sufficit*' of moonlight, which is indispensably requisite; it being the etiquette for the Moon to appear particularly conscious on these occasions. For the adorer, when permitted to pay his vows at the shrine of his Divinity, custom has established in both cases a pretty universal form of prayer.

Thus far the writers of NOVEL and ROMANCE seem to be on a very equal footing; to enjoy similar advantages, and to merit equal admiration. We are now come to a very material point, in which ROMANCE has but slender claims to comparative excellence; I mean the choice of *names* and *titles*. However lofty and sonorous the names of *Amadis* and *Orlando*; however tender and delicate may be those of *Zorayda* and *Roxana*, are they to be compared with the attractive alliteration, the seducing softness, of *Lydia Lovemore*, and *Sir Harry Harlowe*; of *Frederic Freelove*, and *Clarissa Clearstarch*? Or can the simple "*Don Belianis, of*

5

Greece," or the "*Seven Champions of Christendom*", trick out so enticing a title-page, and awaken such pleasing expectations, as the "*Innocent Adultery*," the "*Tears of Sensibility*," or the "*Amours of the Count de D******, and L—y _____?"[5]

Though there is an element of extravagance in his expression it is evident that Canning agrees with Congreve's basic distinction: that 'novels' tend to reflect those areas of life with which the reader is conversant; 'romances' engage in wilder flights of fancy. That Congreve's notion of the difference was still accepted a century later may be seen from the review of Fanny Burney's *Camilla* which appeared in *The British Critic* for November 1796:

> To the old romance, which exhibited exalted personages, and displayed their sentiments in improbable or impossible situations, has succeeded the more reasonable, modern novel; which delineates characters drawn from actual observation, and, when ably executed, presents an accurate and captivating view of real life.[6]

Throughout the eighteenth century 'romance' was seen by some as a term suggesting excessive flights of fancy. This may be seen from the colloquial observations of Steele in *The Spectator*: 'if I do not succeed it shall look like Romance . . .' and 'It would look like Romance to tell you . . .'[7] and from Sterne's comment in *Tristram Shandy*: 'this plea, tho' it might save me dramatically, will damn me biographically, rendering my book, from this very moment, a profess'd ROMANCE, which, before, was a book apocryphal.'[8]

So there is evidence over a long period that the words 'novel' and 'romance' had clearly perceived and separate ideas attached to them. And such sensible distinctions would certainly allow the readers and critics both of the eighteenth century and of the twentieth to generate informed critical opinions: Clara Reeve's 'right judgment of the work'.

Unfortunately, though there is a tradition of clarity of definition, there is vastly more evidence to show that those

6

works now commonly referred to as 'eighteenth century novels' were not perceived as such by the readers or indeed by the major writers of the period, and that, so far from being ready to accept the various works as 'novels', they do not appear to have arrived at a consensus that works such as *Robinson Crusoe*, *Pamela*, *Joseph Andrews*, *Clarissa*, *Tom Jones*, *Peregrine Pickle* and *Tristram Shandy* were even all of the same species.

Some of the confusion was generated by careless use of what, in the best of all possible worlds, could have been employed as key terms. The words 'novel' and 'romance' appear to have acted as if unlike poles of two magnets: the one immediately attracted the other. This verbal tic manifested itself throughout the century. Steele in *The Spectator* wrote, 'But, Child, I am afraid thy Braines are a little disordered with Romances and Novels' (Bond, vol. 2, p. 487); Defoe opened *Moll Flanders* with the remark, 'The world is so taken up of late with Novels and Romances, that it will be hard for a private History to be taken for Genuine . . .',[9] thus further confusing the issue by introducing a new term, 'history', as if it were something distinct. That not all agreed it was a distinct idea is seen from Walpole's letter to Dr Henry: 'I have often said that History in general is a Romance that is believed, and that Romance is a History that is not believed; and that I do not see much other difference between them' (*Letters*, vol. 15, p. 173). Though perhaps flippantly making 'romance' and 'history' synonymous, it has been seen from the letter to Warton that Walpole did distinguish 'romance' and 'novel' even if his correspondents did not: Conway is typical of those who paired the words indiscriminately, writing, 'I remember you buried in romances and novels' (*Letters*, vol. 37, p. 189), and 'I am glad of the mistake which has produced so pretty a piece of imagination as your romantic paragraph; which pleases me so much that I seriously long to see a whole novel, nay, if you will, a romance from the same hand' (*Letters*, vol. 37, p. 363).

Reviewers as well as those who read for pleasure lumped the two terms together. An item in *The London Magazine* noted, 'There is at last a very happy taste sprung up amongst us for *novel* and *romance*' (vol. 18, May 1749, p. 226). The notice of *Peregrine Pickle* in *The Monthly Review* of March 1751 (vol. 4) wrote scornfully of 'that flood of novels, tales, romances, and other monsters of the imagination . . . romances and novels which turn upon characters out of nature, monsters of perfection, feats of chivalry, fairy-enchantments, and the whole train of the marvellous–absurd' (pp. 355-6). Ten years later in the same journal Owen Ruffhead was even more caustic:

> The Genius of Romance seems to have been long since drooping among us; and has, of late, been generally displayed only for the basest purposes; either to raise the grin of Ideotism by its buffoonry, or stimulate the prurience of Sensuality by its obscenity. Novels, therefore, have circulated chiefly among the giddy and licentious of both sexes, who read, not for the sake of thinking, but for want of thought.
>
> So shameful a prostitution has brought this species of writing into such disrepute, that if the more serious and solid Reader is at any time tempted to cast an eye over the pages of Romance, he almost blushes to confess his curiosity. (Vol. 24, 1761, p. 415)

In his *Lectures on Rhetoric and Poetry* (1762) Hugh Blair was less virulently dismissive: 'There remains to be treated of, another species of Composition in prose, which comprehends a very numerous, though, in general, a very insignificant class of Writings, known by the name of Romances and Novels';[10] while Richard Hurd in his *Dissertation on the Idea of Universal Poetry* (1766) queried 'what are we to think of those *novels* and *romances*, as they are called, that is fables constructed on some private and familiar subject, which have been so current, of late, through all Europe?'[11]

Even one of the 'novelists', Richardson, made no attempt to differentiate the two terms, observing of *Clarissa* in his preface, 'It will probably be thought tedious to all such as *dip* into it, expecting a *light Novel*, or *transitory Romance*.'[12] Lord

Chesterfield, after providing a definition of 'novel', proceeded to differentiate it from 'romance' on the grounds of length:

> I am in doubt whether you know what a Novel is: it is a little gallant history, which must contain a great deal of love, and not exceed one or two small volumes. The subject must be a love affair; the lovers are to meet with many difficulties and obstacles to oppose the accomplishment of their wishes, but at last overcome them all; and the conclusion or catastrophe must leave them happy. A Novel is a kind of abbreviation of a Romance; for a Romance generally consists of twelve volumes, all filled with insipid love nonsense, and most incredible adventures.[13]

These ideas were encapsulated by Johnson in his definition of novel in the *Dictionary* of 1755 which supplied the heading for this chapter: 'A small tale, generally of love'. To the twentieth century reader this is not a satisfactory explication: though *Clarissa* may be considered to be about 'love', weighing in as it does at rather more than 200,000 words longer than the Bible, 'small' is hardly apt. However, the notion that in these matters there were giants in those days could be argued from Fanny Burney's description of herself in her advertisement to *Camilla* as 'The Author of this little Work'.[14]

The inaptness of Johnson's definition was recognised at the time. Archibald Campbell's *Lexiphanes* (1767) was devoted to attacking, at times in highly amusing fashion, the ponderousness of Johnson's diction and the shortcomings of the *Dictionary*. In the course of a dialogue with the Critick, Johnson, referred to throughout as J—N, is made to say:

> Without dubiety you misapprehend this dazzling scintillation of conceit in totality, and had you had that constant recurrence to my oraculous dictionary, which was incumbent upon you from the vehemence of my monitory injunctions, it could not have escaped you that the word novel exhibits to all men dignified by literary honours and scientifical accomplishments, two discrepant significations. The one imports that which you have affixed to it, a

romance or fiction, such as the tale of Ajut and Anningait, or the Prince of Abyssinia; but that in which I have at present used it, signifies new, recent, hodiernal.[15]

To Campbell and to the twentieth century reader, though for different reasons, Johnson's definition in the *Dictionary* is unhelpful. From the twentieth century point of view this is because Johnson is clearly not thinking of those works which are now automatically called to mind. This is shown by the examples he adduced to illustrate the word:

> Nothing of a foreign nature; like the trifling *novels* which Ariosto inserted in his poems.
>
> *Dryden*

> Her mangl'd fame in barb'rous pastimes lost,
> The coxcomb's novel and the drunkard's toast.
>
> *Prior*

The sentence from Dryden justifies Johnson's definition; *Orlando Furioso* is peppered with 'short tales' and they are frequently of love. They are not however written in prose, the form now associated with 'novels'.

Johnson's views on the 'novel' were most clearly expressed in *The Rambler*, no. 4 (1750), though it should be noted that at no point during this essay did he use the word. He opened by making a connection between fiction and poetry which accords with his *Dictionary* definition:

> The works of fiction, with which the present generation seems more particularly delighted, are such as exhibit life in its true state, diversified only by accidents that daily happen in the world, and influenced by passions and qualities which are really to be found in conversing with mankind.
>
> This kind of writing may be termed not improperly the comedy of romance, and is to be conducted nearly by the rules of comic poetry. Its province is to bring about natural events by easy means, and to keep up curiosity without the

help of wonder: it is therefore precluded from the machines
and expedients of the heroic romance, and can neither
employ giants to snatch away a lady from the nuptial rites,
nor knights to bring her back from captivity; it can neither
bewilder its personages in desarts, nor lodge them in
imaginary castles.[16]

He provided evidence of the popularity of the form in his
claim that the audience for such works was far more wide-
ranging than for any other literary productions:

Why this wild strain of imagination found reception so
long, in polite and learned ages, it is not easy to conceive;
but we cannot wonder that, while readers could be
procured, the authors were willing to continue it: for when
a man had by practice gained some fluency of language, he
had no further care than to retire to his closet, let loose his
invention, and heat his mind with incredibilities; a book
was thus produced without fear of criticism, without the
toil of study, without knowledge of nature, or acquaintance
with life. (p. 20)

The essay proceeded to draw attention to the two key areas of
eighteenth century criticism: morality and reality, and their
interconnection:

The task of our present writers is very different; it requires,
together with that learning which is to be gained from
books, that experience which can never be attained by
solitary diligence, but must arise from general converse,
and accurate observation of the living world. Their
performances have, as Horace expressed it, *plus oneris
quantum veniae minus*, little indulgence, and therefore more
difficulty. They are engaged in portraits of which every one
knows the original, and can detect any deviation from
exactness of resemblance. Other writings are safe, except
from the malice of learning, but these are in danger from
every common reader; as the slipper ill executed was

censured by a shoemaker who happened in his way at the Venus of Apelles.

But the fear of not being approved as just copyers of human manners, is not the most important concern that an author of this sort ought to have before him. These books are written chiefly to the young, the ignorant, and the idle, to whom they serve as lectures of conduct, and introductions into life. They are the entertainment of minds unfurnished with ideas, and therefore easily susceptible of impressions; not fixed by principles, and therefore easily following the current of fancy; not informed by experience, and consequently open to every false suggestion and partial account.

That the highest degree of reverence should be paid to youth, and that nothing indecent should be suffered to approach their eyes or ears; are precepts extorted by sense and virtue from an ancient writer, by no means eminent for chastity of thought. The same kind, tho' not the same degree of caution, is required in every thing which is laid before them, to secure them from unjust prejudices, perverse opinions, and incongruous combinations of images.

In the romances formerly written, every transaction and sentiment was so remote from all that passes among men, that the reader was in very little danger of making any applications to himself; the virtues and crimes were equally beyond his sphere of activity; and he amused himself with heroes and with traitors, deliverers and persecutors, as with beings of another species, whose actions were regulated upon motives of their own, and who had neither faults nor excellencies in common with himself.

But when an adventurer is levelled with the rest of the world, and acts in such scenes of the universal drama, as may be the lot of any other young man; young spectators fix their eyes upon him with closer attention, and hope by observing his behaviour and success to regulate their own practices, when they shall be engaged in the like part.

For this reason these familiar histories may perhaps be made of greater use than the solemnities of professed

morality, and convey the knowledge of vice and virtue with
more efficacy than axioms and definitions. But if the power
of example is so great, as to take possession of the memory
by a kind of violence, and produce effects almost without
the intervention of the will, care ought to be taken that,
when the choice is unrestrained, the best examples only
should be exhibited; and that which is likely to operate so
strongly, should not be so mischievous or uncertain in its
effects.

The chief advantage which these fictions have over real
life is, that their authors are at liberty, tho' not to invent,
yet to select objects, and to cull from the mass of mankind,
those individuals upon which the attention ought most to
be employ'd; as a diamond, though it cannot be made, may
be polished by art, and placed in such a situation, as to
display that lustre which before was buried among
common stones.

It is justly considered as the greatest excellency of art, to
imitate nature; but it is necessary to distinguish those parts
of nature, which are most proper for imitation: greater care
is still required in representing life, which is so often
discoloured by passion, or deformed by wickedness. If the
world be promiscuously described, I cannot see of what use
it can be to read the account; or why it may not be as safe
to turn the eye immediately upon mankind, as upon a
mirror which shows all that presents itself without
discrimination.

It is therefore not a sufficient vindication of a character,
that it is drawn as it appears, for many characters ought
never to be drawn; nor of a narrative, that the train of
events is agreeable to observation and experience, for that
observation which is called knowledge of the world, will be
found much more frequently to make men cunning than
good. The purpose of these writings is surely not only to
show mankind, but to provide that they may be seen
hereafter with less hazard; to teach the means of avoiding
the snares which are laid by Treachery for Innocence,
without infusing any wish for that superiority with which

the betrayer flatters his vanity; to give the power of
counteracting fraud, without the temptation to practise it;
to initiate youth by mock encounters in the art of necessary
defence, and to increase prudence without impairing
virtue.

Many writers, for the sake of following nature, so mingle
good and bad qualities in their principal personages, that
they are both equally conspicuous; and as we accompany
them through their adventures with delight, and are led by
degrees to interest ourselves in their favour, we lose the
abhorrence of their faults, because they do not hinder our
pleasure, or, perhaps, regard them with some kindness for
being united with so much merit.

There have been men indeed splendidly wicked, whose
endowments threw a brightness on their crimes, and whom
scarce any villainy made perfectly detestable, because they
never could be wholly divested of their excellencies; but
such have been in all ages the great corrupters of the
world, and their resemblance ought no more to be preserved,
than the art of murdering without pain. (pp. 22-3)

Johnson's argument here is very general. Arthur Murphy
revealed that this issue of *The Rambler* represented Johnson's
response to the popularity of *Roderick Random* and *Tom Jones*
which were to be seen as implicitly contrasted here with the
works of Richardson. The contrast is so implicit that the
modern reader would be forgiven for missing it completely
were it not pointed out. For specific criticism one must look
elsewhere.

As literary criticism developed during the eighteenth
century with the rapid growth in monthly periodicals
devoting at times considerable space to literary matters – *The
Monthly Review* devoted some 35,000 words to reviewing
Thomas Amory's *John Buncle* (1756)[17] – so more and more the
theoretical basis of criticism came to be explored. Clara
Reeve has been cited to the effect that the critic needs to be
aware of the form of a work before sensible criticism is
possible; Canning's attempts to define had the same moti-

14

vating force. The most important attempt at categorisation in this area was made by James Beattie in an essay 'On Fable and Romance' in his *Dissertations Moral and Critical* of 1783. This essay is the *locus classicus* of eighteeenth century criticism of prose fiction and is reprinted at length in the next chapter, where it will be seen yet again that though Beattie's attempts at distinguishing different forms of prose fiction were made with a good deal of thought and useful specific illustration, nevertheless the terminology he adopted could be seen as contributing to the confusion of the terms Congreve had so neatly separated.

To illustrate the problem one may take the specific examples of Richardson and Fielding. There were readers and critics who referred to Richardson as a novelist or novel writer and who described his productions as novels. Vicesimus Knox in 1778 declared, 'That Richardson's Novels are written with the purest intentions of promoting virtue, none can deny';[18] and Horace Walpole rather snakily wrote to Mann:

> You tell me of the French playing at whisk – why I found it established when I was last there. I told them they were very good to imitate us in anything, but that they had adopted the two dullest things we have, whisk and Richardson's novels.
>
> (*Letters*, vol. 22, p. 555)

Walpole used the same term of *Pamela*: 'the late singular novel is the universal, and only theme – Pamela is like snow, she covers everything with her whiteness' (*Letters*, vol. 40, p. 29). In 1788 Anna Seward followed Walpole's vocabulary, though not his viewpoint, when writing of *Clarissa*:

> Men eminent for piety, wisdom and virtue, have recommended Richardson's *Clarissa* from the pulpit; a work which Dr. Johnson (so generally unwilling to praise) has been often heard to pronounce, 'not only the first *novel*, but perhaps the first *work* in our language, splendid in point of genius, and calculated to promote the dearest interests of religion and virtue.'[19]

15

'Novel writer' was Hugh Blair's description of Richardson: 'The most moral of all our novel Writers is Richardson, the Author of Clarissa' (*Lectures on Rhetoric and Belles Lettres*, pp. 309-10); and the same term was used by Beattie: 'Yet, like most other novel-writers, he represents some of his wicked characters as more agreeable than was necessary to his plan' ('On Fable and Romance', below, page 54). But almost immediately before this Beattie had written:

> A second species of the Modern Serious Romance is that, which follows *the poetical arrangement*; and, in order to shorten the time of the action, begins in the middle of the story. Such, partly, are *Sir Charles Grandison*, and *Clarissa Harlowe*, by Mr. Richardson. (below, page 52)

Clara Reeve, who so carefully distinguished novel from romance, specifically associated Richardson with the latter: 'The business of Romance is, first, to excite the attention; and, secondly, to direct it to some useful, or at least innocent, end; Happy the writer who attains both these points, like Richardson!' (*Old English Baron*, p. 4). And right at the end of the century John Moore in *A View of the Commencement and Progress of Romance* asserted, 'Richardson introduced a new species of romance.'[20]

Where Richardson's works attracted the two most common critical epithets, *Tom Jones* acted as a magnet to the whole thesaurus. To a large extent this was the inevitable result of Fielding's own attempts to clarify the nature and form of his writings. The title page and dedication both asserted that the work was a 'History',[21] thus denying implicitly, as Defoe had denied explicitly in *Moll Flanders*, that it was either a novel or a romance. Fielding's apparent intention was noted by the anonymous author of *An Essay on the new Species of Writing* (1751)[22] who commented of *Joseph Andrews*, which also contained the word 'History' on its title page:

> As this Sort of Writing was intended as a Contrast to those in which the Reader was even to suppose all the Characters ideal, and every Circumstance quite imaginary, 'twas

thought necessary, to give it a greater Air of Truth, to
entitle it *an History*; and the *Dramatis Personae* (if I may
venture to use the Expression) were christened not with
fantastic high-sounding Names, but such as, tho' they
sometimes bore some Reference to the Character, had a
more modern Termination. (p. 18)

But that not all Fielding's readers were so attentive may be
seen from an article in *The London Magazine* of May 1749
which referred to '*Tom Jones*, or any other modern *romance*'.[23]
Fielding had recognised in the opening sentence of his preface
to *Joseph Andrews* that differing interpretations of key terms
were not only possible, but likely:

As it is possible the mere *English* Reader may have a
different Idea of Romance with the Author of these little
Volumes; and may consequently expect a kind of
Entertainment, not to be found, nor which was even
intended, in the following Pages; it may not be improper to
premise a few Words concerning this kind of Writing,
which I do not remember to have seen hitherto attempted
in our Language.[24]

Fielding's subsequent attempt to provide a definition of the
type of work he was offering to the reading public provided a
number of handles for critics to grasp:

The EPIC as well as the DRAMA is divided into Tragedy
and Comedy. *Homer*, who was the Father of this Species of
Poetry, gave us a Pattern of both these, tho' that of the
latter kind is entirely lost; which *Aristotle* tells us, bore the
same relation to comedy which his *Iliad* bears to Tragedy.
And perhaps, that we have no more Instances of it among
the Writers of Antiquity, is owing to the Loss of this great
Pattern, which, had it survived, would have found its
imitators equally with the other Poems of this great
Original.
    And farther, as this Poetry may be Tragic or Comic, I
will not scruple to say it may be likewise either in Verse or

Prose: for tho' it wants one particular, which the Critic
enumerates in the constituent Parts of an Epic Poem,
namely Metre; yet, when any kind of Writing contains all
its other Parts, such as Fable, Action, Characters,
Sentiments, and Diction, and is deficient in Metre only; it
seems, I think, reasonable to refer it to the Epic; at least, as
no Critic hath thought it proper to range it under any other
Head, nor to assign it a particular Name to itself . . . .

Now a comic Romance is a comic Epic-Poem in Prose;
differing from Comedy, as the serious Epic from Tragedy:
its Action being more extended and comprehensive;
containing a much larger Circle of Incidents, and
introducing a greater Variety of Characters. It differs from
the serious Romance in its Fable and Action, in this; that
as in the one these are grave and solemn, so in the other
they are light and ridiculous: it differs in its Characters, by
introducing Persons of inferiour Rank, and consequently of
inferiour Manners, whereas the grave Romance, sets the
highest before us; lastly in its Sentiments and Diction, by
preserving the Ludicrous instead of the Sublime. (pp. 3-4)

Critical reaction to *Tom Jones* was clearly much influenced by
this statement in *Joseph Andrews*. The review in *The London
Magazine*, though wavering slightly, initially accepted Fielding's term: 'It is intitled, *The History of TOM JONES, a
Foundling*, by Henry Fielding, *Esq*; being a novel, or prose
epick composition . . .', though the effect was somewhat
spoiled by the concluding reference to '*this pretty novel*'.[25]
Arthur Murphy, in his introduction to the 1762 edition of
Fielding's *Works*, not only took over his author's terms but
proceeded to adopt a critical stance very much in accord with
the statement in *Joseph Andrews*:

And now we are arrived at the second grand epoch of Mr.
Fielding's genius, when all his faculties were in perfect
unison, and conspired to produce a complete work. If we
consider *Tom Jones* in the same light in which the ablest
critics have examined the *Iliad*, the *Æneid*, and the *Paradise*

Lost, namely, with a view to the fable, the manners, the sentiments, and the stile, we shall find it standing the test of the severest criticism, and indeed bearing away the envied pride of a complete performance. In the first place, the action has that unity, which is the boast of the great models of composition; it turns upon a single event, attended with many circumstances, and many subordinate incidents, which seem, in the progress of the work, to perplex, to entangle, and to involve the whole in difficulties, and lead on the reader's imagination, with an eagerness of curiosity, through scenes of prodigious variety, till at length the different intricacies and complications of the fable are explained after the same gradual manner in which they had been worked up to a crisis: incident arises out of incident; the seeds of every thing that shoots up, are laid with a judicious hand, and whatever occurs in the latter part of the story, seems naturally to grow out of those passages which preceded; so that, upon the whole, the business with great propriety and probability works itself up into various embarassments, and then afterwards, by a regular series of events, clears itself from all impediments, and brings itself inevitably to a conclusion; like a river, which, in its progress, foams amongst fragments of rocks, and for a while seems pent up by unsurmountable oppositions; then angrily dashes for a while, then plunges under ground into caverns, and runs a subterraneous course, till at length it breaks out again, meanders round the country, and with a clear placid stream flows gently into the ocean. By this artful management, our author has given us the perfection of fable; which, as the writers upon the subject have justly observed, consists in such obstacles to retard the final issue of the whole, as shall at least, in their consequences, accelerate the catastrophe, and bring it evidently and necessarily to that period only, which, in the nature of things, could arise from it; so that the action could not remain in suspense any longer, but must naturally close and determine itself. It may be proper to add, that no fable whatever affords, in its solution, such artful states of suspence, such beautiful turns of surprise, such unexpected incidents, and such sudden discoveries, sometimes apparently embarrassing, but always promising the catastrophe, and eventually promoting the completion of the whole.[26]

The word 'novel' is clearly out of place in such a discussion. Writing in the same year Beattie also saw the propriety of comparing Fielding's works with other epics, though to describe the former he adopted the term 'Comic Epopee':

The difficulty of constructing an Epic or Dramatic fable may appear from the bad success of very great writers who have attempted it. Of Dramatic fables there are indeed several in the world, which may be allowed to have come near perfection. But the beauty of Homer's fable remains unrivalled to this day. Virgil and Tasso have imitated, but not equalled it. That of Paradise Lost is artful, and for the most part judicious: I am certain the author could have equalled Homer in this, as he has excelled him in some other respects: – but the nature of his plan would not admit the introduction of so many incidents, as we see in the Iliad, co-operating to one determinate end. – Of the Comic Epopee we have two exquisite models in English, I mean the *Amelia* and *Tom Jones* of Fielding. The introductory part of the latter follows indeed the historical arrangement, in a way somewhat resembling the practice of Euripides in his Prologues, or at least as excuseable: but, with this exception, we may venture to say, that both fables would bear to be examined by Aristotle himself, and, if compared with those of Homer, would not suffer greatly in the comparison.[27]

Later in the century Henry Pye employed the same term, writing of 'the inimitable comic epopees of Fielding'.[28] Lord Monboddo, on the other hand, though like Murphy and Beattie accepting the arguments relating to epic, comedy and tragedy, stated firmly that *Tom Jones* should be regarded as a poem:

There is lately sprung up among us a species of narrative poem, representing likewise the characters of common life. It has the same relation to comedy that the epic has to tragedy, and differs from the epic in the same respect that comedy differs from tragedy; that is, in the actions and characters, both of which are much nobler in the epic than it it. It is therefore, I think, a legitimate kind of poem; and, accordingly we are told, Homer wrote one of that kind, called *Margites*, of which some lines are preserved. The reason why I mention it is, that we have, in English, a *poem* of that kind, (for so I will call it) which has more of character in it than any work, antient or modern, that I know. The work I mean is, the *History of Tom Jones*, by Henry Fielding.[29]

Beattie's subsequent piece 'On Fable and Romance' inclined to Monboddo's view: 'Prose and Verse are opposite, but Prose and Poetry may be consistent. *Tom Jones*, and *Telemachus*, are epick, or narrative poems, though written in prose; the one Comick, the other Serious and Heroick' (below, page 46).

Fielding provided a clear statement of the nature of his work. Unfortunately much contemporary and modern criticism, in attempts to categorise and rationalise, has chosen to ignore the signpost. Thus we find *Tom Jones* variously described as history, novel, romance, prose epic, comic epopee, poem, and epic or narrative poem. And in many cases the choice of term is used either to justify the subsequent line of criticism or as the culmination of the preceding argument. Critical approaches are inevitably coloured by the perception of the form of the work being criticised.

But if readers and critics are in multiple minds as to what they are reading, what help is to be derived from the authors?

Defoe did not refer to his own works as 'novels' and when he did employ the term it was not in the sense a twentieth century reader would first call to mind. In *Serious Reflections during the life and surprising adventures of Robinson Crusoe with his vision of the angelic world* (1720) he wrote:

Below these we have a Sort of People who will acknowledge a God, but he must be such a one as they please to make him; a fine well bred good natur'd Gentleman like Deity, that cannot have the Heart to damn any of his Creatures to an Eternal Punishment, nor could be so weak as to let the *Jews* crucify his own Son; these men expose Religion, and all the Doctrines of Repentance, and Faith in Christ, with all the Means of a Christian Salvation, as matter of Banter and Ridicule. The Bible they say is a good History in most Parts, but the Story of our Saviour they look upon as a meer Novel, and the Miracles of the New Testament as a Legend of Priestcraft.[30]

'Novel' here is synonymous with Congreve's 'romance'.

Johnson seldom used the word novel as a substantive, not at all in the *Rambler* essay cited above, and none of his contemporary biographers recorded him referring to his own production *Rasselas* (1759) in this way – it was 'book', 'little book' or 'work'. Though when Boswell recorded Lady Macdonald in Johnson's presence referring to it as a novel there was no negative reaction – indeed no reaction at all.[31] Richardson, as will be seen in chapter 3, did not wish his own work to be regarded as fiction, and thus 'novel' would have been a most unsuitable term to use. Fielding, likewise, frequently appears to have avoided using it: his preface to his sister's *David Simple* (1744) employed the terms 'performance', 'work', 'production', 'writings', 'little book' and 'fable'; and declared firmly, '*I have attempted in my Preface to* Joseph Andrews *to prove, that every Work of this kind is in its Nature a comic Epic Poem, of which* Homer *left us a Precedent, tho' it be unhappily lost.*'[32] Sterne at no point in his published work or in his letters ever used the word 'novel': *Tristram Shandy* was referred to as 'this rhapsodical work' (p. 39).

The only great 'novelist' of the eighteenth century who ever admitted to writing a novel was Smollett, who, in the rather curious dedication to *Ferdinand Count Fathom* (1753) which was addressed to himself, provided the reader with a definition of the term:

We live in a censorious age; and an author cannot take too much precaution to anticipate the prejudice, misapprehension and temerity of malice, ignorance and presumption.

I therefore think it incumbent upon me, to give some previous intimation of the plan which I have executed in the subsequent performance, that I may not be condemned upon partial evidence; and to whom can I with more propriety appeal in my explanation, than to you, who are so well acquainted with all the sentiments and emotions of my breast?

A Novel is a large diffused picture, comprehending the characters of life, disposed in different groupes, and exhibited in various attitudes, for the purposes of a uniform plan, and general occurrence, to which every individual figure is subservient. But this plan cannot be executed with propriety, probability or success, without a principal personage to attract the attention, unite the incidents, unwind the clue of the labyrinth, and at last close the scene by virtue of his own importance.

Almost all the heroes of this kind, who have hitherto succeeded on the English stage, are characters of transcendent worth, conducted through the vicissitudes of fortune, to that goal of happiness, which ever ought to be the repose of extraordinary desert. – Yet the same principle by which we rejoice at the remuneration of merit, will teach us to relish the disgrace and discomfiture of vice, which is always an example of extensive use and influence, because it leaves a deep impression of terror upon the minds of those who were not confined in the pursuit of morality and virtue, and while the balance wavers, enables the right scale to preponderate.[33]

His reason for offering this definition is important: 'that I may not be condemned upon partial evidence'. As in the case of *The Old English Baron* the author asserts the necessity of the reader or critic knowing the type of work in hand and thus bringing to it the right criteria. But the definition offered in the third paragraph cited above is not particularly helpful, and though it is true that Smollett was the only major writer of the century to declare he was writing a novel, it may well be argued that his notion of the term was inchoate. Not only that, there is evidence to suggest that he, in common with so many critics, did not make any real distinction between 'novel' and 'romance'. To only one other of his works did he provide prefatory material: *Roderick Random*. There he gave an account of the history of romance and, though declaring that in certain respects his methods differed from those of previous writers of romance, asserted that *Roderick Random* was of the tradition of Cervantes and Le Sage.[34] A reader would find it difficult to justify classifying *Ferdinand Count Fathom* and *Roderick Random* as works of different genres or sub-genres.

To find the eighteenth century novel as perceived in general by the eighteenth century reader one must look to the second rank and the third rate. Though Fielding never considered his own works to be novels he did consider that some writings of others could be so denominated. When in *Tom Jones* Fitzpatrick mistakenly enters the bedroom occupied by Jones and Mrs Waters the ensuing fracas is brought to a halt by Mr Maclachlan who is first described to the reader thus:

> This Gentleman was one of those whom the *Irish* call a Calabalero, or Cavalier. He was the younger Brother of a good Family, and having no Fortune at Home, was obliged to look abroad in order to get one: For which purpose he was proceeding to *Bath* to try his Luck with Cards and the Women.
>
> This young Fellow lay in Bed reading one of Mrs. *Behn's* Novels; for he had been instructed by a Friend, that he would find no more effectual Method of recommending himself to the Ladies than the improving of his Understanding, and filling his Mind with good Literature. (p. 530)

'Good Literature' is here clearly ironic and underlines

Fielding's belief that 'novels' were essentially ephemeral works of dubious value. The works of Mrs Manley and Eliza Haywood may be seen as typifying this class. The former's *The New Atalantis* (1709) was a thinly disguised political and social *roman à clef*, while Mrs Haywood's outpourings earned her Pope's comment 'the libellous Novelist' and a footnote in *The Dunciad* referring to her 'scandalous books'.[35] Horace Walpole saw Mesdames Behn and Haywood as two of a kind, writing to Sir Horace Mann, 'I will write to London for the life of Theodore; though you may depend upon its being a Grub Street piece, without one true fact. Don't let it prevent your undertaking his memoirs – yet I should imagine Mrs Heywood or Mrs Behn were fitter to write his history' (*Letters*, vol. 18, p. 249).

Fielding, for all his efforts, was seen as a novel writer by some of his imitators. One of the earliest writers to see Fielding thus was Francis Coventry in *The History of Pompey the Little; or the life and adventures of a Lap Dog* (1751), which was dedicated to Fielding and explicit in the connection:

To
Henry Fielding, Esq;

SIR,
My design being to speak a word or two in behalf of novel-writing, I know not to whom I can address myself with so much propriety as yourself, who unquestionably stand foremost in this species of composition.

To convey instruction in a pleasant manner, and mix entertainment with it, is certainly a commendable undertaking, perhaps more likely to be attended with success than graver precepts; and even where amusement is the chief thing consulted, there is some little merit in making people laugh, when it is done without giving offence to religion, or virtue, or good manners. If the laugh be not raised at the expence of innocence or decency, good humour bids us indulge it, and we cannot well laugh too often.

Can one help wondering therefore at the contempt, with which many people affect to talk of this sort of

composition? they seem to think it degrades the dignity of
their understandings, to be found with a novel in their
hands, and take great pains to let you know that they never
read them. They are people of too great importance, it
seems, to misspend their time in so idle a manner, and
much too wise to be amused.

Now, tho' many reasons may be given for this ridiculous
and affected disdain, I believe a very principal one, is the
pride and pedantry of learned men, who are willing to
monopolise reading to themselves, and therefore fastidiously
decry all books that are on a level with common
understandings, as empty, trifling, and impertinent . . . I
do not pretend to apply any thing here said in behalf of
books of amusement, to the following little work, imperfect
as it is in all its parts, and how unworthy to be ranked in
that class of writings, which I am now defending. But I
desire to be understood in general, or more particularly,
with an eye to your works, which I take to be master-pieces
and complete models in their kind. They are, I think,
worthy the attention of the greatest and wisest men, and if
any body can read them without entertainment and
instruction, I heartily pity their understandings.[36]

Rather ingenuously, while recognising the way in which the
novel was regarded as an object of no value, 'it degrades the
dignity', Coventry still sees Fielding as 'foremost in this
species of composition' – a compliment Fielding would not
have relished – and also regards his own work as 'unworthy
to be ranked in that class of writings'. That Coventry may
not have had a precise notion of the form in mind may be
argued from his first chapter heading: '*A Panegyric upon Dogs,
together with some Observations on modern Novels and Romances*',
and the general amorphousness of the terminology is reinforced
by such subsequent claims as: 'the Nature of this Work, which
one of my Cotemporaries declares to be an *Epic Poem in Prose*'
and 'I hope the very Superiority of the Character here treated
of, above the Heroes of common Romances, will procure it a
favourable reception' (pp. 5-6).

Of the second rank of writers of fiction in the eighteenth century it might be reasonable to regard Fanny Burney as the first real novelist to recognise herself as such. Her preface to *Evelina* (1778) combined a statement of authorial intention with an assertion of the writer's own position in a tradition:

> *In the republic of letters, there is no member of such inferior rank, or who is so much disdained by his brethren of the quill as the humble Novelist: nor is his fate less hard in the world at large, since, among the whole class of writers, perhaps not one can be named, of whom the votaries are more numerous, but less respectable.*
>
> *Yet, while in the annals of those few of our predecessors, to whom this species of writing is indebted for being saved from contempt, and rescued from depravity, we can trace such names as Rousseau, Johnson*, Marivaux, Fielding, Richardson, and Smollet, no man need blush at starting from the same post, though many, nay, most men, may sigh at finding themselves distanced.*
>
> *The following letters are presented to the public – for such, by novel writers, novel readers will be called, – with a very singular mixture of timidity and confidence, resulting from the peculiar situation of the editor; who, though trembling for their success from a consciousness of their imperfections, yet fears not being involved in their disgrace, while happily wrapped up in a mantle of impenetrable obscurity.*
>
> *To draw characters from nature, though not from life, and to mark the manners of the times, is the attempted plan of the following letters. For this purpose, a young female, educated in the most secluded retirement, makes, at the age of seventeen, her first appearance upon the great and busy stage of life; with a virtuous mind, a cultivated understanding, and a feeling heart, her ignorance of the forms, and inexperience in the manners, of the world, occasion all the little incidents which these volumes record, and which form the natural progression of the life of a young woman of obscure birth, but conspicuous beauty, for the first six months after her* Entrance into the World.
>
> *Perhaps were it possible to effect the total extirpation of novels, our young ladies in general, and boarding-school damsels in particular, might profit from their annihilation: but since the*

distemper they have spread seems incurable, since their contagion bids defiance to the medecine of advice or reprehension, and since they are found to baffle all the mental art of physic, save what is prescribed by the slow regiment of Time, and bitter diet of Experience, surely all attempts to contribute to the number of those which may be read, if not with advantage, at least without injury, ought rather to be encouraged than contemned.

Let me, therefore, prepare for disappointment those who, in the perusal of these sheets, entertain the gentle expectation of being transported to the fantastic regions of Romance, where Fiction is coloured by all the gay tints of luxurious Imagination, where Reason is an outcast, and where the sublimity of the Marvellous rejects all aid from sober Probability. The heroine of these memoirs, young, artless, and inexperienced, is

No faultless Monster, that the World ne'er saw,

but the offspring of Nature, and of Nature in her simplest attire.

In all the arts, the value of copies can only be proportioned to the scarceness of originals: among sculptors and painters, a fine statue, or a beautiful picture, of some great master, may deservedly employ the imitative talents of younger and inferior artists, that their appropriation to one spot, may not wholly prevent the more general expansion of their excellence; but, among authors, the reverse is the case, since the noblest productions of literature, are almost equally attainable with the meanest. In books, therefore, imitation cannot be shunned too sedulously; for the very perfection of a model which is frequently seen, serves but more forcibly to mark the inferiority of a copy.

To avoid what is common, without adopting what is unnatural, must limit the ambition of the vulgar herd of authors; however zealous, therefore, my veneration of the great writers I have mentioned, however I may feel myself enlightened by the knowledge of Johnson, charmed with the eloquence of Rousseau, softened by the pathetic powers of Richardson, and exhilarated by the wit of Fielding, and humour of Smollet; I yet presume not to attempt pursuing the same ground which they have tracked; whence, though they may have cleared the weeds, they have also culled the flowers, and though they have rendered the path plain, they have left it barren.

*The candour of my readers, I have not the impertinence to doubt,
and to their indulgence, I am sensible I have no claim: I have,
therefore, only to entreat, that my own words may not pronounce my
condemnation, and that what I have here ventured to say in regard to
imitation, may be understood, as it is meant, in a general sense, and
not be imputed to an opinion of my own originality, which I have not
the vanity, the folly, or the blindness, to entertain.*

*Whatever may be the fate of these letters, the editor is satisfied
they will meet with justice; and commits them to the press, though
hopeless of Fame, yet not regardless of censure.*

*However superior the capacities in which these great
writers deserve to be considered, they must pardon me
that, for the dignity of my subject, I here rank the authors
of Rasselas and Eloise as Novelists.[37]

This preface, in its statement of authorial intent, is
comparable in importance to Beattie's explication of his
critical position in 'On Fable and Romance'. There are
elements of the formulaic as in the reference to the *'humble
Novelist'* and her denomination of herself as *'editor'* rather than
author, but there is much of major importance. There is the
assertion of a tradition, a tradition moreover in which the
principal figures are named, and it is recognised that some of
these included may cause raised eyebrows. The footnote
justifying the names of Johnson and Rousseau may have been
the result of a realisation that *Rasselas* and *Julie, ou la Nouvelle
Héloise* were not generally seen as novels, or alternatively that
these two literary figures had produced such a range of works
that it was unusual to think of them specifically as writers of
imaginative prose.

Burney's recognition of contemporary critical common-
places may be seen in her tongue-in-cheek reference to the
possibility of *'the total extirpation of novels'* and the beneficial
effects this would have on young ladies. Similarly her slight
misquotation from the Duke of Buckingham's *Essay on Poetry*
may well be an indication of her having read some of the
adverse criticism of *Clarissa*, for the unreality of the 'faultless
Monster' was a point raised by several followers of Fielding.

Two particularly noteworthy matters raised were those relating to characterisation and reality. '*To draw characters from nature, though not from life*' neatly sums up an important distinction, and, when one recalls Defoe's concern to be thought to be drawing from life, a concern also to be found in Richardson's prefaces, is an indication of a major shift in the position of the author.[38] By the date of the publication of *Evelina*, 1778, it had become acceptable to be quite open about one's creation of fiction. A major shift is also apparent in Burney's remarks about the avoidance of imitation. The notion of originality – an idea of comparative unimportance in the first half of the century – came to dominate the literary field after 1750. 1759 saw the publication of Edward Young's *Conjectures on Original Composition*, and in 1767 William Duff produced the far more convincingly argued *Essay on Original Genius; and its various modes of exertion in philosophy and the fine arts, particularly in poetry*. Fanny Burney was obviously attuned to this basic shift in critical attitudes. That she was also aware of long-standing critical positions may be seen from her disabusing the reader who might '*entertain the gentle expectation of being transported to the fantastic regions of Romance*' and her immediately subsequent description of these regions being those '*where Fiction is coloured by all the gay tints of luxurious Imagination, where Reason is an outcast, and where the sublimity of the* Marvellous *rejects all aid from sober Probability*'.

All in all there is evidence here of real thought about the history and the form of fiction, a perception of both the ephemeral and the weighty areas of critical opinion, and *pace* the Petrine '*humble Novelist*', a demonstration of some pride in being part of what she sees as a tradition of distinction.

But that there was still a sense, late in the century, in which 'novel' and 'novelist' were titles of insufficient merit might justifiably be argued from the evidence of such writers as Mary Wollstonecraft who called one of her works *Mary, A Fiction* (1788)[39] and reiterated the term in the opening sentences of both the advertisement, 'In delineating the Heroine of this fiction . . .', and the tale itself, 'Mary, the heroine of this fiction . . .' (p. 1). On the other hand the

posthumous fragmentary *The Wrongs of Women* (1798) was
described in the preface as 'this Novel' (p. 73) and William
Godwin, her husband, added an extract from one of her
letters which claimed, 'it is the delineation of finer sensations,
which, in my opinion, constitutes the merits of our best
novels' (p. 74). Godwin himself in *Things as they are; or, the
Adventures of Caleb Williams* (1794)[40] called the work a
'narrative' in his first preface (p. 1) and referred to himself as
'the humble novelist' in the second preface (p. 2); while in his
account of the composition of the work he used the
expressions 'a narrative of fictitious adventure' and 'a book of
fictitious adventure' (pp. 335-6), avoiding all use of the word
'novel', frequently employing 'tale' and 'story', and observed
of his hero, 'it was necessary to make him, so to speak, the
tenant of an atmosphere of romance' (p. 337).

While Godwin was circumspect about the key terms, one of
his followers, Robert Bage, was not. The title page of his
principal work declared it to be *Hermsprong; or, Man as He is
Not. A Novel* (1796).[41] The resounding assertion of this title
was, however, slightly undercut by subsequent comments
within the text. The suitability of Miss Barton to be the
curate's wife includes the information that 'she was well read,
for her brother had the goodness to bring her all the novels
from the circulating library of the next market town' (p. 46);
while the curate himself recounts the bookseller's response to
the failure of his sermons to sell:

> He thought I might succeed in the novel line. To me,
> however, this does not seem probable; a novel writer ought
> to be well acquainted with human life and character; – I
> know little of either: besides, as novels are now pretty
> generally considered as the lowest of all human
> productions, I know not whether it is for the dignity of my
> cloth to have any thing to do with them. (pp. 49-50)

And this is reinforced by the narrator's own observation,
'surely none but plebeian souls will condescend to read these
humble memoirs' (p. 106). But one needs to consider these

31

views in the light of Bage's strong sense of irony evident throughout *Hermsprong*.

Another of what might loosely be termed the Godwinians, Thomas Holcroft, prefaced *The Adventures of Hugh Trevor* (1794)[42] with a rather earnest discussion of what he was about:

> Every man of determined enquiry, who will ask, without the dread of discovering more than he dares believe, what is divinity? what is law? what is physic? what is war? and what is trade? will have great reason to doubt at some times of the virtue, and at others of the utility, of each of these different employments. What profession should a man of principle, who is anxiously desirous to promote individual and general happiness, chuse for his son? The question has perplexed many parents, and certainly deserves a serious examination. Is a novel a good mode for discussing it, or a proper vehicle for moral truth? Of this some perhaps will be inclined to doubt. Others, whose intellectual powers were indubitably of the first order, have considered the art of novel writing as very essentially connected with moral instruction. Of this opinion was the famous Turgot, who we are told affirmed that more grand moral truths had been promulgated by novel writers than by any other class of men.
>
> But, though I consider the choice of a profession as the interesting question agitated in the following work, I have endeavoured to keep another important inquiry continually in view. This inquiry is, the growth of intellect . . . . (p. 3).

Others, interestingly, had no such intellectual qualms and demonstrated, possibly, the continuity of a tradition to that distinction of Congreve which opened this chapter. The works of Mrs Radcliffe and M. G. Lewis were full of wild and exciting adventures far removed from the day-to-day observations of their readers. Their recognition of this is to be seen on their title pages: *The Mysteries of Udolpho, A Romance* (1794); *The Italian, or the Confessional of the Black Penitents. A Romance*

(1797); and *The Monk. A Romance* (1796). The century opened and closed with a marked measure of agreement on the meaning of one key term at least.

As for the rest of the critical vocabulary, perhaps the best example of the implicit recognition of the importance of terms accompanied by a gesture bordering on despair at the nature of the problem is that provided by Oliver Goldsmith in his advertisement to *The Vicar of Wakefield* (1766),[43] which opened quite simply:

There are an hundred faults in this Thing . . . .

CHAPTER 2

———◆———

'ON FABLE AND ROMANCE'

THE most important eighteenth century critical statement relating to fiction was James Beattie's 'On Fable and Romance' published in his *Dissertations Moral and Critical* (1783).[1] Not only did Beattie make the first extended attempt to categorise different types of fiction, he also nominated specific examples of these types and discussed relevant details from his chosen texts. What is particularly noteworthy is the vocabulary he adopted, which constantly shifted its ground as the essay progressed.

Omitted from the essay printed below are Beattie's extensive digressions on the history and nature of chivalry and feudal government.

> The love of Truth is natural to man; and adherence to it, his indispensable duty. But to frame a fabulous narrative, for the purpose of instruction or of harmless amusement, is no breach of veracity, unless one were to obtrude it on the world for truth. The fabulist and novel-writer deceive nobody; because they do not even pretend that they are true; at least, what they may pretend in this way is considered only as words of course, to which nobody pays any regard. Fabulous narrative has accordingly been common in all ages of the world, and practised by teachers of the most respectable character.

It is owing, no doubt, to the weakness of human nature, that fable should ever have been found a necessary, or a convenient, vehicle for truth. But we must take human nature as it is; and, if a rude multitude cannot readily comprehend a moral or political doctrine, which they need to be instructed in, it may be as allowable, to illustrate that doctrine by a fable, in order to make them attend, and understand it, as it is for a physician to strengthen a weak stomach with cordials, in order to prepare it for the business of digestion. Such was the design of Jotham's parable of the trees chusing a king, in the ninth chapter of the book of Judges: and such that famous apologue, of a contention between the parts of a human body, by which Menenius Agrippa satisfied the people of Rome, that the welfare of the state depended on the union and good agreement of the several members of it. In fact, the common people are not well qualified for argument. A short and pithy proverb, which is easily remembered; or little tales, that appeal as it were to their senses, weigh more with them than demonstration.

We need not wonder, then, to find, that, in antient times, moral precepts were often delivered in the way of proverb or aphorism, and enforced and exemplified by fictitious narrative. Of those fables that are ascribed to Esop, some are no doubt modern, but others bear the stamp of antiquity. And nothing can be better contrived, than many of them are, for the purpose of impressing moral truth upon the memory, as well as the understanding. The disappointment, that frequently attends an excessive desire of accumulation, is finely exemplified in the fable of the dog and his shadow; and the ruinous and ridiculous nature of ambition is with equal energy illustrated in that of the frog and the ox. These little allegories we are apt to undervalue, because we learned them at school; but they are not for that reason the less valuable. We ought to prize them as monuments of antient wisdom, which have long contributed to the amusement and instruction of mankind, and are entitled to applause, on account of the propriety of the invention.

The Greek apologues ascribed to Esop, and the Latin ones of Phedrus, are masterpieces in this way of writing; and have hardly been equalled by the best of our modern fabulists. They are (at least many of them are, for some are trifling) remarkable for the simplicity of the style; and for the attention, which their authors have generally given, to the nature of the animals, and other things, that are introduced as agents and speaker. For in most of the modern fables, invented by Gay, La Fontaine, L'Estrange, Poggio, and others, the contrivance is less natural; and the language, though simple, is quaint, and full of witticism. That a dog should snap at the shadow of a dog, and by doing so lose the piece of flesh that was in his own mouth, is suitable to the character of the animal, and is indeed a very probable story: but that an elephant should converse with a bookseller about Greek authors, or a hare intreat a calf to carry her off on his back, and save her from the hounds, is a fiction wherein no regard is had to the nature of things. In this, as in the higher, sorts of fable, it is right to adhere, as much as may be, to probability. Brute animals, and vegetables too, may be allowed to speak and think: this indulgence is granted, from the necessity of the case; for, without it, their adventures could neither improve nor entertain us: but, with this exception, nature should not be violated; nor the properties of one animal or vegetable ascribed to a different one. Frogs have been seen inflated with air, at least, if not with pride; dogs may swim rivers; a man might taken a frozen viper to his bosom, and be bit to death for his imprudence; a fox might play with a tragedian's headpiece; a lamb and a wolf might drink of the same brook, and the former lose his life on the occasion; but who ever heard of an elephant reading Greek, or a hare riding on the back of a calf?

The wisdom of antiquity was not satisfied with conveying short lessons of morality in these apologues, or little tales. The poets entered upon a more extensive field of fable; in order to convey a more refined species of instruction, and to please by a more exquisite invention, and a higher probability. But I confine myself at present to prose fable.

One of the first specimens of Fabulous History, that appeared in these western parts of the world, is the *Cyropedia* of Xenophon. This work, however, we are not to consider as of the nature of Romance; for the outlines of the story are true. But the author takes the liberty to feign many incidents; that he may set in a variety of lights the character of Cyrus, whom he meant to exhibit as the model of a great and good prince. The work is very elegant and entertaining, and abounds in moral, political, and military knowledge. It is nevertheless, to be regretted, that we have no certain rule for distinguishing what is historical in it, from what is fabulous. The history of Cyrus the Great, the founder of the Persian empire, who has the honour to be mentioned by name in the Old Testament, is surely worth knowing. Yet we are much in the dark in regard to it. The account given of him by Herodotus differs greatly from Xenophon's; and in many cases we know not which to prefer. It is observable however, that Xenophon's description of the manner in which Cyrus took Babylon, by turning aside the course of the Euphrates, and entering, through the empty channel, under the walls of the city, agrees very well with several intimations of that event, which we find in the prophecies of Isaiah, Jeremiah, and Daniel.

Allegorical Fables were not unknown in the days of Xenophon. The Table, or Picture, of Cebes the Theban was written about this time; as well as the Story of Hercules conversing with Virtue and Vice and preferring the honours promised by the former to the pleasures offered by the latter. Cebes's Picture of human life excels in accuracy of description, justness of allegory, and a sweet simplicity of style. The fable of Hercules, as originally written by Prodicus, is lost, and seems not to have been extant in the time of Cicero; but Xenophon gives a full and elegant extract of it, in the beginning of his second book of *Memorabilia*.

Excepting some Allegorical fables scattered up and down in Plato, I do not recollect, among the Classick productions of Greece and Rome, any other remarkable specimens of prose fable: for the heathen mythology, though full of allegories, I am not to touch upon in this place, on account of its connection with poetry; and because my chief purpose is, to inquire into the origin and nature of the Modern Romance.

But, first, it may be proper to observe, that the Oriental nations have long been famous for fabulous narrative. The indolence peculiar to the genial climates of Asia, and the luxurious life which the kings and other great men, of those countries, lead in their seraglios, have made them seek for this sort of amusement, and set a high value upon it. When an Eastern prince happens to be idle, as he commonly is, and at a loss for expedients to kill the time, he commands his Grand Visir, or his favourite, to tell him stories. Being ignorant, and consequently credulous; having no passion for moral improvement, and little knowledge of nature; he does not desire, that they should be probable, or of an instructive tendency: it is enough if they be astonishing. And hence it is, no doubt, that those oriental tales are so extravagant. Every thing is carried on by inchantment and prodigy; by fairies, genii, and demons, and wooden horses, which, on turning a peg, fly through the air with inconceivable swiftness.

Another thing remarkable in these eastern tales, is, that their authors expatiate, with peculiar delight, in the description of magnificence; rich robes, gaudy furniture, sumptuous entertainments, and palaces shining in gold, or sparkling with diamonds. This too is conformable to the character and circumstances of the people. Their great men, whose taste has never been improved by studying the *simplicity* of nature and art, pique themselves chiefly on the *splendour* of their equipage, and the vast quantities of gold, jewels, and curious things, which they can heap together in their repositories.

The greatest, indeed the only, collection that I am

acquainted with, of Oriental fables, is the *Thousand and one tales*, commonly called *The Arabian Nights Entertainment*. This book, as we have it, is the work of Mons. Galland of the French Academy, who is said to have translated it from the Arabick original. But whether the tales be really Arabick, or invented by Mons. Galland, I have never been able to learn with certainty. If they be Oriental, they are translated with unwarrantable latitude; for the whole tenor of the style is in the French mode; and the Caliph of Bagdat, and the Emperor of China, are addressed in the same terms of ceremony, which are usual at the court of France. But this, though in my opinion it takes away from the value of the book, because I wish to see Eastern manners in an Eastern tale, is no proof, that the whole work is by Mons. Galland: for the French are so devoted to their own ceremonies, that they cannot endure any other; and seldom fail to season their translations, even of the gravest and most antient authors, with the fashionable forms of Parisian civility.

As the Arabian Nights Entertainment is a book which most young people in this country are acquainted with, I need not draw any character of it, or remark that it exactly answers the account already given of Oriental fable. There is in it great luxury of description, without any elegance; and great varieties of invention, but nothing that elevates the mind, or touches the heart. All is wonderful and incredible; and the astonishment of the reader is more aimed at, than his improvement either in morality, or in the knowledge of nature. Two things, however, there are, which deserve commendation, and may entitle it to one perusal. It conveys a pretty just idea of the government, and of some of the customs, of those eastern nations; and there is somewhere in it a story of a barber and his six brothers, that contains many good strokes of satire and comick description. I may add, that the character of the Caliph Haroun Alraschid is well drawn; and that the story of forty thieves destroyed by a slave is interesting, and artfully conducted. The voyages of Sinbad claim attention:

they were certainly attended to, by the author of Gulliver's Travels.

Tales in imitation of the Oriental have oft been attempted by English, and other European, authors; who, together with the figurative style, and wild invention of the Asiaticks, (which, being extravagant, are easily imitated) endeavour also to paint the customs and manners of that people. They give us good store of gold and jewels; and eunuchs, slaves, and necromancers in abundance: their personages are all Mahometan, or Pagan, and subject to the despotick government of Caliphs, Visirs, Bashaws, and Emperors; they drink sherbet, rest on sophas, and ride on dromedaries. We have Chinese tales, Tartarian Tales, Persian Tales, and Mogul Tales; not to mention the Tales of the Fairies and Genii; some of which I read in my younger days: but, as they have left no trace in the memory, I cannot now give any account of them.

In the *Spectator*, *Rambler*, and *Adventurer*, there are many fables in the eastern manner; most of them very pleasing, and of a moral tendency. *Rasselas*, by Johnson, and *Almoran and Hamet*, by Hawkesworth, are celebrated performances in this way. The former is admirable in description, and in that exquisite strain of sublime morality by which the writings of this great and good man are so eminently distinguished: – of the latter, the style is rhetorical and solemn, and the sentiments are in general good, but the plan is obscure, and so contrived as to infuse perplexing notions of the Divine Providence; a subject, which the elegant writer seems to have considered very superficially, and very confusedly. – Addison excels in this sort of fable. His vision of Mirzah, in the second volume of the Spectator, is the finest piece of the kind I have ever seen; uniting the utmost propriety of invention with a simplicity and melody of language, that melts the breast, while it charms and soothes the imagination.

Modern Prose Fable (if we omit those sorts of it that have been already hinted at) may be divided into two kinds; which, for the sake of distinction, I shall call the

ALLEGORICAL and the POETICAL. The Allegorical part of
modern prose fable may be subdivided into two species, the
Historical, and the *Moral*; and the Poetical part I shall also
subdivide into the two sorts, the *Serious*, and the *Comick*.
Thus the Prose Fable of the moderns may be distributed
into four species; whereof I shall speak in their order.
1.The Historical Allegory; 2. The Moral Allegory; 3. The
Poetical and Serious Fable; 4. The Poetical and Comick
Fable. These two last I comprehend under the general
term ROMANCE.

I. The FABULOUS HISTORICAL ALLEGORY exhibits real
history disguised by feigned names, and embellished with
fictitious adventures. This sort of fable may also be
subdivided into the *Serious* and the *Comick*.

1. Of the former, the best specimen I know is the *Argenis*;
written in Latin, about the beginning of the last century,
by John Barclay a Scotchman: and supposed to contain an
allegorical account of the Civil Wars of France during the
reign of Henry the third. I have read only part of the work:
and what I read I never took the trouble to decypher, by
means of the key which in some editions is subjoined to it,
or to compare the fictitious adventures of Meleander and
Lycogenes with the real adventures that are alluded to. I
therefore am not qualified to criticise the performance: but
can freely recommend it, as in some places very
entertaining, as abounding in lively description, and
remarkable for the most part, though not uniformly, for the
elegance of the language.

2. We have a *Comick* specimen of the Historical Allegory,
in the *History of John Bull*; a pamphlet written by the
learned and witty Dr. Arbuthnot, and commonly printed
among the works of Swift. It was published in Queen
Anne's time; and intended as a satire on the Duke of
Marlborough, and the rest of the Whig ministry, who were
averse to the treaty of peace that was soon after concluded
at Utrecht. The war, which the Queen carried on against
the French and Spaniards, is described under the form of a
law-suit, that John Bull, or England, is said to have been

engaged in with some litigious neighbours. A candid account of facts is not to be expected in an allegorical tale, written with the express design to make a party ridiculous. The work, however, has been much read, and frequently imitated. It is full of low humour, which in this piece the author affected; but which he could have avoided if he had thought proper; as he undoubtedly possessed more wit and learning, as well as virtue, than any other writer of his time, Addison excepted. In John Bull, great things are represented as mean; the style is consequently burlesque, and the phraseology, and most of the allusions, are taken from low life. There is a key printed, in the late editions, at the foot of each page, to mark the coincidence of the fable with the history of that period.

II. The second species of modern fabulous prose I distinguished by the name of the *Moral Allegory*. Moral and Religious Allegories were frequent in Europe about two hundred and fifty years ago. Almost all the Dramatick exhibitions of that time were of this character. In them, not only human virtues and vices personified, but also angels both good and evil, and beings more exalted than angels, were introduced, acting and speaking, as persons of the drama. Those plays, however, notwithstanding their incongruity, were written for the most part with the laudable design of exemplifying religious or moral truth; and hence were called Moralities. The publick exhibition of them in England ceased about the time of Shakespeare, or in the end of the sixteenth century: but several of the English Moralities are extant, and may be seen in some late collections of Old Plays. In Spain and Italy they continued longer in fashion. When Milton was on his travels, he happened to witness a representation of this kind, written by one Andrieno, and called *Original Sin*; from which, rude as it was, he is said to have formed the first draught of the plan of Paradise Lost.

Those were poetical allegories: but I confine myself to such as are in prose, and assume something of the historical form. – John Bunyan, an unlettered, but ingenious man, of the last century, was much given to this way of writing. His chief work is the *Pilgrim's Progress*; wherein the commencement, procedure, and completion of the Christian life, are represented allegorically, under the similitude of a journey. Few books have gone through so many editions, in so short a time, as the Pilgrim's Progress. It has been read by people of all ranks and capacities. The learned have not thought it below their notice: and among the vulgar it is an universal favourite. I grant, the style is rude, and even indelicate sometimes; that the invention is frequently extravagant; and that in more than one place it tends to convey erroneous notions in theology. But the tale is amusing, though the dialogue be often low: and some of the allegories are well contrived, and prove the author to have possessed powers of invention, which, if they had been refined by learning, might have produced something very noble. This work has been imitated, but with little success. The learned Bishop Patrick wrote the *Parable of the Pilgrim*: but I am not satisfied, that he borrowed the hint, as it is generally thought he did, from John Bunyan. There is no resemblance in the plan; nor does the Bishop speak a word of the Pilgrim's Progress, which I think he would have done, if he had seen it. Besides, Bunyan's tale is full of incident: Patrick's is dry, didactick, verbose, and exceedingly barren in the invention.

Gulliver's Travels are a sort of allegory; but rather Satirical and Political, than Moral. The work is in every body's hands; and has been criticized by many eminent writers. As far as the satire is levelled at human pride and folly; at the abuses of human learning; at the absurdity of speculative projectors; at those criminal or blundering expedients in policy, which we are apt to overlook, or even to applaud, because custom has made them familiar; so far the author deserves our warmest approbation, and his satire will be allowed to be perfectly just, as well as exquisitely severe. His fable is well conducted, and, for the most part, consistent with itself, and connected with probable circumstances. He personates a sea-faring man; and with wonderful propriety supports the plainness and simplicity of the character. And this gives to the whole narrative an air of truth; which forms an entertaining contrast, when we compare it with the wildness of the fiction. The style too deserves particular notice. It is not free from inaccuracy: but, as a model of easy and graceful simplicity, it has not been exceeded by any thing in our language; and well deserves to be studied by every person, who wishes to write pure English. – These, I think, are the chief merits of this celebrated work; which has been more read, than any other publication of the present century. Gulliver has something in him to hit every taste. The statesman, the philosopher, and the critick, will admire his keenness of satire, energy of description, and vivacity of language: the vulgar, and even children, who cannot enter into these refinements, will find their account in the story, and be highly amused with it.

But I must not be understood to praise the whole indiscriminately. The last of the four voyages, though the author has exerted himself in it to the utmost, is an absurd, and an abominable fiction. It is absurd: because, in presenting us with rational beasts, and irrational men, it proceeds upon a direct contradiction to the most obvious laws of nature, without deriving any support from either the dreams of the credulous, or the prejudices of the ignorant. And it is abominable: because it abounds in filthy and indecent images; because the general tone of the satire is exaggerated into absolute falsehood, and because there must be something of an irreligious tendency in a work, which, like this, ascribes the perfection of reason, and of happiness, to a race of beings, who are said to be destitute of every religious idea. – But, what is yet worse, if any thing can be worse, this tale represents human nature itself as the object of contempt and abhorrence. Let the ridicule of wit be pointed at the follies, and let the scourge of satire be brandished at the crimes, of mankind; all this is both pardonable, and praiseworthy; because it may be done with a good intention, and produce good effects. But when a writer endeavours to make us dislike and despise, every one his neighbour, and be dissatisfied with that Providence, who has made us what we are, and whose dispensations towards the human race are so peculiarly, and so divinely beneficent; such a writer, in so doing, proves himself the enemy, not of man only, but of goodness himself; and his work can never be allowed to be innocent, till impiety, malevolence, and misery, cease to be evils.

The Tale of a Tub, at least the narrative part of it, is another Allegorical fable, by the same masterly hand; and, like the former, supplies no little matter, both of admiration, and of blame. As a piece of humourous writing, it is unequalled. It was the author's first performance, and is, in the opinion of many, his best. The style may be less correct, than that of some of his latter works; but in no other part of his writings has he displayed so rich a fund of wit, humour, and ironical satire, as in the Tale of a Tub. The subject is Religion: but the allegory, under which he typifies the Reformation, is too mean for an argument of so great dignity; and tends to produce, in the mind of the reader, some very disagreeable associations, of the most solemn truths with ludicrous ideas. Professed wits may say what they please; and the fashion, as well as the laugh, may be for a time on their side: but it is a dangerous thing, and the sign of an intemperate mind, to acquire a habit of making every thing matter of merriment and sarcasm. We dare not take such liberty with our neighbour, as to represent whatever he does or says in a ridiculous light; and yet some men (I wish I could not say, clergymen) think themselves privileged to take liberties of this sort with the most awful, and most benign dispensations of Providence. That this author has repeatedly done so, in the work before us, and elsewhere, is too plain to require proof. The compliments he pays the Church of England I allow to be very well founded, as well as part of the satire, which he levels at the Church of Rome; though I wish he had expressed both the one and the other with a little more decency of language. But, as to his abuse of the Presbyterians, whom he represents as more absurd and frantick, than perhaps any rational beings ever were since the world began, every person of sense and candour, whether Presbyterian or not, will acknowledge it, if he know any thing of their history, to be founded in gross misrepresentation. There are other faults in this work, besides those already specified; many vile images, and obscene allusions; such as no well-bred man could read, or endure to hear read, in polite company.

III. I come now to the second species of modern prose fable, to which I gave the appellation of *Poetical*, to distinguish it from the former *Allegorical* species. In reading the *Allegorical Prose Fable*, we attend not only to the fictitious events that occur in the narrative, but also those real events that are typefied by the allegory: whereas in the *poetical prose fable* we attend only to the events that are before us. Thus, in the Tale of a Tub, I not only mind what is related of three brothers, Peter, Martin, and Jack, but also keep it constantly in view, that those three brothers are by the author meant to be the representatives of the Romish, English, and Presbyterian churches: whereas when I read Robinson Crusoe, or Tom Jones, I attend singly to the narrative; and no *key* is necessary to make me comprehend the author's meaning.

Considering this as the chief part of my subject, I dispatched the former parts as briefly as I could, that I might have the more time to employ upon it. The rise and progress of the MODERN ROMANCE, or POETICAL PROSE FABLE, is connected with many topicks of importance, which would throw (if fully illustrated) great light upon the history and politicks, the manners, and the literature, of these latter ages. – Observe, that I call this sort of fable *poetical*, from the nature of the invention; and *prose*, because it is not in verse. Prose and Verse are opposite, but Prose and Poetry may be consistent. *Tom Jones*, and *Telemachus*, are epick, or narrative poems, though written in prose; the one Comick, the other Serious and Heroick. (pp. 505-18)

46

This government [feudal government] it was that, among many other strange institutions, gave rise to Chivalry: and it was Chivalry, which gave birth and form to that sort of fabulous writing, which we term *Romance*.

The word is Spanish, and signifies the Spanish Tongue: and the name is suitable enough to the nature of a language whereof the greater part is derived from the antient Latin or Roman. It seems, the first Spanish books were fabulous: and, being called Romance, on account of the tongue in which they were written, the same name was afterward given, by the other nations of Europe, not to Spanish books, which is the proper application of the term, but to a certain class of fabulous writings. (p.522)

Society became more regular, and more secure. The knight-errant was no longer of any use. He was even found troublesome; and the law considered him as a vagrant.

But the old spirit of chivalry was not extinguished: and what remained of it was inflamed by the books called Romances, which were now common in Europe; and, being written in the vulgar tongues, and filled with marvellous adventures, could not fail to be eagerly sought after and read, at a time when books were rare, and men credulous. (pp. 550-1)

Love was not the only theme of the Provensal poets. They occasionally joined their voices to those of the pope, and the monks, and the kings of Europe, to rouse the spirit of crusading. Satire, religious and political, as well as personal, and little tales or novels, with portions of real history, and even theological controversy, were also interwoven in their compositions. (p. 557)

But the final extirpation of chivalry and all its chimeras was now approaching. What laws and force could not accomplish was brought about by the humour and satire of one writer. This was the illustrious Miguel de Cervantes Saavedra. He was born in Madrid in the year one thousand five hundred and forty-nine. He seems to have had every advantage of education, and to have been a master in polite learning. But in other respects fortune was not very indulgent. He served many years in the armies of Spain, in no higher station, than that of a private soldier. In that capacity he fought at the battle of Lepanto, under Don John of Austria, and had the misfortune, or, as he rather thought, the honour, to lose his left hand. Being now disqualified for military service, he commenced author; and wrote many Dramatick pieces, which were acted with applause on the Spanish theatre, and acquired him both money and reputation. But want of economy and unbounded generosity dissipated the former: and he was actually confined in prison for debt, when he composed the first part of *The History of Don Quixote*: a work, which every body admires for its humour; but which ought also to be considered as a most useful performance, that brought about a great revolution in the manners and literature of Europe, by banishing the wild dreams of chivalry, and reviving the taste for the simplicity of nature. In this view, the publication of Don Quixote forms an important era in the history of mankind.

Don Quixote is represented as a man, whom it is impossible not to esteem for his cultivated understanding, and the goodness of his heart: but who, by poring night and day upon the old romances, had impaired his reason to such a degree, as to mistake them for history, and form the design of going through the world, in the character, and with the accoutrements, of a knight errant. His distempered fancy takes the most common occurrences for adventures similar to those he had read in his books of chivalry. And thus, the extravagance of these books being placed, as it were, in the same groups with the appearances of nature and the real business of life, the hideous disproportion of the former becomes so glaring by the contrast, that the most inattentive observer cannot fail to be struck with it. The person, the pretensions, and the exploits, of the errant knight, are held up to view in a thousand ridiculous attitudes. In a word, the humour and satire are irresistible; and their effects instantaneous.

This work no sooner appeared, than chivalry vanished, as now melts before the sun. Mankind awoke as from a dream. They laughed at themselves for having been so long imposed on by absurdity; and wondered they had not made the discovery sooner. It astonished them to find, that nature and good sense could yield a more exquisite entertainment, than they had ever derived from the most sublime phrenzies of chivalry. For, that this was indeed the case: that Don Quixote was more read, and more relished, than any other romance had ever been, we may infer, from the sudden and powerful effects it produced on the sentiments of mankind; as well as from the declaration of the author himself; who tells us, that upwards of twelve thousand copies of the first part were sold, before the second could be got ready for the press: – an amazing rapidity of sale, at a time when the readers and purchasers of books were but an inconsiderable number compared to what they are in our days. 'The very children, (says he) handle it, boys read it, men understand, and old people applaud, the performance. It is no sooner laid down by one, than another takes it up; some struggling, and some entreating, for a sight of it. In fine, (continues he) this history is the most delightful, and the least prejudicial, entertainment, that ever was seen; for, in the whole book, there is not the least shadow of a dishonourable word, nor one thought unworthy of a good catholick.'

Don Quixote occasioned the death of the Old Romance, and gave birth to the New. Fiction henceforth divested herself of her gigantick size, tremendous aspects, and frantick demeanour; and, descending to the level of common life, conversed with man as his equal, and as a polite and chearful companion. Not that every subsequent Romance-writer adopted the plan, or the manner, of Cervantes: but it was from him they learned to avoid extravagance, and to imitate nature. And now probability was as much studied, as it had been formerly neglected.

But before I proceed to the New Romance, on which I shall be very brief, it is proper just to mention a species of

Romantick narrative, which cannot be called either Old or New, but is a strange mixture of both. Of this kind are the *Grand Cyrus*, *Clelia*, and *Cleopatra*; each consisting of ten or a dozen large volumes, and pretending to have a foundation in antient history. In them, all facts and characters, real and fabulous; and all systems of policy and manners, the Greek, the Roman, the Feudal, and the modern, are jumbled together and confounded: as if a painter should represent Julius Caesar drinking tea with Queen Elizabeth, Jupiter, and Dulcinea del Toboso, and having on his head the laurel wreaths of antient Rome, a suit of Gothick armour on his shoulders, laced ruffles at his wrist, a pipe of tobacco in his mouth, and a pistol and tomahawk stuck in his belt. But I should go beyond my depth, if I were to criticize any of those enormous compositions. For, to confess the truth, I never had patience to read one half of the volumes; nor met with a person, who could give me any other account of them, than that they are intolerably tedious, and unspeakably absurd.

The New Romance may be divided into the *Serious* and the *Comick*: and each of these kinds may be variously subdivided.

I. 1. Of *Serious* Romances, some follow *the historical arrangement*: and, instead of beginning, like Homer and Virgil, in the middle of the subject, give a continued narrative of the life of some one person, from his birth to his establishment in the world, or till his adventures may be supposed to have come to an end. Of this sort is *Robinson Crusoe*. The account commonly given of that well-known work is as follows.

Alexander Selkirk, a Scotch mariner, happened, by some accident which I forget, to be left in the uninhabited island of Juan Fernandes in the South Seas. Here he continued four years alone, without any other means of supporting life, than by running down goats, and killing such other animals as he could come at. To defend himself from dangers during the night, he built a house of stones rudely put together, which a gentleman, who had been in it, (for it

was extant when Anson arrived there) described to me as
so very small, that one person could with difficulty crawl in
and stretch himself at length. Selkirk was delivered by an
English vessel, and returned home. A late French writer
says, he had become so fond of the savage state, that he
was unwilling to quit it. But that is not true. The French
writer either confounds the real story of Selkirk with a
fabulous account of one Philip Quarl, written after
Robinson Crusoe, of which it is a paltry imitation; or
wilfully misrepresents the fact, in order to justify, as far as
he is able, an idle conceit, which, since the time of
Rousseau, has been in fashion among infidel and affected
theorists on the continent, that savage life is most natural
to us, and that the more a man resembles a brute in his
mind, body, and behaviour, the happier he becomes, and
the more perfect. – Selkirk was advised to get his story put
in writing, and published. Being illiterate himself, he told
every thing he could remember to Daniel Defoe, a
professed author of considerable note; who, instead of
doing justice to the poor man, is said to have applied these
materials to his own use, by making them the groundwork
of Robinson Crusoe; which he soon after published, and
which, being very popular, brought him a good deal of
money.

Some have thought, that a lovetale is necessary to make
a romance interesting. But Robinson Crusoe, though there
is nothing of love in it, is one of the most interesting
narratives that ever was written; at least in all that part
which relates to the desert island; being founded on a
passion still more prevalent than love, the desire of self-
preservation; and therefore likely to engage the curiosity of
every class of readers, both old and young, both learned
and unlearned.

I am willing to believe, that Defoe shared the profits of
this publication with the poor seaman: for there is an air of
humanity in it, which one would not expect from an author
who is an arrant cheat. In the preface to his second
volume, he speaks feelingly enough of the harm done him

by those who had abridged the first, in order to reduce the price. 'The injury, says he, which those men do to the *proprietors* of works, is a practice all honest men abhor: and they believe they may challenge them to show the difference between that, and robbing on the highway, or breaking open a house. If they cannot show any difference in the crime, they will find it hard to show, why there should be any difference in the punishment.' Is it to be imagined, that any man of common prudence would talk in this way, if he were conscious, that he might himself be proved guilty of that very dishonesty which he so severely condemns?

Be this however as it may, for I have no authority to *affirm* any thing on either side, Robinson Crusoe must be allowed, by the most rigid moralist, to be one of those novels, which one may read, not only with pleasure, but also with profit. It breathes throughout a spirit of piety and benevolence: it sets out in a very striking light, as I have elsewhere observed, the importance of the mechanick arts, which they, who know not what it is to be without them, are so apt to undervalue: it fixes in the mind a lively idea of the horrors of solitude, and, consequently, of the sweets of social life, and of the blessings we derive from conversation, and mutual aid: and it shows, how, by labouring with one's own hands, one may secure independence, and open for one's self many sources of health and amusement. I agree, therefore, with Rousseau, that this is one of the best books that can be put in the hands of children. – The style is plain, but not elegant, nor perfectly grammatical: and the second part of the story is tiresome.

2. A second species of the Modern Serious Romance is that, which follows *the poetical arrangement*; and, in order to shorten the time of the action, begins in the middle of the story. Such, partly, are *Sir Charles Grandison*, and *Clarissa Harlowe*, by Mr. Richardson. That author has adopted a plan of narrative of a peculiar kind: the persons, who bear a part in the action, are themselves the relaters of it. This is

done by means of letters, or epistles; wherein the story is continued from time to time, and the passions freely expressed, as they arise from every change of fortune, and while the persons concerned are supposed to be ignorant of the events that are to follow. And thus, the several agents are introduced in their turns, speaking, or, which is the same thing in this case, writing, suitably to their respective feelings, and characters: so that the fable is partly Epick, and partly Dramatick. There are some advantages in this form of narrative. It prevents all anticipation of the catastrophe; and keeps the reader in the same suspense, in which the persons themselves are supposed to be: and it pleases further, by the varieties of style, suited to the different tempers and sentiments of those who write the letters. But it has also its inconveniences. For, unless the fable be short and simple, this mode of narration can hardly fail to run out into an extravagant length, and to be encumbered with repetitions. And indeed, Richardson himself, with all his powers of invention, is apt to be tedious, and to fall into a minuteness of detail, which is often unnecessary. His pathetick scenes, too, are overcharged, and so long continued, as to wear out the spirits of the reader. Nor can it be denied, that he has given too much prudery to his favourite women, and something of pedantry or finicalness to his favourite men. – Clementina was, no doubt, intended as a pattern of female excellence: but, though she may claim veneration as a saint, it is impossible to love her as a woman. And Grandison, though both a good and a great character, is in every thing so perfect, as in many things to discourage imitation; and so distant, and so formal, as to forbid all familiarity, and, of course, all cordial attachment. Alworthy is as good a man as he: but his virtue is purely human; and, having a little of our own weakness in it, and assuming no airs of superiority, invites our acquaintance, and engages our love.

For all this, however, Richardson is an author of uncommon merit. His characters are well drawn, and distinctly marked; and he delineates the operation of the passions with a picturesque accuracy, which discovers great knowledge of human nature. His moral sentiments are profound and judicious; in wit and humour he is not wanting; his dialogue is sometimes formal; but many of his conversation-pieces are executed with elegance and vivacity. For the good tendency of his writings he deserves still higher praise; for he was a man of unaffected piety, and had the improvement of his fellow-creatures very much at heart.

Yet, like most other novel-writers, he represents some of his wicked characters as more agreeable than was necessary to his plan; which may make the example dangerous. I do not think, that an author of fable, in either prose or verse, should make his bad characters completely bad: for, in the first place, that would not be natural, as the worst of men have generally some good in them: and, secondly, that would hurt his design, by making the tale less captivating; as the history of a person, so very worthless as to have not one good quality, would give disgust or horror, instead of pleasure. But, on the other hand, when a character, like Richardson's *Lovelace*, whom the reader ought to abominate for his crimes, is adorned with youth, beauty, eloquence, wit, and every other intellectual and bodily accomplishment, it is to be feared, that thoughtless young men may be tempted to imitate, even while they disapprove, him. Nor is it a sufficient apology to say, that he is punished in the end. The reader knows, that the story is a fiction: but he knows too, that such talents and qualities, if they were to appear in real life, would be irresistably engaging; and he may even fancy, that a character so highly ornamented must have been a favourite of the author. Is there not, then reason to apprehend, that some readers will be more inclined to admire the gay profligate, than to fear his punishment? – Achilles in Homer, and Macbeth in Shakespeare, are not without great and good qualities, to raise our admiration, and make us take concern in what befals them. But no person is in any danger of being perverted by their example; their criminal conduct being described and directed in such a manner, by the art of the poet, as to show, that it is hateful in itself, and necessarily productive of misery, both to themselves, and to mankind.

I may add, that the punishment of Lovelace is a death, not of infamy, according to our notions, but rather of honour; which surely he did not deserve: and that the immediate cause of it is, not his wickedness, but some inferiority to his antagonist in the use of a small sword. With a little more skill in that exercise, he might, for any thing that appears in the story, have triumphed over Clarissa's avenger, as he had done over herself, and over the censure of the world. Had his crime been represented as the necessary cause of a series of mortifications, leading him gradually to infamy, ruin, and despair, or producing by probable means an exemplary repentance, the fable would have been more useful in a moral view, and perhaps more interesting. And for the execution of such a plan the genius of Richardson seems to me to have been extremely well formed. – These remarks are offered, with a view rather to explain my own ideas of fable, than to detract from an author, who was an honour to his country, and of whose talents and virtues I am a sincere admirer.

His Epistolary manner has been imitated by many novel-writers; particularly by Rousseau in his *New Eloisa*; a work, not more remarkable for its eloquence, which is truly great, than for its glaring and manifold inconsistencies. For it is full of nature and extravagance, of sound philosophy and wild theory, of useful instruction and dangerous doctrines.

II. 1. The second kind of the New Romance is the *Comick*; which, like the first, may, with respect to the arrangement of events, be subdivided into the *Historical* and the *Poetical*.

Of the Historical form are the novels of Marivaux, and *Gil Blas* by M. le Sage. These authors abound in wit and humour; and give natural descriptions of present manners, in a simple, and very agreeable, style. And their works may be read without danger; being for the most part of a moral tendency. Only Le Sage appears to have had a partiality for cheats and sharpers: for these are the people whom he introduces often; nor does he paint them in the odious colours, that properly belong to all such pests of society. Even his hero Gil Blas he has made too much a rogue: which, as he is the relater of his own story, has this disagreeable effect, that it conveys to us, all the while we read him, an idea that we are in bad company, and deriving entertainment from the conversation of a man whom we cannot esteem.

Smollet follows the same historical arrangement in *Roderick Random* and *Peregrine Pickle*: two performances, of which I am sorry to say, that I can hardly allow them any other praise, than that they are humourous and entertaining. He excels, however, in drawing the characters of seamen; with whom in his younger days he had the best opportunities of being acquainted. He seems to have collected a vast number of merry stories; and he tells them with much vivacity and energy of expression. But his style often approaches to bombast; and many of his humourous pictures are exaggerated beyond all bounds of probability. And it does not appear that he knew how to contrive a regular fable, by making his events mutually dependent, and all co-operating to one and the same final purpose. – On the morality of these novels I cannot compliment him at all. He is often inexcusably licentious. Profligates, bullies, and misanthropes, are among his favourite characters. A duel he seems to have thought one of the highest efforts of human virtue; and playing dextrously at billiards a very genteel accomplishment. Two of his pieces, however, deserve to be mentioned with more respect. Count Fathom, though an improbable tale, is pleasing, and upon the whole not immoral. And Sir Launcelot Greaves, though still more has great merit; and is truly original in the execution, notwithstanding that the hint is borrowed from Don Quixote.

2. The second species of the New Comick Romance is

that which, in the arrangement of events, follows the poetical order; and which may properly enough be called the Epick Comedy, or rather the Comick Epick poem: *Epick*, because it is narrative; and *Comick*, because it is employed on the business of common life, and takes its persons from the middle and lower ranks of mankind.

This form of the Comick Romance has been brought to perfection in England by Henry Fielding; who seems to have possessed more wit and humour, and more knowledge of mankind, than any other person of modern times, Shakespeare excepted; and whose great natural abilities were refined by a classical taste, which he had acquired by studying the best authors of antiquity; though it cannot be denied, that he appears on some occasions to have been rather too ostentatious, both of his learning, and of his wit.

Some have said, that Joseph Andrews is the best performance of Fielding. But its chief merit is parson Adams; who is indeed a character of masterly invention, and, next to Don Quixote, the most ludicrous personage that ever appeared in romance. This work, though full of exquisite humour, is blameable in many respects. Several passages offend by their indelicacy. And it is not very easy to imagine, what could induce the author to add to the other faults of his hero's father Wilson the infamy of lying and cowardice; and then to dismiss him, by the very improbable means, to a life of virtuous tranquillity, and endeavour to render him upon the whole a respectable character. Some youthful irregularities, rather hinted at than described, owing more to imprudence and unlucky accident than to confirmed habits of sensuality, and followed by inconvenience, perplexity, and remorse, their natural consequences, may, in a comic tale, be assigned even to a favourite personage, and, by proper management, form a very instructive part of the narration: but crimes, that bring dishonour, or that betray a hard heart, or an injurious disposition, should never be fixed on a character who them [sic] poet or novel-writer means to recommend to our esteem. On this principle, Fielding might be vindicated in regard to all the censurable conduct of Tom Jones, provided he had been less particular in describing it: and, by the same rule, Smollet's system of youthful profligacy, as exemplified in some of his libertines, is altogether without excuse.

Tom Jones and *Amelia* are Fielding's best performances; and the most perfect, perhaps, of their kind in the world. The fable of the latter is entirely poetical, and of the true epick species; beginning in the middle of the action, or rather as near the end as possible, and introducing the previous occurrences, in the form of a narrative episode. Of the former, the introductory part follows the historical arrangement; but the fable becomes strictly poetical, as soon as the great action of the piece commences, that is, if I mistake not, immediately after the sickness of Alworthy: for, from that period, the incidents proceed in an uninterrupted series to the final event, which happens about two months after.

Since the days of Homer, the world has not seen a more artful Epick fable. The characters and adventures are wonderfully diversified: yet the circumstances are all so natural, and rise so easily from one another, and co-operate with so much regularity in bringing on, even while they seem to retard, the catastrophe, that the curiosity of the reader is always kept awake, and, instead of flagging, grows more and more impatient as the story advances, till at last it becomes downright anxiety. And when we get to the end, and look back on the whole contrivance, we are amazed to find, that of so many incidents there should be so few superfluous; that in such variety of fiction there should be so great probability; and that so complex a tale should be so perspicuously conducted, with perfect unity of design. – These remarks may be applied either to *Tom Jones* or to *Amelia*: but they are made with a view to the former chiefly; which might give scope to a great deal of criticism, if I were not in haste to conclude the subject. Since the time of Fielding, who died in the year one thousand seven hundred and fifty-four, the Comick Romance, as far as I am acquainted with it, seems to have been declining apace, from simplicity and nature, into improbability and affectation.

Let not the usefulness of Romance-writing be estimated by the length of my discourse upon it. Romances are a dangerous recreation. A few, no doubt, of the best may be friendly to good taste and good morals; but far the greater part are unskilfully written, and tend to corrupt the heart, and stimulate the passions. A habit of reading them breeds a dislike to history, and all the substantial parts of knowledge; withdraws the attention from nature, and truth; and fills the mind with extravagant thoughts, and too often with criminal propensities. I would therefore caution my young reader against them: or, if he must, for the sake of amusement, and that he may have something to say upon the subject, indulge himself in this way now and then, let it be sparingly, and seldom. (pp. 562-74)

There is a certain amount of ambiguity here both in expression and ideas, but for the most part Beattie demonstrates the major critical approaches of his period.

It is significant that so late in the century his key term, the word used for the whole basis of his categorisation, is 'Romance', and that 'novel' and 'novel-writer' should be so sparingly used, and at times in ways that add to the ambiguity. Thus he early on declares of Xenophon's *Cyropaedia*, 'this work, however, we are not to consider as of the nature of Romance; for the outlines of the story are true . . . it is . . . to be regretted, that we have no certain rule for distinguishing what is historical in it, from what is fabulous' (p.37), and subsequently iterates that 'the proper application of the term [Romance] is . . . to a certain class of fabulous writings' (p.47). Yet having established that there appears to have been a high degree of the historically accurate in *Robinson Crusoe*, he nevertheless continues to observe that it 'must be allowed by the most rigid moralist, to be one of those novels, which one may read, not only with pleasure, but also with profit' (p.52). Beattie's ambivalence of

59

attitude to the relationship of truth and fiction, so very typical of eighteenth century literary criticism, is evident throughout. His argument opens with the statement that 'the fabulist and the novel-writer deceive nobody . . . they do not even pretend that they are true' (p.34), but later claims the fable to be 'a vehicle for truth' (p.35). He praises *Gulliver's Travels* in that 'the whole narrative [has] an air of truth' but almost immediately subsequently condemns Book IV of the same work as 'an absurd, and an abominable fiction' (p.44). Smollett is marked down for being exaggerated beyond all bounds of probability, while Fielding is praised in that in *Tom Jones* 'of so many incidents there should be so few superfluous; and that in such variety of fiction there should be so great probability' (p.58). Problems associated with fiction and truth are explored more fully in the next chapter.

Beattie also homes in on the other crucial element of eighteenth century criticism of prose fiction: the moral quality. His position again indicates a measure of vacillation. That the chief business of fable and romance is 'impressing moral truth' is one of his opening statements, and he talks of the 'laudable design of exemplifying religious or moral truth'. Consistent with this stand is his declaration that the fourth book of *Gulliver's Travels* is 'abominable: because it abounds in filthy and indecent images; because the general tenor of the satire is exaggerated into absolute falsehood; and because there must be something of an irreligious tendency in a work, which, like this, ascribes the perfection of reason and of happiness, to a race of beings, who are said to be destitute of every religious idea' (p.44). Smollett is damned along with Swift; 'of the morality of these novels [*Roderick Random* and *Peregrine Pickle*] I cannot compliment him at all' (p.56). There is a slight hiccough in the logic when of *Tale of a Tub* he comments that the content and style are 'such as no well-bred man could read, or endure to hear read, in polite company' (p.46), where the final three words are reminiscent of Montaigne's distinction between books that 'lie in the Parlour Window' and those one takes to one's 'Closet'.[2] When Beattie comes to Richardson and Fielding he identifies one of the major problems facing those writers who wished to promote moral notions: 'Grandison, though both a good and a great character, is in every thing so perfect, as to forbid all familiarity, and, of course, all cordial attachment. Alworthy is as good a man as he: but his virtue is purely human; and, having a little of our own weakness in it, and assuming no airs of superiority, invites our acquaintance, and engages our love' (p.53). But by the end of his essay Beattie's argument has changed direction somewhat. Initially having seen such works as vehicles of moral truth, he concludes, 'Romances are a dangerous recreation . . . a habit of reading them . . . fills the mind with extravagant thoughts, and too often with criminal propensities.' In this too his essay is a microcosm of eighteenth century critical opinion, as will be seen in chapter 4.

The argument is not restricted to the twin pillars of truth and morality: he also explores such notions as a proper style – *Gulliver's Travels* is 'a model of easy and graceful simplicity, it has not been exceeded by any thing in our language; and well deserves to be studied by every person, who wishes to write pure English' (p.44). The idea of suitability of diction is reinforced by the flat statement, 'I wish to see Eastern manners in an Eastern tale' (p.39), while the concept that there may be some formula for successful fiction is explored and rejected: 'Some have thought, that a lovetale is necessary to make a romance interesting. But Robinson Crusoe, though there is nothing of love in it, is one of the most interesting narratives that ever was written' (p.51). And Beattie's commentary upon the advantages and disadvantages of the epistolary form as used specifically by Richardson is possibly the most succinct to be found in the eighteenth century.

It is clear that Beattie is a man full of ideas relevant to the topic, but who is bedevilled by inadequacies of vocabulary. The works he discusses are variously termed romance, fable, tale, story, history, novel, and performance, terms which are indiscriminately applied within a framework which attempts to rationalise names with expressions such as allegorical prose fable. But the area which evidently poses most problems is that relating to truth. Truth is his starting point – all men desire it; fiction does not pretend to be true, nevertheless it is a vehicle for truth. This becomes initially specifically moral truth, and later religious and moral truth, and in the search after this holy grail untruths are permitted: vegetables may be allowed to speak. He then shifts from truth to probability and introduces the notion of a higher probability, and this device of qualifying and thus confusing key ideas is to be seen particularly with the word *history* which is used in opposition to the fabulous, and thus by implication as a synonym for truth. But it is also used to refer to works of fiction. At one point he resorts to referring to 'real history'; there are similar references to 'real life' and 'real business of life' as if acknowledging that there are unreal states of these ideas. Nature too, one of the great problem words of the century, shifts its ground as often as it does in *Essay on Man*, and is inevitably bound up with truth.

Throughout the succeeding chapters it will be seen that Beattie in this essay combines most of the strengths and weaknesses, perceptions and nelsonian moments, in such a way as to make him the archetypical critic of eighteenth century fiction. What is above all important is that his essay demonstrates the growing realisation of the time that for criticism to be well-founded it was necessary for the critic to recognise the form of the work being criticised. Beattie's is the most careful attempt at distinction and definition that his age produced. What needs to be explored is the extent to which his divisions aid the twentieth century reader.

CHAPTER 3

◆

AMELIA'S NOSE:
PERCEPTIONS OF REALITY

D URING the course of providing a detailed critique of the story her niece Anna had sent to her Jane Austen commented:

> My corrections have not been more important than before; – here & there, we have thought the sense might be expressed in fewer words – and I have scratched out Sir Tho: from walking with the other Men to the Stables &c the very day after his breaking his arm – for though I find your Papa *did* walk out immediately after *his* arm was set, I think it can be so little usual as to *appear* unnatural in a book.[1]

This is very similar to an opinion expressed over a hundred years before by Mrs Manley in her address 'To the reader' prefixed to *The Secret History of Queen Zarah* (1705):

> *For there are Truths that are not always probable; as for Example, 'tis an allowed truth in the* Roman History, *that* Nero *put his Mother to Death, but 'tis a Thing against all Reason and Probability that a Son should embrue his Hand in the Blood of his own Mother; it is also no less probable that a single Captain shou'd at the Head of a Bridge stop a whole Army, although 'tis probable that a small Number of Soldiers might stop, in Defiles, Prodigious Armies, because the Situation of a Place favours the Design, and*

renders them almost equal. He that writes a True History ought to place the Accidents as they Naturally happen, without endeavouring to sweeten them for to procure a greater credit, because he is not obliged to answer for their Probability; but he that composes a History to his Fancy, gives his Heroes what Characters he pleases, and places the Accidents as he thinks fit without believing he shall be contradicted by other Historians, therefore he is obliged to Write nothing that is improbable; 'tis nevertheless allowable that an Historian shows the Elevation of his Genius, when advancing improbable Actions, he gives them the Colours and Appearances capable of Persuading.[2]

The truth of these highly perceptive observations on the disparity between reality and the reader's notion of the proper representations of reality, and between reality and the way in which an author is 'obliged' to present his details, is well seen in the contemporary response to Fielding's *Amelia* (1751).[3] In the opening chapter to Book II Booth begins to recount to Miss Mathews the story of his marriage:

'If the vulgar Opinion of the Fatality in Marriage had ever any Foundation, it surely appeared in my Marriage with my Amelia. I knew her in the first Dawn of her Beauty; and, I believe, Madam, she had as much as ever fell to the Share of a Woman; but though I always admired her, it was long without any Spark of Love. Perhaps the general Admiration which at that Time pursued her, the Respect paid her by Persons of the highest Rank, and the numberless Addresses which were made her by Men of great Fortune, prevented my aspiring at the Possession of those Charms, which seemed so absolutely out of my Reach. However it was, I assure you, the Accident which deprived her of the Admiration of others, made the first great Impression on my Heart in her Favour. The Injury done to her Beauty by the overturning of a Chaise, by which, as you may well remember, her lovely Nose was *beat all to pieces*, gave me an Assurance that the Woman who had been so adored for the Charms of her Person, deserved

a much higher Adoration to be paid to her Mind: For that
she was in the latter Respect infinitely more superior to the
rest of her Sex, than she had ever been in the former.'
(p.66)

This appears to have been based upon truth to life, for
Fielding's first wife, Charlotte Cradock, had had her nose
destroyed also as the result of the overturning of a chaise.
Real though this accident to Charlotte Cradock was, when
the details were transferred to Amelia contemporary critics
would have none of it. The anonymous reviewer in *The London
Magazine* based his objection upon a notion very similar to
that enunciated by Jane Austen:

> A novel, like an epick poem, shou'd at least have the
> appearance of truth; and for this reason notorious
> anachronisms ought to be carefully avoided. In this novel,
> there is a glaring one; for Gibraltar has not been besieged
> since the year 1727, consequently, if Mr. Booth was
> wounded at that siege, and married to his Amelia before it,
> he could neither be a young man, nor his wife a young
> handsome lady, when the masquerades began at Ranelagh,
> which is not above three or four years since. Another
> imperfection, in our opinion, is, that the author should
> have taken care to have had Amelia's nose so completely
> cured, and set to rights, after its being beat all to pieces,
> by the help of some eminent surgeon, that not so much as a
> scar remained, and that she shone forth in all her beauty as
> much after that accident as before, to the unspeakable
> sorrow of all her envious rivals.[4]

Samuel Johnson followed this line of regretting the heroine's
deformity. Mrs Piozzi recorded:

> His attention to veracity was without equal or example:
> and when I mentioned Clarissa as a perfect character; 'On
> the contrary (said he), you may observe there is always
> something which she prefers to truth. Fielding's Amelia
> was the most pleasing heroine of all the romances (he

said); but that vile broken nose never cured, ruined the sale of perhaps the only book, which being printed off betimes one morning, a new edition was called for before night.'[5]

Johnson's attention to veracity was in fact somewhat awry at this point for as W. B. Todd pointed out the initial print run of 5000 copies more than satisfied demand.[6]

Amelia's partial noselessness was not entirely responsible for a public response less than might have been expected after the successes of *Joseph Andrews* and *Tom Jones*, but it was seized upon by Fielding's detractors. Bonnell Thornton made play of the fact that though Booth had described Amelia's nose as 'beat all to pieces' in the passage cited above, nevertheless later in the book the reader is told:

> Amelia sent Booth to call up the Maid of the House, in order to lend her assistance; but before his Return, Mrs. Atkinson began to come to herself; and soon after, to the inexpressible joy of the Serjeant, it was discovered she had no Wound. Indeed, the delicate Nose of Amelia soon made that Discovery, which the grosser Smell of the Serjeant, and perhaps his Fright had prevented him from making; For it now appeared that the red Liquor with which the Bed was stained, tho' it may perhaps run through the Veins of a fine Lady, was not what is properly called Blood; but was, indeed, no other than Cherry Brandy, a Bottle of which Mrs. Atkinson always kept in her Room to be ready for immediate Use; and to which she used to apply for Comfort in all her Afflictions. (p.378)

Neatly adapting Fielding's own words Thornton duly pointed out this contradiction in his *Drury Lane Journal* for 30 January 1752:

> Whereas it has been reported by the *sharp-nos'd* Gentlemen, the Critics, that AMELIA *has no nose*, because her Biographer inform'd us, in the beginning of her History, that *her lovely nose* was beat all to pieces; This is to certify that the said Report is malicious, false, and ill-grounded;

and that the said Author has taken care to obviate it, by telling us, in the said History, when the Cherry Brandy was pour'd over poor Mrs. Atkinson, that AMELIA's *delicate nose soon smelt it out.*[7]

Thornton followed up this relatively temperate attack with a more viciously amusing parody a fortnight later:

Little Betty burst open the door, and ran in, frighten'd out of her seven senses. 'La, Mistress,' says she, 'here's Master com'd home, as drunk as a piper; to be sure, he's in a woundy sad pickle, that sartain: he's all over of a gore of blood, and as nasty! – I wouldn't touch him with a pair of tongs!'

During this, there was a rumbling upon the stairs; when presently Serjeant Atkinson led the suffering Booth in; and, as he held him out at arm's length with one hand, pinch'd his own nostrils close together between his thumb and fore-finger with the other. Amelia was just going to have her own qualms again, but taking heart and another gulp of beer, she flew into her husband's arms, clasp'd him round the middle, and immediately fell a whimpering: nor did she perceive the nasty souse he had been swash'd in, till her delicate nose scented something about him not very savoury.

'Are you hurt, my dear, any wheres?' cried the tender Amelia. 'Hicup,' says Booth, and what he had never been guilty of before, belch'd in her lovely face. She then clap'd him down upon a chair, and was going to wipe his mouth with her muckender: but what was her consternation, when she found his high-arch'd Roman Nose, that heretofore resembled the bridge of a fiddle, had been beat all to pieces! As herself had before lost the handle to her face, she now truly sympathis'd with him in their mutual want of snout.[8]

That Fielding was stung by these, to modern readers, possibly trivial attacks may be seen by the authorial emendations to the second edition of 1762 which introduced into the text explicit references to the surgeon's skill in repairing Amelia's nose.[9]

Throughout the century *Amelia* continued to be cited as an example of an author's failure to recognise that although certain events might well be met with in reality, the reader of imaginative prose works – and certainly the critic of such works – felt it right to limit the areas of life considered to be acceptable. This may be seen in an essay by John Aikin and his sister, the latter being better known by her later married name, Anna Laetitia Barbauld:

> Deformity is always disgusting, and the imagination cannot reconcile it with the idea of a favourite character; therefore the poet and romance-writer are full justified in giving a larger share of beauty to their principal figures than is usually met with in common life. A late genius indeed, in whimsical mood, gave us a lady with her nose crushed for the heroine of his story; but the circumstance spoils the picture; and though in the course of the story it is kept a good deal out of sight, whenever it does recur to the imagination we are hurt and disgusted. It was an heroic instance of virtue in the nuns of a certain abbey, who cut off their noses and lips to avoid violation; yet this would made a very bad subject for a poem or a play. Something akin to this is the representation of any thing unnatural; of which kind is the famous story of the Roman charity, and for this reason I cannot but think it an unpleasing subject for either the pen or the pencil.[10]

The way in which the argument in the final sentence here starts to slide introduces a very important consideration. Though throughout this chapter there have been and will be numerous examples of readers and critics waxing indignant about offences against their perception of the acceptably real, what we must ask is whether the motivation is a concern for accurate representation or for aesthetic representation. The Aikins used the term 'unpleasing' which strongly suggests the latter. And that objections to Amelia sprang from aesthetic considerations may be argued from a comparison with *Tristram Shandy* (1759-67).

Tristram is delivered by Dr Slop the man-midwife and one may presume that Slop is to be understood to be following the general practice of men-midwives of the time. Jean Donnison in *Midwives and Medical Men*[11] observes that deliveries took place in half-darkened rooms; that one male midwife was known to creep in on all fours so that the woman did not know she was being treated by a man; and, morever, 'out of deference to the woman's modesty, the man-midwife commonly worked blind with his hands under a sheet, a practice which sometimes led to serious error' (p.11). Donnison also reproduces a woodcut from an eighteenth century Dutch treatise on midwifery showing a man-midwife with the ends of the sheet firmly attached round his neck in the interests of decency. Slop, having cut his thumb opening the bag of instruments so closely tied up by Obadiah so that he could hear himself whistle, no longer has the accuracy of tactile perception required in such circumstances, mistakes the position of the baby's head and with his forceps smashes the nose flat to Tristram's face. It may be that Sterne's noseless hero was intended to be seen by his readers as a counterpart to Fielding's noseless heroine, in the eighteenth century mode of literary cross-reference which connects, for example, Joseph and Pamela Andrews.

No readers, interestingly, appear to have commented upon the deformity of Sterne's hero. Heroes may be noseless: heroines must not.

It is possible that the true explanation of the objections is to be found neither in matters of reality nor in aesthetics, but in notions of the socially acceptable. Amelia is not the only noseless female in the works of Fielding. In *Tom Jones* Susan the chambermaid is said to have a form

> robust and manlike, and every way made for such
> Encounters. As her Hands and Arms were formed to give
> Blows with great Mischief to an Enemy, so was her Face as

well contrived to receive blows without any great Injury to herself: Her Nose being already flat to her Face . . . .[12]

This deformity, like that of Tristram, was met with a deafening silence.

There is a tension evident between the reader's expectations of a notional representation of reality and the simultaneous, and at times conflicting, expectation of certain literary conventions. Burke made the underlying dichotomy clear in his discussion of the nature of dramatic tragedy:

> But then I imagine we shall be much mistaken if we attribute any considerable part of our satisfaction in tragedy to a consideration that tragedy is a deceit, and its representations no realities. The nearer it approaches the reality, and the further it removes us from all ideas of fiction, the more perfect is its power. But be its power of what kind it will, it never approaches to what it represents. Chuse a day on which to represent the most sublime and affecting tragedy we have; appoint the most favourite actors; spare no cost on the scenes and decorations; unite the greatest efforts of poetry, painting and music; and when you have collected your audience, just at the moment when their minds are erect with expectation, let it be reported that a state criminal of high rank is on the point of being executed in the adjoining square; in a moment the emptiness of the theatre would demonstrate the comparative weakness of the imitative arts, and proclaim the triumph of the real sympathy.[13]

But Burke's estimate of the reaction of a theatre audience when presented with evidence of the disparity of the 'reality' of events on and off stage does not tally with Jane Austen's view of the response of the reader of fiction, nor does it appear to be borne out by such evidence as there is of individual readers' reactions. Writing to Lady Ossory, Horace Walpole recorded his feelings on having read Fanny Burney:

> *Cecilia* I did read, besides its being immeasurably long, and written in Dr Johnson's unnatural phrase, I liked it far less

than *Evelina*. I did delight in Mr Briggs, and in the droll
names he calls the proud gentleman, whose name I forget.
Morris too is well, and Meadows tolerable and Lady
Something Something and Miss Something; but all the rest
are *outrés*. The great fault is that the authoress is so afraid
of not making all her *dramatis personas* act in character, that
she never lets them say a syllable but what is to mark their
character, which is very unnatural, at least in the present
state of things, in which people are always aiming to
disguise their ruling passions, and rather affect opposite
qualities, than hang out their propensities. The old
religious philosopher is a lunatic, and contributing nothing
to the story, might be totally omitted, and had better be so.
But I am most offended at the want of poetical justice. The
proud gentleman and his proud wife ought to be punished
and humbled – whereas his wife is rather exhibited as an
amiable character. To say the truth, the last volume is very
indifferent.[14]

On the one hand Walpole wants the characters to behave in
accordance with the modish conventions of his day: he
objects to Burney's creations as 'very unnatural, at least in
the present state of things'; but simultaneously he craves the
purely literary satisfaction of 'poetical justice' to be visited
upon certain of these characters.[15]

John Aikin and Anna Laetitia Barbauld however demonstrated that there were some readers who were aware of the
subtlety of the distinction involved here. In 1773 they
compared the evocation of pity in the audience of Otway's
Venice Preserved with the reaction of the reader of *Clarissa*:

Let us look at the picture of the old woman in Otway:

– A wrinkled hag with age grown double,
Picking dry sticks, and muttering to herself;
Her eyes with scalding rheum were gall'd and red;
Cold palsie shook her head; her hands seem'd wither'd;
And on her crooked shoulder had she wrapt
The tatter'd remnant of an old strip'd hanging,

71

Which serv'd to keep her carcase from the cold;
So there was nothing of a piece about her.

Here is the extreme of wretchedness, and instead of melting
into pity we turn away with aversion. Indeed the author
only intended it to strike horror. But how different are the
sentiments we feel for the lovely Belvidera! We see none of
those circumstances which render poverty an unamiable
thing. When the goods are seized by an execution, our
attention is turned to *the piles of massy plate, and all the antient
most domestic ornaments*, which imply grandeur and
consequence; or to such instances of their hard fortune as
will lead us to pity them as lovers: we are struck and
affected with the general face of ruin, but we are not
brought near enough to discern the ugliness of its features.
Belvidera ruined, Belvidera deprived of friends, without a
home, abandoned to the wide world – we can contemplate
with all the pleasing sympathy of pity; but had she been
represented as really sunk into low life, had we seen her
employed in the most servile offices of poverty, our
compassion would have given way to contempt and
disgust. Indeed, we may observe in real life that poverty is
only pitied as long as people can keep themselves from the
effects of it. When in common language we say *a miserable
object*, we mean an object of distress which, if we relieve, we
turn away from at the same time. To make pity pleasing,
the object of it must not in any view be disagreeable to the
imagination. How admirably has the author of Clarissa
managed this point? Amidst scenes of suffering which rend
the heart, in poverty, in a prison, under the most shocking
outrages, the grace and delicacy of her character never
suffers even for a moment: there seems to be a charm about
her which prevents her receiving a stain from any thing
which happens; and Clarissa, abandoned and undone, is
the object not only of complacence but veneration.[16]

One may contrast Walpole's views, as a reader, of Fanny
Burney, with Clara Reeve's views of Walpole as a writer,

which she expressed in her preface to *The Old English Baron* (1778):

> Having, in some degree, opened my design, I beg leave to conduct my reader back again, till he comes within view of the Castle of Otranto; a work which, as has already been observed, is an attempt to unite the various merits and graces of the ancient Romances and modern Novel. To attain this end, there is required a sufficient degree of the marvellous, to excite the attention; enough of the manners of real life, to give an air of probability to the work; and enough of the pathetic, to engage the heart in its behalf.
>
> The book we have mentioned is excellent in the last two points, but has a redundancy in the first; the opening excites the attention very strongly; the conduct of the story is artful and judicious; the characters are admirably drawn and supported; the diction polished and elegant; yet, with all these brilliant advantages, it palls upon the mind (though it does not upon the ear); and the reason is obvious, the machinery is so violent, that it destroys the effect it is intended to excite. Had the story been kept within the utmost *verge* of probability, the effect has been preserved, without losing the least circumstance that excites or detains the attention.
>
> For instance, we can conceive, and allow of, the appearance of a ghost; we can even dispense with an enchanted sword and helmet; but then they must keep within certain limits of credibility: A sword so large as to require an hundred men to lift it; a helmet that by its own weight forces a passage through a court-yard into an arched vault, big enough for a man to go through; a picture that walks out of its frame; a skeleton in a hermit's cowl: – When your expectation is wound up to the highest pitch, these circumstances take it down with a witness, destroy the work of imagination, and, instead of attention, excite laughter. I was both surprised and vexed to find the enchantment dissolved, which I wished might continue to the end of the book; and several of its readers have

confessed the same disappointment to me: The beauties are so numerous, that we cannot bear the defects, but want it to be perfect in all respects.[17]

Where in the criticism of *Amelia* the objections had been that the detail, though 'real', had been unsuitable in view of the nature of the work, here the objection is to detail which disappears off the other end of the spectrum of acceptable fictional reality. Clara Reeve's strictures on *The Castle of Otranto* widen the area of discussion. Reality to some eighteenth century readers and critics was not simply the size and shape of the heroine's nose or the degree of the concordance of the behaviour of the characters on the page with that in society, whether high or low. An anonymous pamphleteer in 1751 praised *Joseph Andrews* for the range of its verisimilitude:

> Mr. *Fielding* therefore, who sees all the little Movements by which human Nature is activated, found it necessary to open a new Vein of Humour, and thought the only way to make them lay down *Cassandra*, would be to compile Characters which really existed, equally entertaining with those Chimæras which were beyond Conception. This Thought produced *Joseph Andrews*, which soon became a formidable Rival to the *amazing* Class of Writers; since it was not a mere dry Narrative, but a lively Representation of real Life. For chrystal Palaces and winged Horses, we find homely Cots and ambling Nags; and instead of Impossibility, what we experience every Day.[18]

Just as it was possible to query the real motivation for the Aikins' criticism of *Amelia*, so here it could be argued that again the aesthetic consideration is being passed off as concern for truth. To an inhabitant of mid-eighteenth century London 'homely Cots and ambling Nags' were no more to be experienced every day than were 'chrystal Palaces and winged Horses'. The former, it is true, accorded more closely with the conventional city dweller's view of country life; but

74

this in itself was a subject for debate at the time, the simplistic view of the country being neatly mocked by Johnson in *The Idler*, no. 71.

The British Critic's review of *Camilla* (1796) offered a different line with regard to realistic representation:

> To the old romance, which exhibited exalted personages, and displayed their sentiments in improbable or impossible situations, has succeeded the more reasonable, modern novel; which delineates characters drawn from actual observation, and, when ably executed, presents an accurate and captivating view of real life. To excell in this species of composition are required all the powers of the dramatick writer; an extensive acquaintance with human nature, an acute discernment, an exact discrimination of characters, a correct judgment of probability in situations, an active imagination in devising and combining incidents, with command of language for describing them. There is no species of composition that more forcibly attracts and irresistibly detains attention; and, though the regular manufacture, and regular sale of the most imperfect attempts, by very incompetent writers, are no by means creditable to the taste that encourages so idle a traffic; yet may the better class of novels be allowed to maintain their dignity, and demand a particular examination.
>
> To astonish by the marvellous, and appal by the terrific, have lately been the favourite designs of many writers of novels; who in pursuit of those effects, have frequently appeared to desert, and sometimes have really transgressed the bounds of nature and possibility. We cannot approve of these extravagances. The artful conduct of an interesting plot, and the dramatic delineation of character, are certainly the features that give most dignity to this species of fiction; these are found in great perfection in those English novels which are admitted as models; those of Richardson, Fielding, and Smollet: and their merits cannot be rivalled by any thing imported from the regions of fairy tale.[19]

Arthur Aikin, reviewing Mrs Radcliffe's *The Italian* (1797), seemed, in a notable effort to have his cake and eat it, to be proposing a hierarchical system of truths to life, together with a hierarchical system of the works in which such truths were conveyed:

> The most excellent, but at the same time the most difficult, species of novel-writing consists in an accurate and interesting representation of such manners and characters as society presents; not, indeed, every-day characters, for the interest excited by *them* would be feeble; yet so far they ought to be common characters, as to enable the reader to judge whether the copy be a free, faithful, and even improved sketch from Nature. Such is the *Clarissa* of Richardson, and such is the *Tom Jones* of Fielding. Miss Burney's *Cecilia* is also a striking instance of the higher novel; the more remarkable, indeed, as it displays a knowledge of the world which the forms of society rarely allows women the opportunity of attaining.[20]

Now while it is clear that readers and critics saw the notion of reality as being a proper consideration when discussing literary productions, what of the writers themselves? As so often when one considers the evidence relating to what is so comfortingly referred to as 'the eighteenth century novel', there appear to be as many pegs as one has hats to hang upon them.

Defoe alone provides a whole row of pegs. Frequently the title pages of his works assert the claims of an author who, subsequent research has shown, has little or nothing to do with the writing. *Memoirs of a Cavalier* (1724) was described as being 'Written Threescore Years Ago by an English Gentle-man'[21] and the preface reiterated this assertion of authenticity, claiming that the work in hand followed the manuscript of an unknown author:

> As an evidence that 'tis very probable these Memorials were written many Years ago, the Persons now concerned in the Publication, assure the Reader, that they have had

them in their Possession finished, as they now appear, above twenty Years: That they were so long ago found by great Accident, among other valuable Papers in the Closet of an eminent publick Minister, of no less Figure than one of King William's Secretaries of State.

As it is not proper to trace them any farther, so neither is there any need to trace them at all, to give Reputation to the Story related, seeing the Actions here mentioned have a sufficient Sanction from all the Histories of the Times to which they relate, with this Addition, that the admirable Manner of relating them, and the wonderful Variety of Incidents, with which they are beautified in the Course of a private Gentleman's Story, and such Delight in the reading, and give such a Lustre, as well to the Accounts themselves, as to the Person who was the Actor: and no Story, we believe, extant in the World, ever came abroad with such Advantages.

It must naturally give some Concern in the reading, that the Name of a Person of so much Gallantry and Honour, and so many Ways valuable to the World, should be lost to the Readers: We assure them no small labour has been thrown away upon the Enquiry, and all we have been able to arrive to of Discovery in this Affair is, that a *Memorandum* was found with this Manuscript, in these Words, but not signed by any Name, only the two letters of a Name, which gives us no Light into the matter, which Memoir was as follows.

Memorandum,

I found this Manuscript among my Father's writings, and I understand that he got them as plunder, at, or after, the fight at *Worcester*, where he served as the Major of —'s Regiment of Horse on the Side of the Parliament.

L.K.

As this has been of no Use but to terminate the Enquiry after this Person; so however, it seems most naturally to give an Authority to the Original of the Work, (*viz.*) that it

was born of a Soldier, and indeed it is thro' every Part,
related with so soldierly a Stile, and in the very Language
of the Field, that it seems impossible any Thing, but the
very Person who was present in every Action here related,
could be the Relator of them. (pp.1-2)

This claim was swallowed hook, line and sinker. In the
preface to the undated second edition published somewhere
around 1750 by James Lister at Leeds, evidence of considerable effort having been expended on identifying the supposed
author was manifest:

The Publisher of this Second Edition, to the READER.

The following Historical Memoirs are writ with so much
Spirit and good Sense, that there is no doubt of their
pleasing all such as can form any just Pretensions to either.
However, as upon reading of a Book, 'tis a Question, that
naturally occurs, *Who is the Author?* and as it is too much the
Custom in these Days, to form our Sentiments of a
Performance not from its intrinsic Merit, but from the
Sentiments we form of the Writer, the present Re-
publication of these Memoirs will renew an Enquiry which
has oft been made, *Who wrote them?* Some have imagin'd the
whole to be a Romance: if it be, 'tis a Romance the likest to
Truth that I ever read. It has all the Features of Truth, 'tis
cloath'd with her Simplicity, and adorn'd with her
Charms. Without Hazard I may venture to say, were all
Romance Writers to follow this Author's example, their
Works would yield Entertainment to Philosophers, as well
as serve for the Amusement of Beaux-Esprits. But I am
fully perswaded our Author whoever he was, had been
early concerned in the Actions he relates. 'Tis certain no
Man could have given a Description of his Retreat from
Marston-Moor, to *Rochdale*, and from thence over the Moors
to the *North*, and in so exact a Manner, unless he had really
travel'd over the very Ground he describes. I could point
out many other Instances in the course of the Memoirs,
which Evidence that the Author must have been well

acquainted with the Towns, Battles, Sieges, &c. and a Party in the Action he relates. But as 'tis needless to do this, all that remains is, to trace our Author to his Name.

He says he was second Son to a *Shropshire* Gentleman, who was made a Peer in the Reign of KING CHARLES, the Ist. whose Seat lay eight miles from *Shrewsbury*. This Account suits no one so well as *Andrew Newport*, Esq; second Son to *Richard Newport*, of *High Ercoll*, Esq; which *Richard* was created Lord *Newport, October* 14th, 1642. This *Andrew Newport*, Esq; whom we suppose our Author to be, was after the Restoration made a Commissioner of the Customs, probably in Reward of his Zeal and good Services for the Royal Cause.[22]

As Boulton shows in his edition (p. vii), Andrew Newport was under ten years of age when the Cavalier was serving with Gustavus Adolphus. The identification will not do. It is moreover an almost certainly pointless effort: the *Memoirs*, though based upon some written source material as Boulton points out, are an amalgam of truth and invention which Defoe attempts, initially with great success, to pass off as entirely the former.

Journal of the Plague Year (1722) adopts the same pretence of being based upon an historical manuscript, but omits the paraphernalia of prefatory material and relies on the evidence of the title page:

> Written by a CITIZEN who continued
> all the while in London.
> Never made publick before.[23]

Though it is claimed in the preface to *Moll Flanders* (1722) that the work is based upon Moll's 'own history', and the first paragraph explicitly declares the work to be neither novel nor romance, nevertheless the presence of an editorial persona is admitted:

It is true, that the original of this Story is put into new

Words, and the Stile of the famous Lady we here speak of is a little alter'd, particularly she is made to tell her own Tale in modester Words than she told it at first; the Copy which came first to Hand, having been written in Language, more like one still in *Newgate*, than one grown Penitent and Humble, as she afterwards pretends to be.[24]

A rather less actively involved editorial position had been claimed for *Robinson Crusoe* (1719):

> *If ever the Story of any Man's Adventures in the World were worth making Publick, and were acceptable when Publish'd, the Editor of this Account thinks this will be so.*
>
> *The Wonders of this Man's Life exceed all that (he thinks) is to be found extant; the Life of one Man being scarce capable of a greater Variety.*
>
> *The Story is told with Modesty, with Seriousness, and with a religious Application of Events to the Uses to which wise Men always apply them* (viz.) *to the Instruction of others by this Example, and to justify and honour the Wisdom of Providence in all the Variety of our Circumstances, let them happen how they will.*
>
> *The Editor believes the thing to be a just History of Fact; neither is there any Appearance of Fiction in it: And however thinks, because all such things are dispatch'd that the Improvement of it, as well to the Diversion, as to the Instruction of the Reader, will be the same; and as such, he thinks, without farther Compliment to the World, he does them a great Service in the Publication.*[25]

'*The Editor believes the thing to be a just History of Fact.*' As with Goldsmith's advertisement to *The Vicar of Wakefield*, the use of the word '*thing*' suggests a writer who feels that his work deserves a name, but does not consider that any of the available names is applicable. On top of that one should note the tautological construction of '*just History of Fact*'. Of what is history made if not fact? Defoe here demonstrates an awareness of the semantic shifting of the meaning of 'history' and finds it necessary to reinforce the particular significance he wishes to communicate.

That *Robinson Crusoe* was not so successful as *Memoirs of a Cavalier* in deluding the readership into accepting that the work was 'history' may be deduced from Hugh Blair's remark in his essay 'On fictitious history':

> No fiction, in any language, was ever better supported than the Adventures of Robinson Crusoe. While it is carried on with that appearance of truth and simplicity, which takes a strong hold of the imagination of all readers, it suggests at the same time, very useful instruction; by showing how much the native powers of man may be exerted for surmounting the difficulties of any external situation.[26]

Defoe employed an interesting variation in *Roxana* (1724) where the 'Relator' declared a personal knowledge of the protagonist's relations:

> *The History of this* Beautiful Lady, *is to speak for Itself: If it is not as Beautiful as the Lady herself is reported to be; if it is not as diverting as the Reader can desire, and much more than he can reasonably expect; and if all the most diverting Parts of it are not adapted to the Instruction and Improvement of the Reader, the* Relator says, *it must be from the Defect of his Performance; dressing up the Story in worse Cloaths than the* Lady, *whose Words he speaks, prepar'd it for the World.*
>
> *He takes the Liberty to say, That this* Story *differs from most of the Modern Performances of this Kind, tho' some of them have met with a very good Reception in the World:* I say, *It differs from them in this Great and Essential Article,* Namely, *That the Foundation of This is laid out in Truth of* Fact; *and so the Work is not a Story, but a History . . . .*
>
> *The* Writer says, *He was particularly acquainted with this* Lady's First Husband, *the Brewer, and with his Father; and also, with his Bad Circumstances; and knows that first Part of the Story to be Truth.*
>
> *This may, he hopes, be a Pledge for the Credit of the rest, tho' the Latter Part of her History lay Abroad, and cou'd not so well be vouch'd as the First; yet, as she has told it herself, we have the less Reason to question the Truth of that Part also.*[27]

With *The Life of Mr Duncan Campbell* (1720) multiple involvement was suggested. The title page was sufficiently detailed as to lead the enquiring contemporary reader almost to Campbell's front door:

> The History of the Life and Adventures of Mr. Duncan Campbell, a Gentleman, who, tho' Deaf and Dumb, writes down any Stranger's Name at first Sight; with their future Contingencies of Fortune. Now Living in Exeter Court over against the Savoy in the Strand . . . London: Printed for E. Curll.[28]

There is a notable frontispiece of Campbell painted by Hill and engraved by Price: all the trappings of genuine autobiography. Yet it is not a genuine autobiography. The 'Epistle Dedicatory' appears above the name of Duncan Campbell, but in the epistle the book is declared to have been written by a 'good old Gentleman' rather than by Campbell himself, and the true position was further complicated and obscured by the concluding observation (p. xix):

> I will here say no more, nor hinder you any longer, Gentlemen and Ladies, from the Diversion which my good old Friend, who is now departed this Life, has prepared for you in his Book, which a young Gentleman of my Acquaintance revised, and only subscribe my self,
>
> Yours, &c.
> DUNCAN CAMPBELL.

Duncan Campbell appeared in 1720. Defoe's life span, 1660?-1731, clearly precludes him from being either the deceased 'good old Friend' or the helpful 'young Gentleman'. The 'Epistle Dedicatory' is fiction even if the subsequent *Life* touches truth at some points. That Defoe appears to have delighted in this fusion and confusion of fiction and fact is also evident from *Memoirs of Captain Carleton*, the title most commonly used for a work which originally appeared as *The Memoirs of an English Officer, Who serv'd in the Dutch War in 1672, to the Peace of Utrecht, in 1713. By Capt. George Carleton* (1728).

The book was dedicated to Spencer Compton who, until the previous year, had been Speaker of the House of Commons, and the dedication opened:

> It was my Fortune, my Lord, in my juvenile Years, *Musas cum marte commutare*; and truly I have reason to blush, when I consider the small Advantage I have reaped from that Change. But lest it should be imputed to my Want of Merit, I have wrote these Memoirs, and leave the World to judge of my Deserts. They are not set forth by any fictitious Stories, nor embellished with rhetorical Flourishes; Plain Truth is certainly most becoming the Character of an old Soldier. Yet let them be never so meritorious, if not protected by some noble Patron, some Persons may think them to be of no Value.[29]

In terms of the readership accepting the truth of a work, *Captain Carleton* was particularly successful. Though a number of Defoe's works had been correctly attributed to him by the middle of the eighteenth century, Boswell recorded that *Captain Carleton* was believed genuine by Johnson:

> 'But, (said his Lordship [Lord Eliot],) the best account of Lord Peterborough that I have happened to meet with, is in "Captain Carleton's Memoirs." Carleton was descended of an ancestor who had distinguished himself at the siege of Derry. He was an officer; and, what was rare at that time, had some knowledge of engineering.' Johnson said, he had never heard of the book. Lord Eliot had it at Port Eliot; but, after a good deal of enquiry, procured a copy in London, and sent it to Johnson, who told Sir Joshua Reynolds that he was going to bed when it came, but was so much pleased with it, that he sat up till he had read it through, and found in it such an air of truth, that he could not doubt of its authenticity.[30]

There is however an interesting copy of the first edition of *Captain Carleton* in the Cambridge University Library[31] which contains contemporary marginalia clearly written by a reader who knew: that Carleton was a real person; that he did not write the memoirs himself; and that nevertheless he took a personal interest in their composition. In works like this one is faced with an interweaving of historical record and imagination on such a scale that identifying a suitable critical position from which to view the book is virtually impossible.

It is clear that regardless of the category or categories into which modern criticism may wish to pigeonhole Defoe's works, all the evidence suggests that he saw the denial of fiction as an essential element in his work. This appears to have superseded all other considerations. Bearing in mind Defoe's continuous financial problems as evidenced in his letters,[32] the fact that, apart from the rather weak continuations of *Robinson Crusoe*, he never seems to have made any effort to capitalise upon his successes suggests that the notion of a writer of imaginative prose fiction with a corpus of work was alien to Defoe and possibly also to his contemporaries. One must realise of course that had a work subsequent to, say, *Robinson Crusoe* appeared as being 'by the author of *Robinson Crusoe*' this would have destroyed the authentication of both *Crusoe* and any book upon which such an epithet appeared.

There is an interesting contrast to be made between Defoe and Mrs Manley. The former went out of his way to deny fiction in his work: the latter asserted that her work was not to be taken as fact:

> . . . to remove the Misunderstandings some have conceiv'd, as if this was a Modern History, and related to several Affairs Transacted near Home, to the great Prejudice of the Original Manuscript, which I can assure them is highly Valued at Rome, and whoever refuses to believe, may be satisfied there if they think it worth their while to go thither on Purpose. In the mean time I wou'd have them rest satisfied the whole Story is a Fiction, that there is no such Country in the World as Albigion, nor any such Person now living, or ever was, as Zarah, or the Names Characteris'd, either in This or the First Part.[33]

There is a great irony here, of course, in that Mrs Manley's works were based very closely upon contemporary figures and events, and often came with a key at the end for the benefit of those readers who were not sufficiently in the know. Her assertion of the fictional is designed to reinforce the reader's perception of the factual.

The explicit denial of the fictional status, with the concomitant implicit or explicit assertion of the historical truth of a work, is a device which is to be found throughout the century. Eliza Haywood, a writer whose career spanned a good deal of the first half of the century, in her earlier works adopted the same technique as Defoe, as when in her preface to *The mercenary lover* (1728) she claimed,

> So many Stories, merely the effect of a good Invention, having been published as real Facts, I think it proper to inform my Reader, that the following Pages are fill'd with a sad, but true Account of a Family, living in the Metropolis of one of the finest Islands in the World; and happen'd in the Neighbourhood of a celebrated Church, in the Sound of whose Bells the Inhabitants of that populous City think it an Honour to be born.[34]

But the writer who took the techniques of the denial of fiction to their farthest bourn was Samuel Richardson.

When *Pamela* appeared in 1740 it contained a preface by the 'editor' very similar in apparent intention to Defoe's preliminary material in such works as *Memoirs of a Cavalier*, *Moll Flanders* and *Robinson Crusoe*:

> If to Divert and Entertain, and at the same time to Instruct, and Improve the Minds of the YOUTH of both Sexes:
> If to inculcate Religion and Morality in so easy and agreeable a manner, as shall render them equally delightful and profitable to the younger Class of Readers, as well as worthy of the attention of Persons of maturer Years and Understandings:
> If to set forth in the most exemplary Lights, the Parental, the Filial, and the Social Duties, and that from low to high Life:
> If to paint VICE in its proper Colours, to make it deservedly Odious; and to set VIRTUE in its own amiable Light, to make it truely Lovely:

If to draw Characters justly, and to support them equally:

If to raise a Distress from natural Causes, and to excite Compassion from proper Motives:

If to teach the Man of Fortune how to use it; the Man of Passion how to subdue it; and the Man of Intrigue, how, gracefully, and with Honour to himself, to reclaim:

If to give practical Examples, worthy to be followed in the most critical and affecting Cases, by the modest Virgin, the chaste Bride, and the obliging Wife:

If to effect all these good Ends, in so probable, so natural, so lively a manner, as shall engage the Passions of every sensible Reader, and strongly interest them in the edifying Story:

And all without raising a single Idea throughout the Whole, that shall shock the exactest Purity, even in those tender Instances where the exactest Purity would be most apprehensive:

If these (embellished with a great Variety of entertaining Incidents) be laudable or worthy Recommendations of any Work, the Editor of the Following Letters, which have their Foundation in Truth and Nature, ventures to assert, that all these desirable Ends are obtained in these Sheets: And as he is therefore confident of the favourable Reception which he boldly bespeaks for this little Work; he thinks any further Preface or Apology for it, unnecessary: And the rather for two Reasons, Ist. Because he can Appeal from his own Passions, (which have been uncommonly moved in perusing these engaging Scenes) to the Passions of Every one who shall read them with the least Attention: And, in the next place, because an Editor may reasonably be supposed to judge with an Impartiality which is rarely to be met with in an Author towards his own Works.

The Editor.[35]

This final sentence is quite clearly an attempt to deny fiction. The immense popularity of *Pamela* and a degree of pressure generated by the correspondence triggered off by the work led Richardson to be less assertive in the second edition. The unctuously gratulatory letters prefixed to the first edition were also dropped and replaced by others, some of which were equally laudatory, which contained demands for the identification of the author, very similar to the questioning found in the preface to the second edition of *Memoirs of a Cavalier*. The mask of non-fiction was beginning to slip:

> Yet, I confess, there is *One*, in the World, of whom I think with still greater Respect, than of PAMELA: and That is, of the wonderful AUTHOR of PAMELA. – Pray, Who is he, Dear Sir? and where, and how, has he been able to hide, hitherto, such an encircling and all-mastering Spirit? He possesses every Quality that ART could have charm'd by: yet, he has lent it to, and conceal'd it in, NATURE. – The Comprehensiveness of his Imagination must be truly prodigious! – It has stretch'd out this diminutive mere *Grain* of *Mustard-seed*, (a poor Girl's, little, innocent, Story) into a Resemblance of That *Heaven*, which the Best of Good Books has compar'd it to. – All the Passions are His, in their most close and abstracted Recesses: and by selecting the most delicate, and yet, at the same time, most powerful, of their Springs, thereby to act, wind, and manage, the Heart, *He* moves us, every where, with the Force of a TRAGEDY.[36]

But while the second edition of *Pamela* contained material demonstrating an awareness on the part of several readers, and an accompanying tacit acknowledgment on the part of Richardson, that the work as it stood was not the simple editorial transmission of a series of genuine letters as had initially been claimed, nevertheless in his correspondence Richardson continued to make what to the modern reader may seem both specious and totally unnecessary claims for the historically accurate basis of his story:

> I will now write to your question – Whether there was any original ground-work of fact, for the general foundation of Pamela's story.
> About twenty-five years ago, a gentleman, with whom I was intimately acquainted (but who, alas! is now no more!) met with such a story as that of Pamela, in one of the summer tours which he used to take for his pleasure, attended with one servant only. At

every inn he put up at, it was his way to inquire after curiosities in its neighbourhood, either ancient or modern; and particularly he asked who was the owner of a fine house, as it seemed to him, beautifully situated, which he had passed by (describing it) within a mile or two of the inn.

It was a fine house, the landlord said. The owner was Mr. B. a gentleman of a large estate in more counties than one. That his and his lady's history engaged the attention of every body who came that way, and put a stop to all other enquiries, though the house and gardens were well worth seeing. The lady, he said, was one of the greatest beauties in England; but the qualities of her mind had no equal: beneficent, prudent, and equally beloved and admired by high and low. That she had been taken at twelve years of age for the sweetness of her manners and modesty, and for an understanding above her years, by Mr. B—'s mother, a truly worthy lady, to wait on her person. Her parents, ruined by suretiships, were remarkably honest and pious, and had instilled into their daughter's mind the best principles. When their misfortunes happened first, they had attempted a little school, in their village, where they were much beloved; he teaching writing and the first rules of arithmetic to boys; his wife plain needle-work to girls, and to knit and to spin; but that it answered not; and, when the lady took their child, the industrious man earned his bread by day labour, and the lowest kinds of husbandry.

That the girl, improving daily in beauty, modesty, and genteel and good behaviour, by the time she was fifteen, engaged the attention of her lady's son, a young gentleman of free principles, who, on her lady's death, attempted, by all manner of temptations and devices, to seduce her. That she had recourse to as many innocent stratagems to escape the snares laid for her virtue; once, however, in despair, having been near drowning; that, at last, her noble resistance, watchfulness, and excellent qualities, subdued him, and he thought fit to make her his wife. That she behaved herself with so much dignity, sweetness, and humility, that she made herself beloved of every body, and even by his relations, who, at first despised her; and now had the blessings both of rich and poor, and the love of her husband.

The gentleman who told me this, added, that he had the curiosity to stay in the neighbourhood from Friday to Sunday, that he might see this happy couple at church, from which they never absented themselves: that, in short, he did see them; that her deportment was all sweetness, ease, and dignity mingled: that he never saw a lovelier woman: that her husband was as fine a man, and seemed even proud of his choice: and that she attracted the blessings of the poor. – The relater of the story told me all this with transport.

This, Sir, was the foundation of Pamela's story; but little did I think to make a story of it for the press. That was owing to this occasion.

Mr. Rivington and Mr. Osborne, whose names are on the title page, had long been urging me to give them a little book (which, they said, they were often asked after) of familiar letters on the useful concerns in common life; and, at last, I yielded to their importunity, and began to recollect such subjects as I thought would be useful in such a design, and formed several letters accordingly. And, among the rest, I thought of giving one or two as cautions to young folks circumstanced as Pamela was. Little did I think, at first, of making one, much less two volumes of it. But, when I began to recollect what had, so many years before, been told me by my friend, I thought the story, if written in an easy and natural manner, suitably to the simplicity of it, might possibly introduce a new species of writing, that might possibly turn young people into a course of reading different from the pomp and parade of romance-writing, and dismissing the improbable and marvellous, with which such novels generally abound, might tend to promote the cause of religion and virtue. I therefore gave way to enlargement: and so Pamela became as you see her.[37]

Novels and romances are dismissed in the same sentence, and that the 'marvellous', normally considered a feature of the romance, should be used by Richardson of the novel suggests that he saw no real distinction between the two. His own work he considers to be 'a new species of writing', from which one may draw the inference that such writing requires a new set of rules by which to be judged. On the other hand, that *Pamela* was not entirely divorced from previous works might be deduced from his claim that the 'gentleman, with whom I was intimately acquainted (but who, alas! is now no more!)' is remarkably, and conveniently, like Duncan Campbell's 'good old friend, who is now departed this Life'.

With the second edition of *Pamela* the mask of non-fiction had slipped slightly: with the appearance of *Clarissa* (1747-8) it was firmly back in place. The title page set the tone:

CLARISSA.
OR, THE
HISTORY
OF A
YOUNG LADY:
Comprehending
The most Important Concerns *of* Private LIFE.
And particularly shewing,
The DISTRESSES that may attend the Misconduct
Both of PARENTS and CHILDREN,
In relation to MARRIAGE.

Published by the EDITOR *of* PAMELA.
. . . .

LONDON:
Printed for S. Richardson:
. . . .

M.DCC.XLVIII.

Richardson is not even named as the 'Editor': he is the publisher, yet further removed from the creative state. The preface to volume 1 maintained this pretence by asserting that the work was a 'History' with all the suggestions of accuracy and truth that that word carried in certain circumstances, and by discussing the role of the editor:

> The following History is given in a Series of Letters,
> written principally in a double, yet separate,
> Correspondence;
>   Between Two young Ladies of Virtue and Honour,
> bearing an inviolable Friendship for each other, and
> writing upon the most interesting Subjects: And
>   Between Two Gentlemen of free Lives; one of them
> glorying in his Talents for Stratagem and Invention, and
> communicating to the other, in Confidence, all the secret

Purposes of an intriguing Head, and resolute Heart . . . .

Length will naturally be expected, not only from what has been said, but from the following Considerations:

That the Letters on both Sides are written while the Hearts of the Writers must be supposed to be wholly engaged in their Subjects: The Events at the Time generally dubious: – So that they abound, not only with critical Situations; but with what may be called *instantaneous* Descriptions and Reflections; which may be brought home to the Breast of the youthful Reader: – As also, with affecting Conversations; many of them written in the Dialogue or Dramatic Way.

To which may be added, that the Collection contains not only the History of the excellent Person whose Name it bears, but includes The Lives, Characters, and Catastrophes, of several others, either principally or incidentally concerned in the Story.

But yet the Editor to whom it was referred to publish the Whole in such a Way as he should think would be most acceptable to the Public was so diffident in relation to this Article of *Length*, that he thought proper to submit the Letters to the Perusal of several judicious Friends; whose Opinion he desired of what might be best spared. (pp. iii-v)

Writing to William Warburton in 1748 thanking him for the preface he had contributed to volume 3 of *Clarissa*, Richardson provided an interesting comment upon his reasons for wishing his works to be read as historical records. And he opened his letter by revealing to Warburton that he had not only made certain alterations to the offered preface to maintain the air of truth and his own position as editor, but had also transcribed Warburton's piece so that not even Richardson's own employee in the printing house would be aware of its authorship or the circumstances of its composition. This could be thought to be taking matters a little too far:

19 April 1748

I am infinitely obliged to you, sir, for your Papers. But how shall I take it upon myself? I must, if put to me, by Particulars, suppose it to be suggested to me, at least, by some Learned Friend, so disguising as you may not be suggested to be the Person. And I have transcribed it, that not even my compositor may guess at the Author – But it is really so much above my learning and my ability, that it will not be supposed mine by anybody.

Will you, good Sir, allow me to mention, that I could wish that the Air of Genuineness had been kept up, tho' I want not the letters to be thought genuine; only so far kept up, I mean, as that they should not prefatically be owned not to be genuine: and this for fear of weakening their Influence where any of them are aimed to be exemplary; as well to avoid hurting that kind of Historical Faith which Fiction itself is generally read with, tho' we know it to be Fiction.

(*Selected Letters*, p. 85)

Ignoring the petrine denial of 'I want not the letters to be thought genuine', the final sentence contains a major statement of the eighteenth century concept of reading: 'that kind of Historical Faith which Fiction itself is generally read with, tho' we know it to be Fiction'. To support and reinforce this 'Historical Faith', throughout *Clarissa* Richardson develops the notion of verisimilitude in a number of different and, at times, highly innovative ways. The editorial persona is kept up throughout the seven volumes; there are frequent footnotes providing cross references; there are scholarly annotations: letter IX in volume 4 is headed, 'Not communicated till the history came to be compiled' (p.32), and later one finds the footnote, 'The words thus inclosed [ ] were omitted in the transcript to Mr Lovelace' (vol. 7, p. 247). There are appreciative comments – to Belford's description of Sinclair the bagnio keeper the editor approvingly subjoins:

Whoever has seen Dean Swift's Lady's Dressing-Room, will think this description of Mr. Belford not only more natural but more decent painting, as well as better justified by the design, and by the use that may be made of it. (vol. 7, p. 258n)

There are explications of allusions within the text: when Clarissa writes to Miss Howe, 'Don't you remember the lines of Howard, which once you read to me in my ivy bower?' the alert and omniscient editor adds:

These are the lines the lady refers to:

> From death we rose to life: 'Tis but the same,
> Thro' life to pass again from whence we came.
> (vol. 7, p. 149n)

This footnoting to suggest an editorial presence in addition to the 'true' writer or writers was not new: Swift had made masterly use of the device in *Tale of a Tub*.[38] Where Richardson was innovative was in an area where, among all the writers of imaginative prose in the eighteenth century, he had a unique qualification. Richardson, being a master printer, was in an unrivalled position of control over the minute detail and appearance of his text. It may be argued that Sterne, who became his own publisher during the extended publication of *Tristram Shandy*, was in a comparable position: Sterne's typographical innovations will be discussed in chapter 5. But where Sterne appeared to use the visual element to provoke or amuse his readers, Richardson may be seen to have been employing devices which further reinforce in the reader's mind the notion that the work is a transcript of a genuine correspondence.

To recognise the extent of Richardson's innovations one needs to look at the first edition of *Clarissa*.[39] In volume 2 Clarissa is writing to Miss Howe and transcribes for her correspondent an 'Ode to Wisdom'. Thirteen stanzas of the Ode are printed conventionally, terminating at the bottom of page 50. On a folding sheet, tipped in so that it faces page 50, the reader is provided with the music for the Ode. But this is not mere ornamentation, for the fold-out sheet also contains the words to stanzas 14 to 16 of the Ode. What looks like illustration is an intrinsic part of the text. Furthermore the typeface used for the additional stanzas approximates to handwriting much more than to roman – the reader can be deluded into the assumption that this is Clarissa's hand. This claim might appear rather far-fetched were it not that subsequently type suggestive of handwriting is employed at two key emotional parts of the book. In volume 7, in the middle of a page set up conventionally in roman, one finds four lines of script (see Figure 1). And, even more subtly evocative, one finds in the final volume at the end of the transcript of Clarissa's will, the 'signature' of Clarissa Harlowe almost as if it were a facsimile (see Figure 2).

The type face used here is a version of one called Grover's Scriptorial. It had been quite specifically designed to represent handwriting, and for a period of twenty years had been used by Ichabod Dawks for his *Newsletter* so that his subscribers could feel that they were being supplied individually with the latest news of importance.[40] Richardson, as a master printer, cannot but have been aware of the implications and results of employing Grover's Scriptorial at these emotional high points of his text.

Not all his devices were equally successfully employed. Lovelace indignantly writes to Belford enclosing a letter from Anna Howe to Laetitia Beaumont:

> Thou wilt see the margin of this cursed letter crouded with indices [☞]. I put them to mark the places devoted for vengeance, or requiring animadversion. (vol. 4, pp. 327-8)

In the left-hand margins of the ensuing sixteen and a half pages there are 106 little printer's hands, which the reader may rather sourly feel probably constituted the entire stock of this ornament in Richardson's printing shop. The device certainly gives the pages a certain visual immediacy, and the profusion may be intended to represent Lovelace's lack of control. Fortunately it is not repeated.

To set against this, one must note the most successful of these typographical efforts at realistic representation. In volume 5 Lovelace sends a letter to Belford containing what purport to be transcriptions of Clarissa's jottings which she had cast aside. They are introduced with the comment:

198   *The* HISTORY *of*

My deareſt Miſs Howe,   *Wedn. near* 3 *o'Clock.*

YOU muſt not be ſurprized—nor grieved—that Mrs.
Lovick writes for me.   Altho' I cannot obey you,
and write with my *pen*, yet my *heart* writes by hers—Accept it ſo—It is the neareſt to obedience I can !

And now, what *ought* I to ſay ?   What *can* I ſay ?—
But why ſhould you not know the truth ?   Since ſoon you
muſt—very ſoon.

Know then, and let your tears be thoſe, if of pity, of
joyful pity !   for I permit you to ſhed a few, to imbalm, as
I may ſay, a fallen bloſſom—Know then, that the good
doctor, and the pious clergyman, and the worthy apothe-
cary, have juſt now, with joint benedictions, taken their
laſt leave of me :   And the former bids me hope—Do, my
deareſt, let me ſay *hope*—for my enlargement before to-
morrow ſun-ſet.

Adieu, therefore, my deareſt friend !   Be this your con-
ſolation, as it is mine, that in God's good time we ſhall
meet in a bleſſed Eternity, never more to part ! —Once
more, then, adieu and be happy !—Which a generous nature cannot be, unleſs to its power, it makes others ſo too.

*God for ever bleſs you ! prays, dropt on my bended
Knees, altho' ſupported upon them,*

Your Grateful, Obliged, Affectionate,

Clar. Harlowe.

When I had tranſcribed and ſealed this letter, by her
direction, I gave it to the meſſenger myſelf ; who told me
that Miſs Howe waited for nothing but his return, to ſet
out for London.

Thy ſervant is juſt come ; ſo I will cloſe here.   Thou
art a mercileſs maſter.   The two fellows are *battered* to
death by thee, to uſe a female word ; and all female words,
tho' we are not ſure of their derivation, have very ſignifi-
cant meanings.   I believe, in their hearts, they wiſh the
angel in the heaven that is ready to receive her, and thee
at thy proper place, that there might be an end of their
flurries ; another word of the ſame gender.

What

Figure 1   *Clarissa*, vol. 7, p. 198.

Miſs Clariſſa Harlowe. 309

But if I am to be interred in town, let only the uſual Burial-ſervice be read over my corpſe.

If my body be permitted to be carried down, I bequeath ten pounds to be given to the poor of the pariſh, at the diſ-cretion of the church-wardens, within a fortnight after my interrment.

If any neceſſary matter be omitted in this my Will; or if any thing appear doubtful or contradictory, as poſſibly may be the caſe; ſince, beſides my inexperience in theſe matters, I am now at this time very weak and ill; having put off the finiſhing hand a little too long, in hopes of obtaining the laſt forgiveneſs of my honoured friends; in which caſe I ſhould have acknow-leged the favour with a ſuitable warmth of duty, and filled up ſome blanks which I left to the very laſt (*a*), in a more agree-able manner to myſelf, than now I have been enabled to do----In caſe of ſuch omiſſions and imperfections, I deſire that my couſin Morden will be ſo good as to join with Mr. Belford in conſidering them, and in comparing them with what I have more explicitly written; and if, after *that*, any doubt remain, that they will be pleaſed to apply to Miſs Howe, who knows my whole heart: And I deſire that their conſtruction may be eſtabliſhed: And I hereby eſtabliſh it, provided it be unanimous, and direct it to be put in force, as if I had ſo written and de-termined myſelf.

And Now, O my bleſſed REDEEMER, do I, with a lively faith, humbly lay hold of Thy meritorious Death and Suf-ferings; hoping to be waſhed clean in Thy precious Blood from all my ſins: In the bare hope of the happy conſe-quences of which, how light do thoſe ſufferings ſeem (grie-vous as they were at the time) which I confidently truſt will be a means, by Thy Grace, to work out for me a more exceeding and eternal weight of glory!

Clariſsa Harlowe.

Signed, ſealed, publiſhed, and declared, the day and year above-written, by the ſaid Clariſſa Harlowe, as her LaſtWill andTeſtament; contained in ſeven ſheets of paper, all written with her own hand, and every ſheet ſigned and ſealed by herſelf, in the preſence of Us,
John Williams,
Arthur Bedall,
Elizabeth Swanton.

(*a*) p. 133, of this Volume.

LET-

Figure 2 *Clarissa*, vol. 7, p. 309.

But some of the scraps and fragments, as either torn thro', or flung aside, I will copy, for the novelty of the thing, and to shew thee how her mind works, now she is in this whimsical way. (vol. 5, p. 234)

Of the fragments 'Paper X' is the most interesting (see Figure 3). The relatively random presentation of the lines seems to be an attempt to duplicate the wild jottings of the disturbed heroine. The difficulties of setting up the forme to produce such an arrangement of lines on the page are such that only an author who was also his own printer could have ensured that the finished product approximated to his conception.

When one gets to the end of *Clarissa*, there is a 'Postscript' in which the editorial image wavers slightly:

The Letters and Conversations, where the Story makes the slowest progress, are presumed to be characteristic. They give occasion likewise to suggest many interesting Personalities, in which a good deal of the Instruction essential to a work of this nature, is conveyed. And it will, moreover, be remembred, that the Author, at his first setting out, appraised the Reader, that the story was to be looked upon as the Vehicle only to the Instruction.

To all which we may add, that there was frequently a necessity to be very circumstantial and minute, in order to preserve and maintain that Air of Probability, which is necessary to be maintained in a Story designed to represent real Life; and which is rendered extremely busy and active by the plots and contrivances formed and carried on by one of the principal Characters. (vol. 7, pp. 431-2)

At long last the 'Editor' has become the 'Author'; what had been described to Warburton as the 'Air of Genuineness' has become the 'Air of Probability'; and a 'Story designed to represent real Life' is an implicit admission of invention.

On the other hand, three years later the third edition of *Clarissa* appeared claiming on its title page, 'In which Many Passages and some Letters are restored from the Original

Miſs Clariſſa Harlowe.   239

PAPER X.

LEAD me, where my own Thoughts themſelves may loſe me,
 Where I may doze out what I've left of Life,
Forget myſelf; and that day's guilt! ——
Cruel remembrance! --- how ſhall I appeaſe thee?

——Oh! you have done an act
That blots the face and bluſh of modeſty;
     Takes off the roſe
From the fair forehead of an innocent love,
And makes a bliſter there! ——

     Then down I laid my head,
Down on cold earth, and for a while was dead;
And my freed Soul to a ſtrange ſomewhere fled!
     Ah! ſottiſh ſoul! ſaid I,
When back to its cage again I ſaw it fly,
     Fool! to reſume her broken chain,
And row the galley here again!
Fool! to that body to return,
Where it condemn'd and deſtin'd is to *mourn*.

O my Miſs Howe! if thou haſt friendſhip, help me,
And ſpeak the words of peace to my divided ſoul,
     That wars within me,
And raiſes ev'ry ſenſe to my confuſion.
     I'm tott'ring on the brink
Of peace; and thou art all the hold I've left!
Aſſiſt me in the pangs of my affliction!

When honour's loſt, 'tis a relief to die:
Death's but a ſure retreat from infamy.

     Then farewel, youth,
     And all the joys that dwell
With youth and life!
     And life itſelf, farewel!

For life can never be ſincerely bleſt.
Heaven puniſhes the *Bad*, and proves the *Beſt*.

AFTER all, Belford, I have juſt ſkimm'd over theſe
tranſcriptions of Dorcas; and I ſee there is method
                                             and

Figure 3 *Clarissa*, vol. 5, p. 239.

Manuscript', and for the benefit of those who had already bought sets of the first two editions Richardson issued a single additional volume entitled *Letters and Passages Restored from the Original Manuscripts of the History of Clarissa* (1751).[41] One might argue that 'Original Manuscript' was ambiguous, being able to refer to those of the author as well as those of an editor. Nevertheless the effect of the wording must have been to reinforce the reader's notion of the latter.

Thus on the one hand we have a readership whose expectations of works of fiction are circumscribed by at times conflicting but nevertheless strongly held opinions of what constituted reality of characterisation, appearance and setting, regardless of whether the work concerned was openly denominated fiction or not; while on the other hand we have certain writers whose concern for satisfying or gulling their readers leads to the denial of any fictional element to their works. The whole concept of the supposed element of reality and the reader's response was neatly caught by Sterne in *Tristram Shandy*:

> Was every day of my life to be as busy a day as this, – and to take up, – truce –
>
> I will not finish that sentence till I have made an observation upon the strange state of affairs between the reader and myself, just as things stand at present – an observation never applicable before to any one biographical writer since the creation of the world, but to myself – and I believe will never hold good to any other, until its final destruction – and therefore, for the very novelty of it alone, it must be worth your worships attending to.
>
> I am this month one whole year older than I was this time twelve-month; and having got, as you perceive, almost into the middle of my fourth volume – and no farther than to my first day's life – 'tis demonstrative that I have three hundred and sixty-four days more life to write just now, than when I first set out; so that instead of advancing, as a common writer, in my work with what I have been doing at it – on the contrary, I am just thrown so many volumes

back – was every day of life to be as busy a day as this –
And why not? – and the transactions and opinions of it to
take up as much description – And for what reason should
they be cut short? as at this rate I should just live 364 times
faster than I should write – It must follow, an' please your
worships, that the more I write, the more I shall have to
write – and consequently, the more your worships read, the
more your worships will have to read.

Will this be good for your worships eyes?[42]

This is pushing the reader's 'Historical Faith' to its limit.

In *Peregrine Pickle* (1751) Smollett presented the reader with
a somewhat different problem. Chapter 88, entitled 'The
Memoirs of a Lady of Quality', occupies well over 100 pages
of the text, and purports to be the autobiography of Lady
Vane whose marital problems had been notorious for many
years. The events recounted are scandalous, but on the
evidence of contemporary comment in letters and reports in
the monthly journals such as *The Gentleman's Magazine* they
also appear to be fairly accurate. It was widely believed at
the time that this chapter had indeed been written by Lady
Vane. Smollett compounded this by advertising prior to
publication:

> That the publick may not be imposed on, we are
> authorized to assure them, that no Memoirs of the above
> Lady, that may be obtruded on the World, under any
> Disguise whatever, are genuine, except what is comprised
> in this Performance.[43]

This advertisement was the result of the fact that word had
got out that Smollett intended to include Lady Vane's
memoirs in his work, and in true eighteenth century style
various other hacks had rushed to get their versions out first.
Smollett's denial that the other publications were genuine
carries the corollary that his own satisfied this requirement.
And readers clearly believed him: Walpole wrote to Horace
Mann:

My Lady Vane has literally published the memoirs of her own life, only suppressing part of her lovers, no part of the success of the others with her: a degree of profligacy not to be accounted for; she does not want money, none of her stallions will raise her credit; and the number, all she had to brag of, concealed![44]

Smollett's use of the word 'genuine' suggests the essential truth of the work, but to this day critics are undecided as to whether or not this is the case. Paul-Gabriel Boucé observes, 'Though it is probable that Smollett wrote these Memoirs himself, it is equally probable that he kept very close to the account Lady Vane gave him of her past';[45] while James L. Clifford is similarly cautious:

> Who wrote these memoirs? No one seems to know. Did Smollett write them down from Lady Vane's dictation? Or were they the lady's own composition, corrected, possibly, by someone else? From stylistic evidence alone it seems likely that, whatever the source, the final version was done by the same hand that shaped the rest of the novel.[46]

A contemporary reader, Lady Luxborough, revealed the uncertainty this confusion had sown:

> Peregrine Pickle I do not admire . . . but the thing which makes the book sell, is the History of Lady V——, which is introduced (in the last volume, I think) much to her Ladyship's dishonour; but published by her *own* order, from her *own* Memoirs, given to the author for that purpose; and by the approbation of her *own* Lord. What was ever equal to this fact, and how can one account for it?[47]

That this large and essentially irrelevant slab of narrative should have been inserted into an apparently fictional work does indeed leave the reader wondering how to account for it. But it is not the only such example. Chapter 106 is a very thinly disguised summary of a near-contemporary event –

the trial between James Annesley and Richard, Earl of Anglesey which had taken place in 1744. As with 'The Memoirs of a Lady of Quality', the chapter makes no essential contribution to the furtherance of the narrative or characterisation of the work as a whole. Whereas Defoe and Richardson had at least manifested an air of consistency in their presentation of their writings as truth, Smollett is not merely inconsistent but, by the advertisement and the frequent sniping references to contemporaries with whom he conceived himself to be at loggerheads, positively parades the inconsistency. Lady Luxborough's query does not appear to have a rational answer, and the notion of the boundaries between truth and fiction takes another blow.

The intrusion into fictional works of material written by persons other than the author of the whole requires the reader to view the interpolation in a rather different light. There are several such interpolations in *Tristram Shandy*. The 'memoire presenté à Messieurs les Docteurs de SORBONNE', which discusses the possibilities and problems of baptising a child *in utero*, is perfectly genuine and in the second edition, as if to underline this point, Sterne provided a footnote reference so that readers could check the truth of the matter. Unlike Lady Vane's Memoirs, the medical and ethical deliberations of the Sorbonne are relevant to their context: a child is due and the birth is sufficiently beset with danger to warrant immediate baptism without permitting even the time the father needs to button his breeches. The 'memoire' has a multiple effectiveness: it ties in with the development of such plot as the book offers, with the constant sniping at the wilder shores of Roman Catholicism, with Sterne's manifest delight in exposing the lunacies of the learned; and it provides the author with yet another opportunity to seize upon to share a private joke with the reader in the know. Perhaps above all the recognition that this is an interpolation requires the reader to consider the effect of context upon reaction: the serious becomes comic though in itself remaining exactly the same.

'The Abuses of Conscience', a sermon which occupies

much of volume 2 of *Tristram Shandy*, was written by Sterne, but in a neat inversion of what one might have thought to be the conventional use of interpolation he goes out of his way to confuse the matter of authorship. After Trim has read the sermon, the narrator comments:

> Ill-fated sermon! Thou wast lost, after this recovery of thee, a second time, dropp'd thro' an unsuspected fissure in thy master's pocket, down into a treacherous and tatter'd lining, – trod deep into the dirt by the left hind foot of his Rosinante, inhumanly stepping upon thee as thou falledst; – buried ten days in the mire, – raised up out of it by a beggar, sold for a halfpenny to a parish-clerk, – transferred to his parson, – lost for ever to thy own, the remainder of his days, – nor restored to his restless MANES till this very moment, that I tell the world the story.
>
> Can the reader believe, that this sermon of *Yorick*'s was preach'd at an asssize, in the cathedral of *York*, before a thousand witnesses, ready to give oath of it, by a certain prebendary of that church, and actually printed by him when he had done, – and within so short a space as two years and three months after *Yorick*'s death. – *Yorick*, indeed, was never better served in his life! – but it was a little hard to maletreat him before, and plunder him after he was laid in his grave. (pp. 166-7)

'The Abuses of Conscience' was preached by Laurence Sterne at York Minster on 29 July 1750 as the Assize Sermon. He was at that time Prebendary of North Newbold. The sermon was printed on 7 August 1750. The fictional narrator, Tristram Shandy, is asserting that the historical figure, Laurence Sterne, stole a sermon written by one of his own creations. And for the local York reader who might well have heard and remembered the Assize Sermon this also provides a method of precisely dating Yorick's death. Fact and fiction meld again.

An equally odd interpolated passage is to be found in *Clarissa*. The 'Ode to Wisdom' mentioned above (page 93) was written not by Richardson but by Elizabeth Carter, and he apparently had not had her permission to print the poem. Having been publicly reproved by *The Gentleman's Magazine* Richardson removed the first thirteen stanzas from the second edition but, because he retained the fold-out sheet of music, the stanzas thereon were still printed without permission. He then managed to obtain the author's consent for the poem to reappear in its entirety, and restored the whole to the third edition.[48] Whilst providing yet more evidence of Richardson's obsessive tinkering with his text, this particular instance also creates a problem as to how one assesses reader response to such a passage which has acquired an element of infamy as a result of a dispute external to the work in which it appeared, and which drew attention to a previously unexpected plurality of authorship.

By way of coda to this section, one may note that in *The Castle of Otranto* Horace Walpole developed a variant on the mode of denial of authorship used by Mrs Manley. The first volume of her *Secret Memoirs* (1709) claimed on the title page to have been 'Written Originally in Italian', a claim qualified in the corresponding spot in volume 2 to 'Written Originally in Italian, and Translated from the Third Edition of the French'. The title page of the first edition of *Otranto* also claimed the work to be a translation:

THE

CASTLE of OTRANTO

A

STORY.

Translated by

WILLIAM MARSHAL, GENT.

From the Original ITALIAN of

ONUPHRIO MURALTO,

CANON of the Church of St. NICHOLAS

at OTRANTO.

LONDON:

Printed for THO. LOWNDS in Fleet-Street.

MDCCLXV.

And just as Defoe and Richardson had buttressed the claims of their title pages with extended arguments in prefaces, so too Walpole used a preface to specificate his:

> The following work was found in the library of an ancient catholic family in the north of England. It was printed at Naples, in the black letter, in the year 1529. How much sooner it was written does not appear. The principal incidents are such as were believed in the darkest ages of christianity; but the language and conduct have nothing that favours of barbarism. The style is the purest Italian. If the story was written near the time when it is supposed to have happened, it must have been between 1095, the aera of the first crusade, and 1243, the date of the last, or not long afterwards. There is no other circumstance in the work that can lead us to guess at the period in which the scene is laid; the names of the actors are evidently fictitious, and probably disguised on purpose: yet the Spanish names of the domestics seem to indicate that this work was not composed until the establishment of the Arragonian kings in Naples had made Spanish appellations familiar in that country. The beauty of the diction, and the zeal of the author, [moderated however by singular judgment] concur to make me think that the date of the composition was little antecedent to that of the impression. Letters were then in their most flourishing state in Italy, and contributed to dispel the empire of superstition, at that time so forcibly attacked by the reformers. It is not unlikely that an artful priest might endeavour to turn their own arms on the innovators; and might avail himself of his abilities as an author to confirm the populace in their ancient errors and superstitions. If this was his view, he has certainly acted with signal address. Such a work as the following would enslave a hundred vulgar minds beyond half the books of controversy that have been written from the days of Luther to the present hour.
>
> The solution of the author's motives is however offered as a mere conjecture. Whatever his views were, or

whatever effects the execution of them might have, his work can only be laid before the public at present as a matter of entertainment. Even as such, some apology for it is necessary. Miracles, visions, necromancy, dreams, and other preternatural events, are exploded now even from romances. That was not the case when our author wrote; much less when the story itself is supposed to have happened. Belief in every kind of prodigy was so established in those dark ages, that an author would not be faithful to the *manners* of the times who should omit all mention of them. He is not bound to believe them himself, but he must represent his actors as believing them.

If this *air* of the *miraculous* is excused, the reader will find nothing else unworthy of his perusal. Allow the possibility of the facts, and all the actors comport themselves as persons would do in their situation. There is no bombast, no similies, flowers, digressions, or unnecessary descriptions. Every thing tends directly to the catastrophe. Never is the reader's attention relaxed. The rules of the drama are almost observed throughout the conduct of the piece. The characters are well drawn, and still better maintained. Terror, the author's principal engine, prevents the story from ever languishing; and it is so often contrasted by pity, that the mind is kept up in a constant vicissitude of interesting passions.[49]

It was noted earlier (pages 70-1) that in his views on *Cecilia* Walpole, as a reader, was rather ambivalent about his expectations of fictional representations of reality; here, as a writer, the ambivalence is still present. 'The names of the actors are evidently fictitious' is immediately qualified by 'and probably disguised on purpose', while his observations on the necessity to 'be faithful to the manners of the times' is very much at one with his strictures on Fanny Burney's failure to have her characters behave in a natural way 'in the present state of things'.

Whereas Defoe and Richardson attempted to pass themselves off as editors and were thus able to praise their own performance, rather fulsomely in the latter's case, Walpole's persona is merely the translator, which also allows him to praise though he does qualify this self-congratulation:

> It is natural for a translator to be prejudiced in favour of his adopted work. More impartial readers may not be so much struck with the beauties of this piece as I was. Yet I am not blind to my author's defects. I could wish he had grounded his plan on a more useful moral than this; that *the sins of the fathers are visited on their children to the third and fourth generation.* I doubt whether in his time, any more than at present, ambition curbed its appetite of dominion from the dread of so remote a punishment. And yet this moral is weakened by that less direct insinuation, that even such anathema may be diverted by devotion to saint Nicholas. Here the interest of the monk plainly gets the better of the judgment of the author. However, with all its faults, I have no doubt but the English reader will be pleased with a sight of this performance. The piety that reigns throughout, the lessons of virtue that are inculcated, and the rigid purity of the sentiments, exempt this work from the censure to which romances are but too liable. Should it meet with the success I hope for, I may be encouraged to re-print the original Italian, though it will tend to depreciate my own labour. Our language falls far short of the charms of the Italian, both for variety and harmony. The latter is peculiarly excellent for simple narrative. It is difficult in English *to relate* without falling too low or rising too high; a fault obviously occasioned by the little care taken to speak pure language in common conversation. Every Italian or Frenchman of any rank piques himself on speaking his own tongue correctly and with choice. I cannot flatter myself with having done justice to my author in this respect: his style is as elegant as his conduct of the passions is masterly. It is a pity that he did not apply his talents to what they were evidently proper for, the theatre. (p. 5)

In the concluding paragraph of the preface he offered the

same claim for the essential truth of the work as had been offered by so many others:

> I will detain the reader no longer but to make one short remark. Though the machinery is invention, and the names of the actors imaginary, I cannot but believe that the groundwork of the story is founded on truth. The scene is undoubtedly laid in some real castle. The author seems frequently, without design, to describe particular parts. *The chamber*, says he, *on the right hand; the door on the left hand; the distance from the chapel to Conrad's apartment:* these and other passages are strong presumptions that the author had some certain building in his eye. Curious persons, who have leisure to employ in such researches, may possibly discover in the Italian writers the foundation on which our author has built. If a catastrophe, at all resembling that which he describes, is believed to have given rise to this work, it will contribute to interest the reader, and will make *The Castle of Otranto* a still more moving story. (pp. 5-6)

Defoe and Richardson had both claimed that the reader would be able to deduce the essential truths of their works by recognising the accurate representation of human nature presented. Walpole employed a rather more subtle literary argument: the 'truth' of the work will be evident because the choice of words is such as to convey that the topography of the action is set in a possibly identifiable building.

Just as the success of *Pamela* had contributed to flushing Richardson out of hiding, so too with *Otranto*. The second edition of 1765 opened with an apology for having misled the public, and developed into a commentary upon the work's relation to what Walpole considered to be reality, both in fact and in fiction:

> The favourable manner in which this little piece has been received by the public, calls upon the author to explain the grounds on which he composed it. But before he opens those motives, it is fit that he should ask pardon of his readers for having offered his work to them under the

borrowed personage of a translator. As diffidence of his own abilities, and the novelty of the attempt, were his sole inducements to assume that disguise, he flatters himself he shall appear excusable. He resigned his performance to the impartial judgment of the public; determined to let it perish in obscurity, if disapproved; nor meaning to avow such a trifle, unless better judges should pronounce that he might own it without a blush.

It was an attempt to blend the two kinds of romance, the ancient and the modern. In the former all was imagination and improbability: in the latter, nature is always intended to be, and sometimes has been, copied with success. Invention has not been wanting; but the great resources of fancy have been dammed up, by a strict adherence to common life. But if in the latter species Nature has cramped imagination, she did but take her revenge, having been totally excluded from old romances. The actions, sentiments, conversations, of the heroes and heroines of ancient days were as unnatural as the machines employed to put them in motion.

The author of the following pages thought it possible to reconcile the two kinds. Desirous of leaving the powers of fancy at liberty to expatiate through the boundless realms of invention, and thence of creating more interesting situations, he wished to conduct the mortal agents in his drama according to the rules of probability; in short, to make them think, speak and act, as it might be supposed mere men and women would do in extraordinary positions. He had observed, that in all inspired writings, the personages under the dispensation of miracles, and witnesses to the most stupendous phenomena, never lose sight of their human character: whereas in the productions of romantic story, an improbable event never fails to be attended by an absurd dialogue. The actors seem to lose their senses the moment the laws of nature have lost their tone. As the public have applauded the attempt, the author must not say he was entirely unequal to the task he had undertaken: yet if the new route he has struck out shall

have paved a road for men of brighter talents, he shall own
with pleasure and modesty, that he was sensible the plan
was capable of receiving greater embellishments than his
imagination or conduct of the passions could bestow on it.
(pp. 7-8)

We arrive at the inevitable question: was there any
identifiable force generating this obsession gripping both
readers and writers with the representation of the real?

CHAPTER 4

—————◆—————

'ROMANCES, CHOCOLATE, NOVELS, AND THE LIKE INFLAMERS'

Budgell, *Spectator*, no. 365

THOUGH most of Defoe's prefaces, as has been seen, manifest an anxiety to assure the reader that what follows is a true record, with *Colonel Jack* (1722) truth is clearly subordinated to moral didacticism and the claims made for the latter are on the grand scale:

> It is so customary to write Prefaces to all Books of this Kind to introduce them with the more Advantage into the World, that I cannot omit it, tho' on that Account, 'tis thought, this Work needs a *Preface* less than any that ever went before it; the pleasant and delightful Part speaks for it self; the useful and instructive Part is so large, and capable of so many improvements, that it would imploy a Book, large as it self, to make Improvements suitable to the vast Variety of the Subject.
>
> Here's Room for just and copious Observations, on the Blessing, and Advantages of a sober and well govern'd Education, and the Ruin of so many Thousands of Youths of all Kinds, in this Nation, for want of it; also how much publick Schools, and Charities might be improv'd to prevent the Destruction of so many unhappy Children, as, in this Town, are every Year Bred up for the Gallows.
>
> The miserable Condition of unhappy Children, many of whose natural Tempers are docible, and would lead them

111

to learn the best Things rather than the worst, is truly deplorable, and is abundantly seen in the History of this Man's Childhood; where, though Circumstances form'd him by Necessity to be a Thief, a strange Rectitude of Principles remain'd with him, and made him early abhor the worst Part of his Trade, and at last wholly leave it off: If he had come into the World with the Advantage of Education, and been well instructed how to improve the generous Principles he had in him, what a Man might he not have been.

The various Turns of his Fortunes in the World, make a delightful Field for the Reader to wander in; a Garden where he may gather wholesome and medicinal Plants, none noxious or poisonous; where he will see Virtue and the Ways of Wisdom, every where applauded, honoured, encouraged, rewarded; Vice and all Kinds of Wickedness attended with Misery, may Kinds of Infelicities, and, at last, Sin and Shame going together, the Persons meeting with Reproof and Reproach, and the Crimes with Abhorrence.

Every wicked Reader will here be encouraged to a Change, and it will appear that the best and only good End of a wicked mispent Life is Repentance; that in this, there is Comfort, Peace, and often times Hope, and that the Penitent shall be return'd like the Prodigal, *and his latter End be better than his Beginning*.

While these Things, and such as these, are the Ends and Designs of the whole Book, *I think*, I need not say one Word more as an Apology for any part of the rest, no, nor for the whole; if Discouraging every thing that is Evil, and encouraging every thing that is vertuous and good; I say, If these appear to be the whole Scope and Design of the Publishing this story, no Objection can lye against it, neither is it of the least Moment to enquire whether the Colonel hath told his own Story true or not; If he has made it a *History* or a *Parable*, it will be equally useful, and capable of doing Good; and in that it recommends it self without any other *Introduction*.[1]

112

This asserts fairly firmly that the prime motivation of *Colonel Jack* is moral, and it is surprising to find in the preface to a work by Defoe the statement, 'neither is it of the least Moment to enquire whether the Colonel hath told his own Story true or not.' What one has come to regard as the matter of paramount importance to Defoe is denied.

Neither the editor of the standard edition of *Colonel Jack* nor the definitive bibliography of Defoe's works[2] points out that *Colonel Jack* was extensively revised, and the revisions made to the work's preface make all the more remarkable the denial of the overriding truth of the narrative. Phrases are changed in order to enhance the moral claims made. 'The Advantages of Education' becomes 'the Advantage of a virtuous Education'; 'What a Man might he not have been' is given a stronger religious thrust with 'what a Figure might he not have made, either as a man, or a Christian'. 'Every wicked Reader' becomes a 'vicious Reader', and that Defoe does not appear to have thought 'wicked' a strong enough term is suggested by the further alteration of 'wicked mispent Life' to 'impious mispent Life'. The final paragraph is completely rejigged:

> A Book founded on so useful a Plan, calculated to answer such valuable Purposes as have been Specified, can require no Apology: Nor is it of any Concern to the Reader, whether it be an exact historical Relation of real Facts, or whether the Hero of it intended to present us, at least in part, with a moral Romance: On either Supposition it is equally Serviceable for the Discouragement of Vice, and the Recommendation of Virtue.[3]

The original idea is expanded into two separate propositions: whether the work presented is 'an exact historical Relation of real Facts' which lays heavy tautological emphasis on the notion of reality – or whether this is a 'moral Romance'. The true explanation is made with some force: 'it is equally Serviceable for the Discouragement of Vice, and the Recommendation of Virtue.' From a writer who prefaced so many of his works with asseverations of authenticity this is a very important apparent shift.

One difficulty with Defoe is deciding in what spirit to take some of his editorial assertions. The preface to *Moll Flanders*, for example, contains a crucial ambiguity:

> It is true that the original of this Story is put into new Words, and the stile of the famous Lady we here speak of, is a little alter'd, particularly she is made to tell her own tale in modester Words than she told it at first; the Copy which first came to Hand, having been written in Language more like one still in *Newgate*, than one grown Penitent and Humble, as she afterwards pretends to be.[4]

'Pretends' here allows the reader to opt for one of two possible meanings: the dominant modern meaning with its associations of the sham; or, as the editor of the Oxford edition of the work appears to prefer, 'proposes' or 'aspires to'. Other passages from the preface and the body of the work need to be considered in relation to this word. The preface also includes the claim that 'there is not an ill thing mention'd, but it is condemn'd, even in the Relation, nor a vertuous just Thing, but it carries its Praise along with it' (p.3), a claim which is, in the light of several episodes in the book, highly debatable. Within the body of Moll's memoirs it is noticeable that she only brings up the subject of repentance either at moments when she is in imminent danger of being caught or punished, or, at the end of the work, when the vast wealth which she has acquired allows the luxury of affirmations of penitence.

Such a reading is of the sort which comes under attack in the preface to *Roxana* where, after the quasi-formulaic asseveration of the proper interpretation of the work, the reader who does not accept this synoptic view is sharply assailed:

> In the Manner she has told the Story, it is evident she does not insist upon her Justification in any one Part of it; much less does she recommend her Conduct, or indeed any Part of it, except her Repentance, to our Imitation: On the contrary, she makes frequent Excursions in a just censuring

and condemning her own Practice: How often does she reproach herself in the most passionate Manner; and guide us to just Reflections in the like Cases?

It is true She met with unexpected Success in all her wicked Courses; but even in the highest Elevations of her Prosperity she makes frequent Acknowledgements, That the Pleasure of her Wickedness was not worth the Repentance; and that all the Satisfaction she had, all the Joy in the View of her Prosperity, no, nor all the Wealth she rowl'd in; the Gaiety of her Appearance; the Equipages, and the Honours, she was attended with, cou'd quiet her Mind, abate the Reproaches of her Conscience, or procure her an Hour's Sleep, when just Reflections kept her waking.

The Noble Inferences that are drawn from this one Part, are worth all the rest of the Story; and abundantly justify (as they are the profess'd Design of) the Publication.

If there are any Parts in her Story which being oblig'd to relate a wicked Action, seem to describe it too plainly, the Writer says, all imaginable Care has been taken to keep clear of Indecencies and immodest Expressions; and 'tis hop'd you will find nothing to prompt a vicious Mind, but everywhere much to discourage and expose it.

Scenes of Crime, can scarce be represented in such a Manner but some may make a Criminal Use of them; but when Vice is painted in its Low-priz'd Colours, 'tis not to make People in love with it, but to expose it; and if the Reader makes a wrong Use of the Figures, the Wickedness is his own.[5]

Whether or not such claims of inherent moral value in the work are to be accepted must ultimately rest with the individual reader – Defoe's works, as modern criticism has shown, have many handles.

Though Defoe so often claims his works to be true and to be useful guides to the proper conduct of life, in this combination he was not entirely in line with contemporary critical opinion. John Dennis, writing on Shakespeare,

digressed to consider the different effects on the reader of fact
and fiction:

> For the just Fiction of a Fable moves us more than an
> Historical Relation can do, for the two following Reasons:
> First, by reason of the Communication and mutual
> Dependence of its Parts. For if Passion springs from
> Motion, then the Obstruction of that Motion or a counter
> Motion must obstruct and check the Passion: And
> therefore an Historian and a Writer of Historical Plays
> passing from Events of one nature to Events of another
> nature without a due Preparation, must of necessity stifle
> and confound one Passion by another. The second Reason
> why the Fiction of a Fable pleases us more, than an
> Historical Relation can do is, because in an Historical
> Relation we seldom are acquainted with the true Causes of
> Events, whereas in a feign'd Action which is duly
> constituted, that is, which has a just beginning, those
> Causes always appear. For 'tis observable that in both a
> Poetical Fiction and an Historical Relation, those Events
> are the most entertaining, the most surprizing, and the
> most wonderful, in which Providence most plainly appears.
> And 'tis for this Reason that the Author of a just Fable,
> must please more than the Writer of an Historical
> Relation. The Good must never fail to prosper, and the
> Bad must be always punish'd: Otherwise the Incidents,
> and particularly the Catastrophe which is the grand
> Incident, are liable to be imputed rather to Chance, than
> to Almighty Conduct and to Sovereign Justice.[6]

This question of whether truth or fiction is the more effective
in the reinforcement of a moral message is one to which
writers constantly return throughout the century. Mrs
Manley, upon whom so many looked with scorn, claimed in
her preface to *The Secret History of Queen Zarah* to have adopted
a very moral line in her story:

> '*Tis an indispensible Necessity to end a Story to satisfie the Disquiets
> of the Reader, who is engag'd to the Fortunes of those People whose*

Adventures are described to him; 'tis depriving him of a most delicate
Pleasure, when he is hindred from seeing the Event of an Intrigue,
which has caused some Emotion in him, whose Discovery he expects,
be it either Happy or Unhappy; the chief End of History is to
instruct and inspire into Men the Love of Vertue, and Abhorrence of
Vice, by the Examples propos'd to them; therefore the Conclusion of
a Story ought to have some Tract of Morality which may engage
Virtue; those People who have a more refin'd Vertue are not always
the most Happy; but yet their Misfortunes excite their Readers Pity,
and affects them; although Vice be not always punish'd yet 'tis
describ'd with Reasons which shew its Deformity, and make it
enough known to be worthy of nothing but Chastisements.[7]

Once again the vocabulary adopted presents problems. What
is meant by her use of 'History'? Is this work to be seen as
fact or fiction? As actual or plausible? A term which, if
definitive, would be a most useful critical tool is cheerfully
appropriated by both sides. *The Secret History of Queen Zarah* is
based upon historical detail, but it is presented in a mode
which suggests fiction. Divisions are constantly blurred and
critical positions become more and more untenable.

Mrs Manley's equally despised compeer, Eliza Haywood,
also made claims for the improving tendencies of fiction, and
did so throughout her long career, in the early stages of which
the moral comment was part of the body of the text. The
opening paragraph of *Idalia: or, the unfortunate mistress. A novel*
was openly moralising:

If there were a Possibility that the Warmth and Vigour of
Youth could be temper'd with a due Consideration, and
the Power of Judging rightly; how easy were it to avoid the
Ills which most of us endure? How few would be unhappy?
With what Serenity might the *Noon* of Life glide on, would
we account with reason for our *Morning* Actions! We hear,
indeed, daily Complaints of the Cruelty of *Fate*, but if we
examine the Source, we shall find almost all the Woes we
languish under are self-caus'd; and that either to pursue
the Gratification of some unruly Passion, or by the

Performance of an incumbent Duty, those Mistakes which
so fill the World derive their Being; and would more justly
merit *Condemnation* than *Compassion*, were not the fault too
Universal.[8]

Twenty-five years later, possibly as a result of the influence of
Richardson's extensive prefatory material to his works, *Life's
Progress through the passions: or, the adventures of Natura* appeared
with a full-blown 'Introduction' of considerable interest as a
statement of the writer's creed:

I have often heard it observed by the readers of biography,
that the characters are generally too high painted; and that
the *good* or *bad* qualities of the person pretended to be
faithfully represented, are displayed in stronger colours
than are to be found in nature. To this the lovers of
hyperbole reply, that *virtue* cannot be drawn too beautiful,
nor *vice* too deformed, in order to excite in us an ambition
of imitating the *one*, and a horror at the thoughts of
becoming any way like the *other*. – The argument, at first,
seems to have some weight, as there is nothing, not even
precept itself, which so greatly contributes whether to
rectify or improve the mind, or the prevalence of example:
but then it ought to be considered, that if the pattern laid
down before us, is so altogether angelic, as to render it
impossible to be copied, emulation will be in danger of
being swallowed up in an unprofitable admiration; and on
the other hand, if it appears so monstrously hideous as to
take away all apprehensions of ever resembling it, we
might be too apt to indulge ourselves in errors which would
seem small in comparison with those presented to us. –
There never yet was any one man, in whom all the *virtues*,
or all the *vices*, were summed up; for, though reason and
education may go a long way toward curbing the passions,
yet I believe experience will inform, even the *best* of men,
that they will sometimes launch out beyond their due
bounds, in spite of all the care that can be taken to restrain
them; nor do I think the very *worst*, and most wicked, does

118

not feel in himself, at some moments, a propensity to good, though it may be possible he never brings it into practice; at least, this was the opinion of the antients, as witness the poet's words:

> *All men are born with seeds of* good *and* ill;
> *And each shoot forth, in more or less degree;*
> One *you may cultivate with care and skill,*
> *But from the* other *ne'er be wholly free.*

The human mind may, I think, be compared to a chequer-work, when light and shade appear by hand; and in proportion as either of these is most conspicuous, the man is alone worthy of promise or censure; for none there are who can boast of being wholly bright.

I believe by this the reader will be convinced he must not expect to see a faultless figure in the hero of the following pages; but to remove all possibility of a disappointment on that score, I shall farther declare, that I am an enemy to all *romances, novels,* and whatever carries the air of them, tho' disguised under different appellations; and as it is a *real,* not *fictitious* character I am about to present, I feel myself obliged, for the reasons I have already given, as well as to gratify my own inclinations, to draw him such as he was, not such as some sanguine imaginations might wish him to have been.

I flatter myself, however, that truth will appear not altogether void of charms, and the adventures I take upon me to relate, not be less pleasing for being within the reach of probability, as such as might have happened to any other as well as the person they did. – Few there are, I am pretty certain, who will not find some resemblance of himself in one part or another of his life, among the various and surprizing turns of fortune, which the subject of this little history experienced, as also be reminded in what manner the passions operate in every stage of life, and how far the constitution of the *outward frame* is concerned in the emotions of the *internal faculties.*

These are things surely very necessary to be considered,

and when they are so, will, in a great measure, abate that unbecoming vehemence, with which people are apt to testify their admiration, or abhorrence of actions, which it very often happens would lose much of their *eclat* either way, were the secret springs that gave them motion, seen into with the eye of philosophy and reflection.

But this will be more clearly understood by a perusal of the facts herein contained, from which I will no longer detain the attention of my reader.[9]

Mrs Haywood here adopted the via media in her attitude to the proper moral level of characterisation – somewhere between the faultless and the vicious. Despite her prolific output of volumes designated 'novel' on their title pages, she had recognised that in the 1740s this was no longer a term to apply to one's work, and so declared: 'I am an enemy to all *romances, novels*, and whatever carries the air of them, tho' disguised under different appellations'; she jumped on the evidently successful Richardsonian bandwagon – 'it is a *real*, not a *fictitious* character I am about to present'; and the actions were advertised as 'within the reach of probability'. And if there is any reader so obtuse as to have failed to realise the essential propriety, the final paragraph of the work re-emphasised Mrs Haywood's overt stance:

> Thus have I attempted to trace nature in all her mazy windings, and shew life's progress thro' the passions, from the cradle to the grave. – The various adventures which happened to *Natura*, I thought, afforded a more ample field, than those of any one man I ever heard, or read of; and flatter myself, that the reader will find many instances, that may contribute to rectify his own conduct, by pointing out those things which ought to be avoided, or at least more carefully guarded against, and those which are worthy to be improved and imitated. (p. 231)

Mesdames Manley and Haywood consistently, and Defoe occasionally, made large moral claims for their works which are open to considerable dispute, and it may be reasonable to suppose that such claims were formulaic in an effort not to lose readers – a neat proleptic inversion of the modern practice of providing salacious cover illustrations to relatively innocuous works in order to attract readers.

The extent to which works of fiction did or did not have beneficial effects on their readership was frequently debated both in general terms and in relation to specific titles. Goldsmith, writing to his brother about the upbringing of his nephew, adopted a highly idiosyncratic attitude. Whereas most of the disputants accepted the premise that in general reading of fiction had adverse moral effects, Goldsmith condemned the habit on the grounds that it induced an over-heightened sense of virtue:

> Above all let him [Goldsmith's nephew] never touch a romance or novel, those paint beauty in colours more charming than nature, and describe happiness that man never tastes. How delusive, how destructive therefore are those pictures of consummate bliss, they teach the youthful mind to sigh after beauty and happiness which never existed, to despise the little good which fortune has mixed in our cup, by expecting more than she ever gave. And in general take the word of a man who has seen the world, and studied human nature more by experience than precept, take my word for it I say that books teach us very little of the world . . . .
>
> I had learn'd from books to love virtue, before I was taught from experience the necessity of being selfish.[10]

Other writers, such as John Hawkesworth, adopted a more conventional viewpoint, that writers of fiction had a moral imperative, and in a paper in the *Adventurer*, Hawkesworth developed his argument to consider the nature of an effective interrelationship between imagination and instruction:

> But it is justly expected of the writer of fiction, who has unbounded liberty to select, to vary and to complicate, that his plan should be complete, that he should principally consider the moral tendency of his work, and that when he relates events he should teach virtue.
>
> The relation of events becomes a moral lecture, when vicious actions produce misery, and vicious characters

incur contempt; when the combat of virtue is rewarded with honour, and her sufferings terminate in felicity; but though this method of instruction has been often recommended, yet I think some of its peculiar advantages have been still overlooked, and for that reason not always secured.

Facts are easily comprehended by every understanding: and their dependance and influence upon each other are discovered by those, who would soon be bewildered in a series of logical deductions: they fix that volatility which would break away from ratiocination; and the precept becomes more forcible and striking as it is connected with example. Precept gains only the cold approbation of reason, and compels an assent which judgment frequently yields with reluctance, even when delay is impossible: but by example the passions are roused; we approve, we emulate, and we honour or love; we detest, we despise, and we condemn, as fit objects are successively held up to the mind: the affections are, as it were, drawn out into the field: they learn their exercise in a mock fight, and are trained for the service of virtue.

Facts, as they are most perfectly and easily comprehended, and as they are impressed upon the mind by the passions, are tenaciously remembered, though the terms in which they are delivered are presently forgotten; and for this reason the instruction that results from facts is more easily propagated: many can repeat a story, who would not have understood a declamation; and though the expression will be varied as often as it is told, yet the moral which it was intended to teach will remain the same.

But these advantages have not always been secured by those who have professed 'to make a story the vehicle of instruction', and to 'surprise levity into knowledge by a show of entertainment;' for instead of including instruction in the events themselves, they have made use of events only to introduce declamation and argument. If the events excite curiosity, all the fine reflections which are said to be interspersed, are passed over; if the events do not excite curiosity, the whole is rejected together, not only with disgust and disappointment, but indignation, as having allured by a false promise, and engaged in a vain pursuit. These pieces, if they are read as a task by those for whose instruction they are intended, can produce none of the effects for which they were written; because the instruction will not be necessarily remembered with the facts; and because the story is so far from recommending the moral, that the moral is detested as interrupting the story. Nor are those who voluntarily read for instruction, less disappointed than those who seek only entertainment; for he that is eager in the pursuit of knowledge, is disgusted when he is stopped by the intervention of a trivial incident or a forced compliment, when a new personage is introduced, or a lover takes occasion to admire the sagacity of a mistress.[11]

This may be a suitable point at which to offer a *caveat lector*. It has been suggested earlier that those critics and readers who raised the matter of adherence to reality might have been at base rather more preoccupied with aesthetic or social concerns. It is possible to suggest similarly that those who raised the pennant of morality did so to distract attention from their true motivations.

In his 'Sermon on the causes of the present wretched condition of Ireland' Swift talked of the provision and function of charity schools:

In those schools children are, or ought to be, trained up to read and write, and cast accounts; and those children should, if possible, be of honest parents, gone to decay through age, sickness, or other unavoidable calamity, by the hand of God; not the brood of wicked strollers; for it is by no means reasonable, that the charity of well-inclined people should be applied to encourage the lewdness of those profligate, abandoned women, who crowd our streets with their borrowed or spurious issue.

In those hospitals which have good foundations and

rents to support them, whereof, to the scandal of
Christianity, there are very few in this kingdom; I say, in
such hospitals, the children maintained ought to be only of
decayed citizens, and freemen, and be bred up to good
trades. But in these small parish charity-schools which
have no support, but the casual goodwill of charitable
people, I do altogether disapprove the custom of putting
the children 'prentice, except to the very meanest trades;
otherwise the poor honest citizen, who is just able to bring
up his child, and pay a small sum of money with him to a
good master, is wholly defeated, and the bastard issue,
perhaps, of some beggar, preferred before him.[12]

Literacy is to be confined to those groups who will put it to a
socially acceptable proper use. It is to be denied to the rest of
society. Throughout the century the question of the correct
use of literacy recurred in a variety of different forms. It was
a particularly dominant element in the discussion of fiction,
and often disguised as moral concern:

It must be a matter of real concern to all considerate
minds, to see the youth of both sexes passing so large a
part of their time in reading that deluge of familiar
romances, which, in this age, our island overflows with.
'Tis not only a most unprofitable way of spending time, but
extremely prejudicial to their morals, many a young person
being entirely corrupted by the giddy and fantastical
notions of love and gallantry, imbibed from thence. There
is scarcely a month passes, but some worthless book of this
kind, in order to catch curiosity by its novelty, appears in
the form of two volumes 12mo. price five or six shillings,
and they are chiefly the offspring, as I take it, of the
managers of the circulating libraries, or their venal
authors. Some few of them, indeed, have come from better
pens, but the whole together are an horrible mass of hurtful
insignificance, and, I suppose, may amount now to above
an hundred volumes; I speak at the lowest.[13]

Circulating libraries, which provided ready access to fiction, came in for attack, both serious and ironic:

> *Mrs. Malaprop.* There's a little intricate hussy for you!
>
> *Sir Anthony.* It is not to be wondered at ma'am, – all this is the natural consequence of teaching girls to read. Had I a thousand daughters, by Heaven! I'd as soon have them taught the black art as their alphabet!
>
> *Mrs. Mal.* Nay, nay, Sir Anthony, you are an absolute misanthropy.
>
> *Sir Ant.* In my way hither, Mrs. Malaprop, I observed your niece's maid coming forth from a circulating library! – She had a book in each hand – they were half-bound volumes with marble covers! – From that moment I guessed how full of duty I should see her mistress!
>
> *Mrs. Mal.* These are vile places, indeed!
>
> *Sir Ant.* Madam, a circulating library in a town is as an evergreen tree of diabolical knowledge! It blossoms through the year! – and depend on it, Mrs. Malaprop, that they who are so fond of handling the leaves, will long for the fruit at last.[14]

Those who, it was felt, were abusing their access to literacy (and the library) and were in most danger of harm were adolescent females. This is a recurrent observation in the criticism of the times. The young female reader is the key reader in the eyes of the critics who are usually middle-aged males. And at times it is quite evident that these elderly males are rather too interested in the sexual excitement they imagine the unattended young virgins to be deriving from their unsupervised and solitary reading.

Henry Pye, subsequently Poet Laureate, demonstrated that his critical perceptions were on the level of his poetry, though more memorable, when he asserted:

> The only persons of the present day, who at all devote their attention with ardor and perseverance to the reading

compositions of fictitious distress, (and I believe their
number, especially among the higher ranks, decreases
every day,) are those usually called romantic young
women, who dedicate much of their time to the study of the
numerous tales, with which the press continually furnishes
our circulating libraries ... the general effect of novel-
reading on the gentler sex is too obvious to be doubted; it
excites and inflames the passion which is the principal
subject of the tale, and the susceptibility of the female
votary of the circulating library, is proverbial. But we
must, in the first place, recollect, that the passion of love is
very different in itself from terror and pity, though it may
be the cause of circumstances replete with both; and it is
the tendency to this passion, and not to those of pity and
terror, which is encreased by this kind of reading. Beside, it
is not perhaps so much the passion itself that is enflamed,
as the wish to feel it is created by this study. A desire of
resembling the fictitious heroine of a novel, has often
induced a young mind to enquire for those sensations,
which, without such a search, might have continued for
some time dormant in the bosom. So far, therefore, is love
from being blunted by imitative fiction, that such fiction is
often an efficient cause of its being first excited.[15]

A contributor to *The Gentleman's Magazine* made the same
point:

they have a tendency still more fatal, they bring young
readers acquainted with the worst part of the female sex,
habituate them to loose principles and immodest practices,
and thus send them into the world debauched, at least in
heart, at an age which should be adorned with simplicity
and innocence. Concern for the female character makes
this remark not foreign to our subject.[16]

The eighteenth century young lady was deliberately excluded
from certain areas of knowledge – she was not taught Greek,
and there was little opportunity of acquiring Latin.[17] The

division between the proper modes and areas of education for the two sexes was maintained for a considerable period – think of Jane Austen's descriptions of the upbringing of Tom and Edmund Bertram as against that of their sisters Maria and Julia.

It is, of course, easy to disparage eighteenth century society in this matter. But, consider:

> *Would you approve of your young sons and daughters – because girls can read as well as boys – reading this book?*

That was not an eighteenth century question. It was put to the jury by the prosecuting counsel at the trial of Penguin Books for publishing an obscene work, *Lady Chatterley's Lover*, in 1960.[18]

The subjects of female education and society's attitude to literacy cannot be adequately discussed here, but throughout this chapter they must be borne in mind as possible explanations of the tone and content of many of the apparently morally concerned opinions.

Regardless of the true motivation, one has to accept that the notion of morality as the true litmus test for literary works was very seriously debated and is the most frequently occurring theme to be found not only in published criticism but also in the statements of the writers themselves and in the private correspondence of their readers. This is perhaps best to be seen in the curious way in which, then as now, so many critics and readers polarised themselve into two mutually exclusive camps: the admirers of Richardson and those of Fielding. I use the word 'curious' in view of the fact that Fielding himself, though having made much capital out of the unwitting prurience and blasphemy manifested in *Pamela*, wrote Richardson a highly complimentary letter while reading *Clarissa*, a letter which clearly shows the way in which Fielding felt works of fiction made moral points:

> The Circumstance of the Fragments is Great and Terrible; but her [Clarissa's] Letter to Lovelace is beyond any thing I have ever read. God forbid that the Man who reads this with dry Eyes should

be alone with my Daughter when she hath no Assistance within Call.[19]

On the other hand Richardson appears to have lost few opportunities to denigrate the works and character of his fellow-writer both in conversation and correspondence which had wide circulation. Frequently critics and readers judged the one by the standards or in terms of the other. Thus Boswell recorded:

> Fielding's characters, though they do not expand
> themselves so widely in dissertation, are as just pictures of
> human nature, and I will venture to say, have more
> striking features, and nicer touches of the pencil; and
> though Johnson used to quote with approbation a saying of
> Richardson's, 'that the virtues of Fielding's heroes were the
> vices of a truly good man,' I will venture to add, that the
> moral tendency of Fielding's writings, though it does not
> encourage a strained and rarely possible virtue, is ever
> favourable to honour and honesty, and cherishes the
> benevolent and generous affections. He who is as good as
> Fielding would make him, is an amiable member of society,
> and may be led on by more regulated instructors, to a
> higher state of ethical perfection.[20]

An outstandingly neutral position was adopted by a French author, Barthe, extracts from whose novel *La jolie Femme* were translated for *The Gentleman's Magazine* in 1770. This was one of the few published opinions to recognise that both writers had produced works of great moral worth, which impinged on their readers in very different ways:

> The works of *Richardson* are dear to me; I know none in
> which genius is more discernible. The illusion is lasting,
> and complete: What art must he have had to produce it!
> When I read *Clarissa*, I am of the family of the Harlowes. I
> am interested for one, I hate another, I am indifferent for a
> third. By turns, I could embrace and fight with Lovelace.
> His pride, his gaiety, his drollery charm and amuse me: his

genius confounds me, and makes me smile; his wickedness astonishes and enrages me; but at the same time, I admire as much as I detest him; he is the Cromwell of women. I interrupt the unhappy Clarissa, in order to mix my tears with hers: I accost her, as if she was present with me. No Author, I believe, ever metamorphosed himself into his characters so perfectly as Richardson; we forget, we no longer see, the hand which puts so many secret springs in motion; sometimes we are tempted to suspect that the letters were intercepted. If you add to so many perfections those excellent morals diffused through all the work, that soul of virtue and sensibility which animates whatever it touches, you must confess that to exhibit such pictures is to be a benefactor to mankind: Above all, *Grandison* is the book which most inspires virtue, Plutarch and Plato not excepted.

Fielding may justly be styled his rival. No man in the world (without excepting Molière) was better acquainted with the shades which diversify characters; and he is the Author who has best seized the manners of the people, though it is said that they generally form the nation. A living picture animated with its caprices, its passions, its follies; a true, singular pencil; a simple, lively moral, which naturally results from various scenes; all this insures to Fielding a distinguished place among those Writers whose fertile imagination has drawn Nature as she really is. Less sublime, less pathetic than Richardson, but more chearful, more original, he engages us as much as the other makes us weep. If the one has opened all the treasures of morality, the other, with a wise œconomy, has insinuated it with an imperceptible art into the soul of those who would not receive it. The one paints with large strokes, attracts the heart on every side, and imperiously hurries it away; the other, by varied, chosen, delicate touches, brings smiles on the lips, and tears into the eyes. Indeed he soon dries them; but this transition is so managed as not to be abrupt. His style has the same effect as that ancient music, whose art made the soul pass gently, or, as it were, insensibly, from

129

joy to sorrow; thus producing various and even opposite emotions. In short, Richardson is more grand, more formed on models which will live throughout all ages; the other is more simple, more instructive, and his admirers being less idolatrous, he will have, perhaps, a still greater number of readers.[21]

Barthe's eulogy of Lovelace underlines one of Richardson's major problems – in wishing to portray Clarissa as a paragon of virtue he is forced into showing her as overcoming, or at least countering, the epitome of vice. But at the same time the latter must simultaneously be presented as a character such that Clarissa's attraction to him is explicable. In this area Richardson plays with fire.

Vicesimus Knox is more representative of those who weighed the two writers against each other and found one morally defective:

That Richardson's Novels are written with the purest intentions of promoting virtue, none can deny. But in the accomplishment of this purpose scenes are laid open, which it would be safer to conceal, and sentiments excited, which it would be more advantageous to early virtue not to admit. Dangers and temptations are pointed out; but many of them are dangers which seldom occur, and temptations by which few in comparison are assaulted. It is to be feared, the moral view is rarely regarded by youthful and inexperienced readers, who naturally pay the chief attention to the lively description of love, and its effects; and who, while they read, eagerly wish to be actors in the scenes which they admire.

The cultivated genius of Fielding entitles him to a high rank among the classics. His works exhibit a series of pictures drawn with all the descriptive fidelity of a Hogarth. They are highly entertaining, and will always be read with pleasure; but they likewise disclose scenes, which may corrupt a mind unseasoned by experience.[22]

Of these two colossi of mid-eighteenth century fiction it was Fielding who was most frequently condemned for failing to reach (or preach) the moral standards required. This may in part be attributed to Richardson's influence, for he was assiduous in the dissemination of the message that his works were above all intended to be agents for good. This is to be seen not only in his public assertions such as the prefatory material to *Pamela* discussed at some length in chapter 3, but also in many items in his vast correspondence with his readers. Two of his letters to George Cheyne *re Pamela* may serve as indicators of his methods:

I am endeavouring to write a Story, which shall catch young and airy Minds, and when Passions run high in them, to shew how they may be directed to laudable Meanings and Purposes, in order to decry such Novels and Romances, as have a Tendency to inflame and corrupt: and if I were to be too spiritual, I doubt I should catch none but Grandmothers, for the Granddaughters would put my Girl indeed in better Company, such as that of the graver Writers, and *there* they would leave her; but would still pursue those Stories, that pleased their Imaginations without informing their Judgments. And the principal Complaints against me by many, and not Libertines neither, are, that I am too grave, too much of a Methodist, and make Pamela too pious. I have in View, however, to avoid inflaming Descriptions and to turn even the Fondness of ye Pair to a kind of intellectual Fondness; for I never make them rise in their Fondness of each other, but for some laudable Behaviour or Conduct; *Benevolence* on *his* side, which obliges her; or *Gratitude* on *her*'s, and when she hopes he is govern'd by the best and most solid Motives: And if on these Occasions there is so much Grossness in a Kiss between a Man and his Wife, which from Man to Man, in the like Incidents, wou'd have been expressed in *more than common* Words, in a *Pressure of the Hand*, and *Tenderness of Expression*, to manifest their reciprocal Gratitude and Pleasure, what shall we say? – To be sure there is no Writing on these Subjects to please such a Gentleman as that in the Tatler, who cou'd find Sex in a *laced shoe*, when there was none in the Foot, that was to wear it. And what wou'd such an one have said to pass now through Covent-Garden, under Twenty Hoop-petticoats, hanging over his Head at the Habit-Shops?

131

In my scheme I have generally taken Human Nature *as it is*; for it is to no purpose to suppose it Angelic, or to endeavour to make it so. There is a Time of Life, in which the Passions will predominate; and Ladies, any more than Men, will not be kept in Ignorance; and if we can properly mingle Instruction with Entertainment, so as to make the latter *seemingly* the *View*, while the former is *really* the End, I imagine it will be doing a great deal . . . .

To say, that these Tender Scenes should be *suppos'd* rather than *described*, is not answering my Design, when the Instruction lies *in them*, and when I wou'd insinuate to my *younger Readers*, that even their tenderest Loves should be govern'd by Motives of Gratitude for laudable Obligations; and I have been told I am in Danger of *leaving Nature*, and being too refin'd for Practice on some of these Occasions. But I hope not! If I meet not with Minds too delicate on one hand, or too gross on the other; I presume too much on my *Intention*; but indeed so little, at times, on my Capacity, that I cannot express my Diffidence.

As to the Difference between the Sexes, I leave that Matter as I find it, because I think it necessary in my Plan to avoid all Notions not generally receiv'd or allowed.[23]

This letter had been written in answer to Cheyne's rather startling advice, on having read the first two volumes of *Pamela*, 'You ought to avoid Fondling – and Gallantry, Tender Expressions not becoming the Character of Wisdom, Piety and conjugal Chastity especially in the Sex.' Volumes 3 and 4 caused a brisk *volte face* and Cheyne wrote to suggest that they contained rather too much preaching and too little which might excite the emotions of the reader.

Richardson's reply was informative:

As to the Opinion of the Critics you mention that ye last two Volumes of ye History of Pamela are Defective in Incidents; I must own I am so great an Enemy to the French Marvellous, that I only aimed to give the Piece such a Variety, as should be consistent with Probability, and the general Tenor of a genteel Married Life. I aimed, as far as my poor Talents wou'd permit, to *instruct*, rather than to Surprize; and I labour'd hard to rein in my Invention, and made it a Rule with me to avoid unnecessary Digressions, & Foreign Episodes; and indeed had so much Matter upon my Hands to give

probable Instances of what a good Wife, a tender Mother, a faithful
Friend, a Kind Mistress, and a worthy Neighbour shou'd do
(including the first parts of Education, which might fall under the
Mother's eye) that being resolved to comprise the Whole in two
Volumes, four in all, I had great Difficulty so to touch so many
Subjects distinctly and intelligibly to ye common understandings,
and so had not Field for Excursions of Fancy & Imagination.
Besides, Sir, the four Volumes were to be consider'd as one Work.
The two First were to include the Storms, the Strategems, and all
that could indanger Virtue, and ingage the Attention of the Reader,
for its Distresses – The succeeding of course were to be more calm,
serene, and instructive, and such as should be Exemplary, as I may
say: For I always had it in View, I have the Vanity to repeat, to
make the Story rather *useful* than *diverting*; and if I cou'd perform it
in such a manner as should entertain, it was all I aimed at. The
cause of Virtue and Religion, was what I wish'd principally to serve;
and I hoped it wou'd be allowed to be a New, and in some sort, an
Original Piece; which I had in vain endeavour'd to put better Heads
upon before I undertook it myself. I am better pleased it has your
Approbation with regard to ye *Morality* than if it had diverted more
by a greater Variety of Incidents, without deserving that Character,
altho' its Reception had been to produce me Thousands of
Pounds.[24]

These two letters, which are in many ways entirely typical,
make a variety of important points about Richardson's views
of the nature and purposes of prose fiction in general and his
own in particular. His dismissive reference to 'such Novels
and Romances, as have a Tendency to inflame and corrupt'
reinforces the idea already put forward that he did not take
kindly to the thought that his own works could be described
by either of these terms, and thus aligns him very firmly
alongside Fielding in this matter. His choice of 'inflame' to
describe the effects of certain works upon their readers ties in
with the assertiveness of the title page of *Pamela* which
declares the work to be:

A Narrative which has its Foundation in TRUTH and
NATURE; and at the same time that it agreeably
entertains, by a Variety of curious and affecting

INCIDENTS, is entirely divested of all those Images, which, in too many Pieces calculated for Amusement only, tend to inflame the Minds they should instruct.

And this links Richardson to Budgell's earlier juxtapositioning of 'Romances, Chocolate, Novels, and the like Inflamers'.[25] Chocolate, in sharp distinction to its modern connotation of a dish for a good night's rest, had a reputation in the eighteenth century and earlier of being a potent aphrodisiac. It was an ingredient of Spanish Fly, and serious warnings were issued as to its effects. Helge Rubinstein records that Casanova drank it rather than champagne, and cites examples of attacks made upon the habit of drinking such a potent substance:

> The theologian Johannes Franciscus Rauch published a Disputation in 1624 in which he inveighed against the immoderate use of chocolate by the monks, claiming that it was a violent inflamer of passions, and that if monks had been forbidden to drink it, the scandals with which the holy order had been branded might have been groundless. At about the same time the English physician, Henry Stubbs, writes of Chocolate in *The Indian Nectar*:
>
>> And as *Chocolate* provokes other Evacuations through the several *Emunctories* of the body, so it doth that of *Seed*, and becomes *provocative to lust* upon no other account . . . .[26]

The notion of the novel as sexually inflaming linked to the hypotheticised or actual readership of lonely maidens increased the temperature of the language of criticism.

Though Richardson was so anxious to promote his work as the antithesis of inflaming, he was aware of reader reaction to his works, and that responses were both favourable and antagonistic: the view 'too much of a Methodist' is precisely that expressed by Walpole (below, page 167). By meeting such criticism directly and in correspondence with readers, Richardson stands out even in an age when writers were devoted to ensuring their readers got it right by his determination to ensure that his readers judge correctly. To the modern reader, faced with works of such literary and physical magnitude as *Pamela, Clarissa* and *Sir Charles Grandison*, the prospect of working through six volumes of letters may be rather daunting. It is, however, extremely illuminating.

Richardson's works appeared in a quasi-serial fashion: *Pamela*'s four volumes appeared in two stages; the seven volumes of *Clarissa* appeared in three stages; and writing to Clairaut prior to the publication of *Sir Charles Grandison* he revealed his reasons for timing publication in this way:

> I think to publish it at three several times; because there are some few Surprises in different Parts of it, which, were the Catastrophe known, would be lessen'd, and take off the Ardor of such Readers as should happen to approve of the Piece.[27]

Once more the vocabulary is revelatory: 'Ardor' has a connotation of burning, inflaming. Richardson's constant recourse to this element of diction suggests a real concern on his part as to the disparity between the intended and the actual effects of his writings. Ironically, in view of his constant and public protestations, it is possible to regard him as the true inflamer of the century. The fire scene in *Clarissa* quite obviously excited much of his readership in a way which would have appalled him. This paradoxical quality in Richardson's work was brilliantly caught by Fielding in *Shamela*, and Richardson's own tacit recognition of the inflammatory nature of his work may be seen in the extensive revisions which he made to *Pamela*, and the constant tinkering which went on with the text of *Clarissa*.[28] This manipulation of text was closely allied with his attempted manipulation of reader response which took place not only in the text itself, but before, during and after publication in his letters. The letters serve as invaluable commentary.

In the first of the letters to Cheyne above he harps on the topic discussed in the previous chapter: the idea of reality. The claim here is, 'I have generally taken Human Nature *as it is*; for it is to no purpose to suppose it Angelic, or to endeavour to make it so.' This is repeated in the second letter in which he says his intention was 'to give probable Instances' and wished to be 'consistent with Probability'. His reasons are similar to those of Defoe in the prefaces to *Moll Flanders* and *Roxana* – that the apparent truth of the relation will work a stronger moral instruction upon the reader. In the first letter to Cheyne the thrust of the argument is, 'If we can properly mingle Instruction with Entertainment, so as to make the latter *seemingly* the *View*, whilst the former is *really* the End, I imagine it will be doing a great deal', while the second letter states, 'I always had it in View, I have the Vanity to repeat, to make the Story rather *useful* than *diverting*: and if I cou'd perform it in such a manner as should entertain, it was all I aimed at', an argument which shifts the emphasis slightly, and raises a number of problems about the interrelationship of 'reality', morality and entertainment.

One of these problems became more evident when one sets Richardson's views of his own works against his view of Fielding's. Writing to Mrs Donellan, he expresses an opinion which conflicts with that expressed to Cheyne:

> You guess that I have not read *Amelia*. Indeed I have read but the first volume. I had intended to go through with it; but I found the characters and situations so wretchedly low and dirty, that I imagined I could not be interested for any one of them; and to read and not to care what became of the hero and heroine, is a task that I thought I would leave to those who had more leisure than I am blessed with.
>
> Parson Young sat for Fielding's parson Adams, a man he knew, and only made a little more absurd than he is known to be. The best story in the piece, is of himself and his first wife. In his *Tom Jones*, his hero is made a natural child, because his own first wife was such. Tom Jones is Fielding himself, hardened in some places, softened in others. His Lady Bellaston is an infamous woman of his former acquaintance. His Sophia is again his first wife. Booth, in his last piece, again himself; Amelia, even to her noselessness, is again his first wife. His brawls, his jarrs, his gaols, his spunging-houses, are all drawn from what he has seen and known. As I said (witness also his hamper plot) he has little or no invention: and admirably do you

observe, that by several strokes in his *Amelia* he designed to be good, but knew not how, and lost his genius, low humour, in the attempt.[29]

Fielding lacks imagination: he introduces into his works characters identifiable with those in real life. This is to be seen as a short-coming in works of fiction. But remember Richardson's letter to Aaron Hill about the originals of *Pamela* (above, pages 87-9). The argument is specious and designed to lead up to the real point: that Fielding's work is immoral. Immoral because the characters and circumstances are 'wretchedly low and dirty'. There is an element of the nelsonian about this when one thinks of the justification offered to Cheyne in response to the argument that 'Tender Scenes should be suppos'd rather than described.'

The effectiveness of Richardson's dissemination of the view that Fielding's works were ethically unacceptable may be seen in the way his correspondents passed on his opinions. Sarah Chapone wrote to Elizabeth Carter:

> Mr — tells me that you are a friend to Fielding's Amelia. I love the woman, but for the book – it must have merit, since Miss Carter and some few more good judges approve of it. Are you not angry with the author, for giving his favourite character such a lord and master? and is it quite natural that she should be perfectly happy and pleased with such a wretch? A fellow without principles, or understanding, with no other merit in the world but a natural good temper, and whose violent love for his wife could not keep him from injuring her in the most essential points, and that in circumstances that render him utterly inexcusable. Can you forgive his amour with that dreadful, shocking monster, Miss Mathews? Are we to look upon these crimes as the failings of human nature, as Fielding seems to do, who takes his notions of human nature from the most depraved and corrupted part of it, and seems to think no characters natural, but such as are a disgrace to the human species? Don't you think Booth's sudden conversion a mere botch to save the author's credit as a moral writer? And is there not a tendency in all his works, to soften the deformity of vice, by placing characters in an amiable light, that are destitute of every virtue except good nature? Was not you tired with the two first volumes? What think you of

Mrs. Bennet and her story? Pray let me have your sentiments at large on this book, for I am uneasy to know how it comes to pass that you like it, and I do not. The last volume pleased me very well; Doctor Harrison's character is admirable; the scene between Colonel James and his lady, excellent; that in which colonel James's challenge comes to the hands of Amelia is extremely affecting; the conversation between the Lord and Doctor Harrison, the doctor's letter, and the comments of the bucks upon it, I also admire very much. And now, I think, I have mentioned all that I can praise in the whole book; but it would take up more paper than I have left to point out one half of the pages that disgusted me.[30]

The same elements appear: there is discussion of the extent to which the characters are 'natural', that is 'real'; there is the *donnée* that an author should have 'credit as a moral writer'; and there is the conclusion that by the standards of morality Fielding's works fail. There is an admission that Fielding's characters could be seen as truthful representations, but are representations of 'the most depraved and corrupted part' of humanity. And again it is possible to refine this particular critical approach: there is to be morality, and this morality is to be based upon reality, but those areas of life which are to be seen as providing the acceptable examples of reality are restricted. This is entirely in keeping with Richardson's frequent explanations and justifications of his principles of selection of material.

When Elizabeth Carter attempted to defend her appreciation of *Amelia* Sarah Chapone returned to the attack with renewed vigour:

I am extremely obliged to you for gratifying my curiosity with your reasons for speaking so favourably of Amelia, though, at the same time, I am not a little mortified to find that I cannot assent to all you say. I am afraid I have less mercy in my disposition than you, for I cannot think with so much lenity of the character of Booth, which, though plainly designed as an amiable one by the author, is in my opinion contemptible and wicked. 'Rather frail than wicked!' Dear Miss Carter! that is what I complain of, that Fielding contrives to gloss over gross and monstrous faults in such a manner that even his virtuous readers shall call them frailties. How bad may be the consequence of such representations to those who are interested in the deception, and glad to find that their favourite vices are kept in countenance by a character which is designed to engage the esteem and good wishes of the reader. Had I not reason to accuse the author of 'softening or hiding the deformity of vice,' when infidelity, adultery, gaming, and extravagance, (the three last accompanied with all the aggravation that the excellence of a wife and the distress of a young family could give them) are so gently reproved, even by Miss Carter? 'His amour with Miss Mathews,' you say, 'however blameable, was attended with some alleviating circumstances:' what these were I am unable to discover. I think none but an abandoned heart, incapable of the least delicacy, and lost to the love of virtue and abhorrence of vice, could have entertained any thoughts but of horror and detestation for that fiend of a woman, after hearing her story.[31]

But just as not all eighteenth century expressed opinion on the nature of fictional representations of reality were in accord, what constituted acceptable morality varied. The review of *Amelia* in *The Monthly Review* thought its moral message one of its great strengths:

But be it said, to the honour of the *English*, and to Mr. Fielding, in particular, that he never thought so ill of the public, as to make his court to it at the expence of the sacred duties of morality. Wherever the obligation of painting the corruptions of mankind, and the world, *not as it should be, but as it really exists*, forces him into descriptions in which his actors depart from the paths of virtue and prudence, he is sure to make examples of them, perhaps more salutary, than if he had made them too rigidly adhere to their duty. Their follies and vices are turned so as to become instructions in the issue of them, and which make a far more forcible impression than merely speculative maxims and dry sentences. *Longum iter est per præcepta, breve et efficax per exempla*. Sen. Epist. 6.
By this means too the author imitates nature in inforcing its capital laws; by the attractions of pleasure he puts morality into action; it is alive, and insinuates its greatest

truths into the mind, under the colours of amusement and
fiction. Readers are, by the magic of this association, made
to retain what has at once instructed and diverted them,
when they would be apt to forget what has perhaps no
more than wearied, or *dulled* them. The chief and capital
purport of this work is to inculcate the superiority of
virtuous, conjugal, love, to all other joys; to prove that
virtue chastens our pleasures, only to augment them; that
the paths of vice, are always those of misery, and that
virtue, even in distress, is still a happier bargain to its
votaries, than vice, attended with all the splendor of
fortune. So just, so refined a morality, would alone, with a
candid and ingenuous reader, compensate for almost any
imperfections in the execution of this work, some parts
whereof will doubtless appear, amidst its beauties, to stand
in need of an apology: *for example*, where the characters are,
however exact copies of nature, chosen in too low, and
disgustful a range of it, and rather too often repeated, and
too long dwelt upon. The humours of an inn-keeper, an
inn-keeper's wife, a gaoler, a highwayman, a bailiff, a street
walker, may, no doubt, with great propriety find their
place in those novels, of which the matter is taken out of
common life; it would even be an absurd affectation to omit
them, in compliance to a false delicacy, which calls every
thing *low*, that does not relate to a high sphere of life,
especially when they present themselves so naturally as in
many places of this author's works. But when they occur
too often, when the ingredients are not sparingly mixed,
they will disgust even those, who, from their distance in
rank or circumstance from these subjects, may be curious
to have some idea of them, and can only come at it in such
descriptions.[32]

The Richardsonian view of the unacceptably low is countered
here: 'false delicacy, which calls every thing *low*, that does not
relate to a high sphere of life'.[33] And praise is offered to
Fielding for managing to combine so effectively the real, 'the
world, not as it should be, but as it really exists', the

140

entertaining, and the instructively moral: 'by the attractions of pleasure he puts morality into action.'

As time went on the supporters of Fielding switched from their relatively defensive posture. In 1785 Richard Cumberland launched a witty attack upon the morality of *Clarissa*:

The novel, which of all others is formed upon the most studied plan of morality, is *Clarissa*, and few young women I believe are put under restriction by their parents or others from gratifying their curiosity with a perusal of this author: guided by the best intentions, and conscious that the moral of his book is fundamentally good, he has taken all possible pains to weave into his story incidents of such a tragical and affecting nature, as are calculated to make a strong and lasting impression on the youthful heart. The unmerited sufferings of an innocent and beautiful young lady, who is made a model of patience and purity; the unnatural obduracy of her parents; the infernal arts of the wretch who violates her, and the sad catastrophe of her death, are incidents in this affecting story better conceived than executed: failing in this most essential point, as a picture of human nature, I must regard the novel of *Clarissa*, as one of the books, which a prudent parent will put under interdiction; for I think I can say from observation, that there are more artificial pedantic characters assumed by sentimental Misses, in the vain desire of being thought *Clarissa Harlows* [*sic*], than from any other source of imitation whatsoever: I suspect that it has given food to the idle passion for those eternal scribblings, which pass between one female friend and another, and tend to no good point of education. I have a young lady in my eye, who made her will, wrote an inscription for the plate of her own coffin, and forswore all mankind at the age of sixteen. As to the characters of Lovelace, of the heroine herself, and the heroine's parents, I take them all to be beings of another world. What Clarissa is made to do, and what she is allowed to omit, are equally out of the regions of nature. Fathers and mothers who may oppose the

inclinations of their daughters, are not likely to profit from
the examples in this story, nor will those daughters be
disposed to think the worse of their own rights, or the
better of their parents, for the black and odious colours in
which these unnatural characters are painted. It will avail
little to say that Clarissa's miseries are derivable from the
false step of her elopement, when it is evident that
elopement became necessary to avoid compulsion. To
speak with more precision my opinion in the case, I think
Clarissa dangerous only to such young persons whose
characters are yet to be formed, and who from natural
susceptibility may be prone to imitation, and likely to be
turned aside into errors of affectation. In such hands, I
think a book so addressed to the passions and wire-drawn
into such prolixity, is not calculated to form either natural
manners or natural style; nor would I have them learn of
Clarissa to write long pedantic letters 'on their bended
knees,' and beg 'to kiss the hem of their ever-honoured
Mamma's garment,' any more than I would wish them to
spurn at the addresses of a worthy lover, with the pert
insult of a Miss Howe.

The natural temper and talents of our children should
point out to our observation and judgment the particular
mode in which they ought to be trained; the little tales told
to them in infancy, and the books to be put into their
hands in a forwarder age, are concerns highly worth
attending to. Few female hearts in early youth can bear
being softened by pathetic and affecting stories without
prejudice. Young people are all imitation, and when a girl
assumes the pathos of Clarissa without experiencing the
same afflictions, or being put to the same trials, the result
will be a most insufferable affectation and pedantry.[34]

Cumberland takes the argument advanced by his opponents
and attempts to convert them into a suitably self-destructing
petard. The mocking tone opens with the implied assertion
that the main audience for *Clarissa* is composed of malleable
young ladies. He denies the truth of the characterisation, 'As

to the characters of Lovelace, of the heroine herself, and the heroine's parents, I take them all to be beings of another world', and of the actions, 'What Clarissa is made to do, and what she is allowed to omit, are equally out of the regions of nature.' Notions of reality recur here, a reality which is equated with 'the regions of nature', a highly elastic term. But what makes Cumberland's point interesting is the conception that it is not just what is done which offends this limitation, but also, though sadly he does not expand upon the idea, one has to consider what has been omitted. There is a further twist to the limitation of the literary real – not only must characters not do the unacceptable; they must equally satisfy certain expectations. This thought is essentially one developed towards the end of the century, and will be looked at in more detail in chapter 6. Cumberland does not try to push the argument to the point of asserting that a reading of *Clarissa* would result in the reader being induced to behave immorally, he merely believes the young lady would be inclined to adopt 'a most insufferable affectation and pedantry'.

One of the explanations offered for the polarisation of the supporters of Richardson and of Fielding is that the former too often lack a sense of humour. That there may be some truth in this could be argued from the response Cumberland's *jeu d'esprit* elicited from Anna Seward:

Mr. CUMBERLAND tells the public, that he knew a young female, whose head was turned by reading *Clarissa*; and who, in the rage of imitation, insisted upon having her coffin in her bed-chamber!

Insane people have always some reigning idea. That the coffin of Clarissa should *once* have proved that reigning idea, is surely a very contemptible reason for interdicting this noble composition, as inimical to the morals, and discretion of youth.

Many religious enthusiasts have fancied they had prophetic and apostolic inspiration. At the Cathedral of one of our celebrated provincial towns, some twenty years ago, I often used to see a man, whom many of the present inhabitants remember. It was his custom to stand, during service, before the rails of the altar. He had read about our Saviour, till he fancied *himself* that sacred character, and a native resemblance of face, and figure to the prints of Jesus, aided the phrenzy. He had trained the growth of his dark beard in the Jewish fashion, and his hair, parted upon his forehead, hung in equal ringlets down each side the front part of his neck. He was thin, and pale, with a remarkable air of placid dignity. The mildness this maniac constantly preserved, rendered him inoffensive.

With the same reason might the SCRIPTURE be censured as a dangerous study upon that instance, as this admirable work, because one romantic delirious fool bespoke her coffin, without the reasons which impelled Clarissa to take that singular step.

It is curious to hear the author of our most sentimental comedies, speak with contempt over the unerring sentiments which enrich these volumes. It would be happy for the rising, and for the future generation, if our young women *would* imitate the principles, and the conduct of Clarissa, though not perhaps in bespeaking their coffin: a circumstance for which she apologizes, confessing it a sally of mournful enthusiasm, and too scrupulous delicacy; excusable *only* from the peculiarity of her situation, and from being obliged to chuse a *male* executor. Recommending Clarissa's conduct as an example, I desire it may be remembered that her flight with Lovelace was involuntary, and that her meeting and corresponding with him, was merely from the persecutions she endured, and in the hope of preventing the most fatal mischiefs between him and her brother. She, however, repents of the last two circumstances, as forming a deep error, imploring Heaven that its consequences may *warn* her sex against being rash enough to repose the smallest degree of confidence in a libertine; who, as she says, to be a libertine must have got over and defied all moral restraints.

It is from the pen of a *father* that we see the unfeeling, the

144

pointless sneer upon the exemplary duty, the contrite
affection of a dying daughter, because she writes *on her knees*
to supplicate pardon for what she considers a great fault,
that prohibited correspondence (though she had been
impelled into the commission of it by the cruelty of her
family) and to invoke blessings upon them, who had shown
no mercy to her!

In contradiction to experience, and with great illiberality,
Mr. CUMBERLAND asserts, that encouraging young women
to correspond with each other, tends to no good point of
education. *Every* good habit is capable of being perverted to
bad uses. Because numerous books of evil tendency are
extant, we might as wisely resolve that our daughters
should not learn to *read*, as that, because they may write
frivolous, and improper letters, they should be precluded
from the *certain* advantages of a well-regulated epistolary
intercourse with their young friends. Discreet parents will,
in a great degree, suggest the subjects of these letters, and
invite from time to time, a communication of their
contents, by expressing pleasure in their perusal. Such an
intercourse forms the style of young people, gives them
habits of reflection, awakens intellectual emulation, and
supplies them with resources, which have an inevitable
tendency to abate the desire of dissipation, enables them to
be rational and pleasing companions to men of sense when
they marry, to fill the parental and monitory duties with
dignity and delight, to the certain improvement of the
future generation.

If women intrigue more in France than in England,
though their understandings are better cultivated, it is
because their inclinations are never consulted in their
marriage engagements: and because infamy is less
consequent than it is *here*, upon a violation of those
engagements. But the French women are Lucretias
compared to the Italians; a superiority which arises from
the companionable qualities of the former, and the unlettered
ignorance of the latter, that delivers up all the powers of
their imagination to the influence of one reigning idea.

Whoever has successfully studied the nature of the human mind, knows, that to store it with a *variety* of ideas, to render it capable of perceiving the value of knowledge, and the charms of genius, is to render it less subservient to the influence of the senses.

After Mr. CUMBERLAND has expressed his desire of banishing the finest moral work of this age, from the libraries of our youth, and the pen from the fingers of our women; he proceeds to inveigh more justly against that mode of education, too prevailing within these last twenty years, which can never enlarge the flock of ideas, or inspire any taste for intellectual pleasures. Upon this plan, a girl's time, in that important period, which divides infancy from womanhood, is every hour of it engrossed by the French grammar, the harpsichord, the dancing, and the drawing-master.

When young ladies *thus*, and *only* thus accomplished, become mistresses, in any degree of their own time, whether single, or married, there is no probability, alas! that they will devote it to the voluminous pages of the moral, the pious RICHARDSON. They have no imaginations that can awaken to a perception of his genius – no hearts that can soften at his pathos – no understanding to perceive the undeviating truth, and good sense of his observations.

The *Female Quixotte* [*sic*] is an admirable satire upon the *now* totally exploded study of the old romances, and gave the death's wound to that declining taste. But to satirize, with any probability of *good* effect, the CLARISSA, or the GRANDISON, is impossible. People of judgment will not attempt it, and injudicious people will attempt it in *vain*.

To read novels frequently, and indiscriminately, is a most pernicious habit. There are no means so effectual of rendering them distasteful as an early familiarity with the effusions of RICHARDSON's genius. They will exalt the understanding above endurance of the trash, daily pouring out from the circulating libraries. Who that has read MILTON wastes the midnight taper over the vapid fustian of Sir RICHARD BLACKMORE?[35]

146

Anna Seward appears to have equated morals with manners, for where Cumberland had drawn attention to the 'affectation and pedantry' which *Clarissa* might induce, this is interpreted as 'interdicting this noble composition, as inimical to the morals'. The comparison of *Clarissa* with the Bible not only suggests that Seward was over-reacting but may be compared with those moments in *Pamela* when, possibly unwittingly, Richardson had made his eponymous heroine describe herself in terms more fittingly emanating from the mouth of the Virgin Mary. Seward's reaction may, astonishingly, have been typical of certain readers: it is reported of Colley Cibber that he 'had been thrown into such violent raptures by a sight of the original draft of the novel that he had – or said he had – a Vision of Heaven'.[36]

One might also recall the extravagant claims prefixed to *Colonel Jack*. There is the usual nod in the direction of the question of reality in her remark that Cumberland's views are 'in contradiction to experience', but the dominating message of this essay is that *Clarissa* is a supreme work of moral didacticism and the tone of this message is almost as flattering as Richardson's own: 'the finest moral work of this age'; 'the moral, the pious RICHARDSON', 'the effusions of Richardson's genius'; while the works of others are 'trash'. As Cumberland was asserting the superiority of Fielding, some of Seward's readers at this point might well have understood 'trash' to be directed to that writer as well as to the shelves of the circulating libraries. It is also worth considering Seward's remarks relating to literacy and female education: 'Because numerous books of evil tendency are extant, we might as wisely resolve that our daughters should not learn to read ... a girl's time, in that important period, which divides infancy from womanhood, is every hour of it engrossed by the French grammar, the harpsichord, the dancing, and the drawing-master.' Her waspishness reveals the depth of concern.

It was not just the devoutly aggressive Richardsonian followers who queried the propriety of Fielding's works. The anonymous author of *An Essay on the New Species of Writing*, some of whose sensible critical insights have been cited above (pages 16-17), also animadverted on this topic.

These Remarks could hardly make a just Claim to that
Impartiality, I have all along been so great a Stickler for,
was I entirely to pass over in Silence the few Mistakes our
Author has been guilty of in the Conduct of his several
Performances. But I shall be very little inclin'd to enlarge
on so disagreeable a Part of the Critic's Office. First then
for *Joseph Andrews* – We are told, that the chief End of these
Pieces is the Extirpation of Vice, and the Promotion of
Virtue; to say the Truth, which the general Bent of them
always tends to. But we fear this grand Rule has in some
Places been too much disregarded. As the Works of Mr.
Fielding are in every Body's Hands, there ought not to be a
Line in them which should cause the modestest Lady a
single Blush in the Perusal. This Delicacy of Stile and
Sentiment has been quite neglected in some Dialogues
between the wanton Lady *Booby* and most innocent *Joseph
Andrews*; and more particularly so in one Chapter, which
must occur to the Remembrance of every Reader
conversant with these Works. We may venture to say this
one Chapter has been prejudicial to the young People of
both Sexes, and that more Readers have look'd upon the
Innocence of *Joseph Andrews* as Stupidity, than the
Wantonness of Lady *Booby* as guilt. Lewdness is too mean a
Branch of Humour (if indeed it is a Branch of Humour) for
a Man of Mr. *Fielding*'s Sense to have Recourse to: and we
hope that he will henceforth leave it to those barren
Writers of Comedy who have no other Way of pleasing, but
a scandalous Coincidence with the deprav'd Taste of a
vicious Audience.[37]

Yet again, as the litmus paper of literature is morality so that
morality is that of 'the modestest lady'. Some ladies however
managed to read works such as *Tom Jones*, and so far from
feeling in some way besmirched as a result, felt that it had
been an educative experience. Madame du Deffand expressed
this point of view in a letter to Walpole:

Je viens de relire *Tom Jones*, dont le commencement et la fin m'ont charmée. Je n'aime que les romans qui peignent les caractères, bons et mauvais. C'est là où l'on trouve de vraies leçons de morale; et si on peut tirer quelque fruit de la lecture, c'est de ces livres-là; il me font beaucoup d'impression; vos auteurs [sont] excellents dans ce genre, et les nôtres ne s'en doutent point. J'en sais bien la raison, c'est que nous n'avons point de caractère. Nous n'avons que plus ou moins d'éducation, et que nous sommes par conséquent imitateurs et singes les uns des autres.[38]

The dominance of the moral judgment of fiction was of course to be found outside the great central battlefield of the century. A typical short notice of some representative 'trash' may be found in the *Analytical Review*'s comments upon Ann Hilditch's *Mount Pelham* which are here quoted in their entirety:

> Much ado about nothing. We place this novel without any reservation, at the bottom of the second class. The language is affected; and it has all the faults we have before enumerated. The morality is rather lax; for the author, a female, says, 'so gentle, so forgiving, is the nature of a virtuous female; and so prone are we to love the offender, yet detest the offence.' This is the varnish of sentiment to hide sensuality.[39]

If a work could be entirely dismissed on moral grounds it was also true that a work considered deficient in every other regard could be thoroughly recommended because it was morally valuable. Thus the *Monthly Review* commenting on *The Vicar of Wakefield*:

> With marks of genius equal, in some respects, to those which distinguish our most celebrated novel-writers, there are in this work, such palpable indications of the want of a thorough acquaintance with mankind, as might go near to prove the Author totally unqualified for success in this species of composition, were it not that he finds such resources in his own extraordinary natural talents, as may,

in the judgment of many readers, in a great measure, compensate for his limited knowledge of men, manners, and characters, as they really appear in the living world. – In brief, with all its faults, there is much rational entertainment to be met with in this very singular tale: but it deserves our warmer approbation, for its moral tendency; particularly for the exemplary manner in which it recommends and enforces the great obligations of universal BENEVOLENCE: the most amiable quality that can possibly distinguish and adorn the WORTHY MAN and the GOOD CHRISTIAN![40]

The moral response to one of the major figures of eighteenth century fiction – Sterne – may serve to show the confusion which can be generated when the reaction to the supposed level of morality of works of fiction is inextricably bound up with conceptions of the morality perceived to be governing the private lives of their authors. *The Royal Female Magazine* greeted the first two volumes of *Tristram Shandy* with the observations that the book:

affects (and not unsuccessfully) to please, by a contempt of all the rules observed in other writings, and therefore cannot justly have its merits measured by them. It were to be wished though, that the wantonness of the author's wit had been tempered with a little more regard to delicacy, throughout the greatest part of his work.[41]

In passing one should note the belief that for works to be adequately compared it is necessary that they be of the same type, but for the moment it is the second sentence, with its moral judgment, which matters. The publication of *Tristram Shandy* produced some virulent reactions. Mrs Delaney, the wife of the Dean of Down, wrote to her sister:

The Dean is indeed very angry with the author of Tristram, etc. and those who will not condemn the work as it deserves; it *has not* and *will not* enter this house, especially now your account is added to a very bad one we had heard before.[42]

Three weeks later she wrote again:

> D.D. is not a little offended with Mr. Sterne; his book is read here as in London, and seems to divert more than it offends, but as neither I nor any of my particular set have read it, or shall read it, I know nothing more of it than what you have said about it. Mrs. Clayton and I had a furious argument about reading books of a bad tendency; I stood up for preserving a purity of mind, and discouraging works of *that kind* – *she* for trusting to her *own strength* and *reason*, and bidding defiance to any injury such books could do her; but as I *cannot presume* to depend on my own strength of mind, I think it safest and best to *avoid* whatever may prejudice it.[43]

That Mrs Delaney felt she was entitled to condemn the book twice despite not having read one word, nor it would seem even having set eyes on the work, is even more extreme than Richardson's denunciation of *Amelia* above (page 136) having read only the first volume. It is indicative of the strength of feeling in this matter that here we have two ladies arguing about the propriety of a book which one of them at least has not read – whether Mrs Clayton has or not is not revealed; and that earlier in this chapter there have been examples of correspondents such as Sarah Chapone making mighty efforts to influence others against particular literary productions on the grounds of their unsuitability for female eyes. Another of Richardson's correspondents, Lady Bradshaigh, writing to the man himself about Sterne's works, widened her attack to include Sterne the man:

> It is a pity a man of so much humour, cou'd not contain himself within the bounds of decency. Upon the whole, I think the performance, mean, *dirty Wit*. I may add *scandelous*, considering the *Man*. But what shall we say, that the writing such a book, shou'd recommend the author to the great favour of a R^t. Rev^d. It will not be improper, here, to add another *scandelous*, and that *Tristram Shandy* shou'd clear the way for a large Edition of Yorick's Sermons. In my opinion, the worst that ever appear'd in print, if they are all answerable to the first three, for I look'd no farther. But why shou'd I tire you with this man, who is, I dare say, as unworthy as man can be.[44]

It was not just that *Tristram Shandy* was a book which contained a variety of dubious jokes; it had been written by a clergyman. And what made matters worse was that he was a clergyman with pretensions: he also wrote sermons. Lady Bradshaigh, having read just the first three, considered them 'the worst that ever appear'd in print', a judgment not shared by many. The usual objection to Sterne's *Sermons* was provoked not by their content, but by their title page which led Owen Ruffhead to declare in *The Monthly Review*:

> Before we proceed to the matter of these sermons, we think it becomes us to make some animadversions on the manner of their publication, which we consider as the greatest outrage against Sense and Decency, that has been offered since the first establishment of Christianity – an outrage which would scarce have been tolerated even in the days of paganism.[45]

Lady Bradshaigh's remarks ended on the personal note that as a result of reading some of Sterne's works she felt him to be a 'man, who is, I dare say, as unworthy as man can be'. Richardson's own approbation of Mrs Donellan's comment upon Fielding, 'he designed to be good, but knew not how', suggests that in his coterie the personality of an author was a valid element in the criticism of his writings.

The point at which personality obtrudes most remarkably is in *A genuine letter from a Methodist preacher in the country to Laurence Sterne, M.A.*[46] This pamphlet, which has been ascribed, probably wrongly, to George Whitfield, opened the attack by commenting upon the unsuitability of Sterne's book when one considered his occupation:

> I must inform you that I have read the history of *Tristram Shandy* and I cannot conceive how it was possible for a divine of the church of England to write so prophane a book; – a book penned by the Devil himself; and calculated, above all other books, to advance the interests of the Prince of Darkness, to lead mankind astray from the paths of righteousness, and conduct them towards the bottomless pit. (p. vii)

152

This developed into a direct personal onslaught:

Oh *Sterne!* thou art scabby, and such is the leprosy of thy mind that it is not to be cured like the leprosy of the body, by dipping nine times in the river Jordan. Thy prophane history of *Tristram Shandy* is as it were an anti-gospel, and seems to have been penned by the hand of Antichrist himself . . . Sterne, Sterne! if thou hadst been full of the Holy Ghost, thou would'st never have written that prophane book, *The Life and Opinions of Tristram Shandy*, to judge of which, one would think the author had a cloven foot.

Thou art puffed up with spiritual pride, and vanity of human learning has led thee aside into the paths of prophaneness.

Thou hast even been so far elated as to give the likeness of thyself before thy sermons, but, though it is the likeness of something upon earth, I shrewdly doubt that it will never be the likeness of any thing in heaven.

Return therefore to grace, before it is too late; throw aside Shakespear, and take up the word of God. (pp. 2, 20)

It is impossible for the twentieth century reader to appreciate fully the responses of the contemporary reader of these works in relation to moral beliefs. And one must not forget that this manner of reading and judging literary productions was not confined to fiction.

The examples quoted so far have been from published criticism or from correspondence. In both cases, it could be argued, the writers' opinions may be misleading in that there is the possibility of an element of self-projection. The ladies writing to Richardson would naturally wish to have Richardson perceive them to be proper readers. As an example of a reader apparently unconcerned with the image of himself, one may turn to the diaries of Thomas Turner, an obscure inhabitant of a small Sussex village, a failed schoolteacher who became the local shopkeeper. He filled 116 volumes with his diary; cannot have conceived himself to have been of sufficient interest for these volumes to have been written with a view to publication; and appears to have been recording solely for his own benefit. He is a truly ordinary reader. And how does he record his responses?

Read the 13th Book [of Pope's translation of the Odyssey], after supper; I think the soliloquy which Ulysses makes when he finds the Phoenicians have in his sleep left him on his native shore of Ithaca, with all his treasure, contains a very good lesson of morality.[47]

But moral beliefs and responses were often coloured by other matters, and that this was recognised, may be seen from Johnson's comments on *The Beggar's Opera*:

> Of this performance, when it was printed, the reception was different according to the different opinion of its readers. Swift commended it for the excellence of its morality, as a piece that had "placed vices of all kinds in the strongest and most odious light"; but others, and among them Dr. Herring, afterwards Archbishop of Canterbury, censured it as giving encouragement not only to vice but to crimes, by making a highwayman the hero, and dismissing him at last unpunished. It has even been said, that, after the exhibition of the *Beggar's Opera*, the gangs of robbers were evidently multiplied.
>
> Both these decisions are surely exaggerated. The play, like many others, was plainly written only to divert, without any moral purpose, and is therefore not likely to do good.[48]

It is remarkable that Johnson, a critic normally highly attuned to moral matters, could have been so dismissive of this element of Gay's work. But the same blindness is to be found in his observations on Swift's poems:

> In the poetical works of Dr. Swift there is not much upon which the critic can exercise his powers. They are often humorous, almost always light, and have the qualities which recommend such compositions, easiness and gaiety.[49]

One wonders which poems he could have been reading.

It is beyond question that the changes in the mores of society have been so great, the decline of the influence of the Anglican church so vertiginous, the acceptance of 'trash' so common, that most of the nuances immediately recognised in the eighteenth century are no longer visible. Nevertheless, in view of the overriding importance attached to the moral element in literature by eighteenth century readers and critics, and above all by the writers themselves, any critical approach to these writings which pays no attention to the Christian ethic may rightly be regarded as both partial and flawed.

CHAPTER 5

---◆---

MOTLEY EMBLEMS AND MUCH WANTED STANDARDS

TRISTRAM *Shandy* makes great use of visual effects, both actual and implied. Volume 1, which also contains an all-black leaf to commemorate the death of Yorick, concludes with the narrator addressing the reader:

> What these grave perplexities of my uncle *Toby* were, – 'tis impossible for you to guess; – if you could, – I should blush; not as a relation, – not as a man, – nor even as a woman, – but I should blush as an author; inasmuch as I set no small store by myself upon this very account, that my reader has never yet been able to guess at any thing. And in this, Sir, I am of so nice and singular a humour, that if I thought you was able to form the least judgment or probably conjecture to yourself, of what was to come in the next page, – I would tear it out of my book.[1]

The reader of the twentieth century edition turns the page and sees at the head of the next that here starts Volume 2.

> I have begun a new book, on purpose that I might have room enough to explain the nature of the perplexities in which my uncle *Toby* was involved, from the many discourses and interrogations about the siege of *Namur*, where he received his wound.[2]

156

But Sterne's contemporary was faced with the free endpaper. The whole point of the observation is that there is no 'next page' to be torn out: there is another volume to be opened. Sterne's use of typographic quirks ranges widely. There is the simple use of a cross to reinforce the action described:

What could Dr. *Slop* do? – He cross'd himself + – Pugh!
but the Doctor, Sir, was a Papist. (p. 122)

The Queen went directly to her oratory, musing all the way, as she walked through the gallery, upon the subject; turning it this way and that way in her fancy – *Ave Maria* + – what can *La Fosseuse* mean? said she, kneeling down upon the cushion. (p. 411)

There are asterisks which are grouped to allow of intelligent substitution by the reader:

The chamber-maid had left no ******* *** under the bed: Cannot you contrive, master, quoth *Susannah*, lifting up the sash with one hand, as she spoke, and helping me up into the window seat with the other, – cannot you manage, my dear, for a single time to **** *** ** *** ******?
I was five years old. (p. 449)

There are also groupings for which no one, as yet, has provided any adequate substitution:

– Do, my dear Jenny, tell the world for me, how I behaved under one, the most oppressive of its kind which could befall me as a man, proud, as he ought to be, of his manhood –
'Tis enough, said'st thou, coming close up to me, as I stood with my garters in my hand, reflecting upon what had *not* pass'd – 'Tis enough, Tristram, and I am satisfied, said'st thou, whispering these words in my ear, **** ** **** *** ******; _ **** ** **** – any other man would have sunk down to the center – (p. 624)

A woodblock is used to illustrate the progress of the plot so

[152]

C H A P. XL.

I Am now beginning to get fairly into
my work; and by the help of a
vegitable diet, with a few of the cold
feeds, I make no doubt but I fhall be
able to go on with my uncle *Toby*'s ftory,
and my own, in a tolerable ftraight line.
Now,

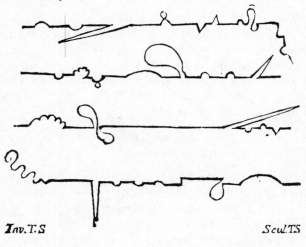

Inv.T.S   *Scul.TS*

Thefe

Figure 4   *Tristram Shandy*, vol. 6, p. 152.

158

[17]

Nothing, Trim——ſaid my uncle Toby, muſing——

Whilſt a man is free—cried the Corporal, giving a flouriſh with his ſtick thus——

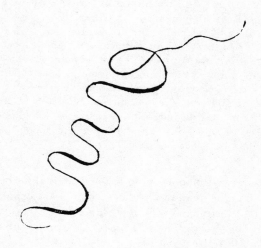

Vᴏʟ. IX.   C

Figure 5   *Tristram Shandy*, vol. 9, p. 17.

far (see Figure 4); and another block is employed to provide a
visual representation of the path traced by Trim's stick in his
attempt to explain his notion of freedom (see Figure 5).

Sterne's realisation of the importance of the visual element
in his work is clear from a letter he sent to his friend Richard
Berenger whom he employed as an intermediary to elicit an
illustration from Hogarth:

> You bid me tell You all my Wants – What the Devil in Hell can
> the fellow want now? – By the Father of the Sciences (you know his
> Name) I would give both my Ears (if I was not to loose my Credit
> by it) for no more than ten Strokes of *Howgarth*'s witty Chissel, to
> clap at the front of my next edition of *Shandy*. –
> The Vanity of [a] pretty Girl in the Hey day of her Roses &
> Lillies, is a fool to that of [an] Author of my Stamp – Oft did Swift
> sigh to Pope in these Words – Orna me – Write something of Yours
> to mine, to transmit us down together hand in hand to futurity. The
> loosest Sketch in Nature, of Trim's reading the Sermon to my Father
> &c; w^d do the Business – & it w^d mutually illustrate his System and
> mine – But my dear Shandy with what face – I would hold out my
> lank Purse – I would Shut my Eyes –, & You should put in your
> hand, & take out what you liked for it –.[3]

That Sterne had planned from the very start that the passage
referred to, the reading of the sermon by Corporal Trim,
should be illustrated by Hogarth may be deduced from the
fact that the description of Trim at this point (pp.140-2) is
full of subtle references to Hogarth's *Analysis of Beauty* which
had appeared in 1753. The illustration acquired, Sterne's
recognition of its publicity value may be seen from the
advertisements for the second edition of *Tristram Shandy* which
announced with typographical emphasis 'with a Frontispiece
by Mr. HOGARTH'. Hogarth's second contribution to the
work, the cut of Walter Shandy arriving rather too late at the
christening of his son which, illustrating a scene in volume 4,
is usually to be found as the frontispiece to volume 3, seems
to have been the first occasion in English publishing when an
imaginative prose work was illustrated in its first edition by a
representation of a moment of the action.[4]

By way of comic contrast with the Hogarth contributions, in volume 6 there is a blank page which is prefixed by the observation:

> To conceive this right, – call for pen and ink – here's paper ready to your hand. – Sit down, Sir, paint her [the widow Wadman] to your own mind – as like your mistress as you can – as unlike your wife as your conscience will let you – 'tis all one to me – please but your own fancy in it. (p. 566)

The blank page for the reader's depiction of widow Wadman is a remarkably early example of the active encouragement of reader participation in the process of creation.

There are occasions when Sterne's bibliographical curiosities are, necessarily, inadequately conveyed by any modern edition. The twenty-fifth chapter of volume 6 opens:

> No doubt, Sir – there is a whole chapter wanting here – and a chasm of ten pages made in the book by it – but the book-binder is neither a fool, or a knave, or a puppy – nor is the book a jot more imperfect, (at least upon that score) – but, on the contrary, the book is more perfect and complete by wanting the chapter, than having it, as I shall demonstrate to your reverences in this manner – I question first by the bye, whether the same experiment might not be made as successfully upon sundry other chapters – but there is no end, an' please your reverences, in trying experiments upon chapters – we have had enough of it – So there's an end of that matter. (p. 372)

Modern editions do usually omit the ten pages specified, but the first edition omits only nine numbers in the pagination, with the result that for the whole of the rest of the volume the recto pages, in total contravention of a long-standing tradition, are provided with even numbers. This does not affect the reader's appreciation of the words, but it does add to the air of dislocation fostered in the book.

Sterne's supreme device is equally unconcerned with words. Volume 3 contains a marbled leaf which is introduced as 'the next marbled page (motly emblem of my work!)' (p.268). What is not generally recognised today is that owing to the very nature of the hand marbling process every marbled page in *Tristram Shandy* is different. *Tristram Shandy* is unique in that every copy is necessarily unique. The page may be 'motly emblem of the work' but it must be realised that this is a case of 'to every copy its own motly emblem'.[5]

Typographical bizarreries were not invented by Sterne. Swift in *Tale of a Tub* made frequent use of groups of asterisks to indicate moments of hiatus in the manuscript; as has been shown above in chapter 3, Richardson also employed a variety of the less usual elements of the printing house stock. But Sterne operates on the grand scale – the examples provided above are examples, they by no means constitute a complete list.

What is remarkable is the almost total absence of response. One or two reviewers did comment upon the use of asterisks. *The Grand Magazine* published a review in the form of a dialogue in the course of which one of the speakers said:

> He has discovered a new method of talking bawdy astronomically; and has made *four stars* (which, perhaps, may stand for the four Satellites of *Jupiter*) convey ideas which have set all the maidens a madding, have tickled the whole bench of bishops, and put all his readers in good humour.[6]

But those elements, notably the marbled page, which to the modern reader appear so startlingly innovative elicited not a single observation in any published criticism of the time, nor does any reference occur in the letters of such prolific correspondents as Horace Walpole. The only near-contemporary response I know of is in a copy of the 'New Edition' of 1768 in my possession where an apparently indignant owner has written across the page concerned:

> M[r]. Tristram Shandy might much better imploy himself in wrighting than sending a Marble Paper leaf into the World.

Not, you will notice, surprise at finding this unexpectedly colourful ornament in the book, but a complaint about the absence of what the reader expected to find: words.

From this one might deduce that the contemporary reader might have been more responsive to *A Sentimental Journey*. Whereas *Tristram Shandy* made much play of the visual, *A Sentimental Journey* opens and closes with two remarkably inventive *literary* devices.

> – They order, said I, this matter better in France –
> – You have been in France? said my gentleman, turning
> quick upon me with the most civil triumph in the world.[7]

No one has yet discovered an earlier example in English of a work of prose fiction which opens with direct speech: one may compare such formulaic openings as that to *Robinson Crusoe*, 'I was born in the Year 1632, in the City of York . . . .' But Sterne does not make just a simple switch to direct speech; there is a double shift here, for the reader is pitchforked into the middle of a conversation – one suspects Sterne is taking Mr Horace's rule of *in medias res* absolutely literally, in direct contrast to *Tristram Shandy* which opens almost equally literally *ab ovo* – and moreover it is a conversation of which we do not learn the subject. What 'this matter' may be is never disclosed. No contemporary chose to comment upon this detail which was apparently not noticed until 1977.[8]

Similarly silently received was the final page (see Figure 6). The total absence of punctuation after 'Chambre's' could, rather anachronistically, be described as Joycean – and it is a detail which too few modern editions accurately represent. The effect of the aposiopestic break is to trap the reader. Had there been a full stop then conventional grammar would require the reader to understand that the part grasped is the girl's hand. But had there been a dash – a typographical addition made after Sterne's death and perpetuated in far too many versions – then the reader is to assume that any element of the girl's dress or anatomy may be conjured up, with the exception of her hand. Total absence of punctuation allows for total freedom of interpretation; one may even continue reading and accept 'END', which is both possibly apposite in its own right and possibly indicative of an affected pun on 'hand'.

Yet no one saw fit to comment on this either. Why?

Here is a writer of immense popularity producing innovative ideas, both literary and bibliographic, and his readers do not seem to have noticed. This is inconceivable. Alternatively one can only believe that they did notice what Sterne was doing, but saw no necessity to pass any remarks on the matter. If this is true, then the perception of 'an eighteenth century novel' needs radical revision.

For a considerable period of the eighteenth century two armed grenadiers in full uniform stood on the stage of the major London theatres. Our best evidence for this is an unnamed and amateurish painting of a performance of *Macbeth* at Covent Garden in 1765 where the two grenadiers are clearly visible standing to attention on either side of Macbeth, Banquo and the three witches. The artist was providing an accurate representation of what he saw. There are a small number of written references to this practice – but they are so tantalisingly few that it is not known when the practice started, when it finished, or even why it took place. There are a very large number of pictorial representations of dramatic performances in the eighteenth century. Apart from the unnamed amateur effort not one shows the grenadiers – they appear either not to have been seen or to have been eliminated from critical vision. In this case what to the twentieth century observer is well worth remark was to the eighteenth century entirely commonplace. Even when Fielding wishes to portray the simplicity of Partridge in his reaction to the visit to the theatre where he sees Garrick in *Hamlet*, the author does not go to the point of having his character see the soldiers.[9]

There are, I would suggest, two reasons why contemporary responses do not include comments upon elements seized upon by observers of another age: either, as with the grenadiers, the matter is entirely commonplace, or, as in the

[208]

—(I was going to have added, that I would not have trefpafs'd againft the remoteft idea of decorum for the world)—

—But the Fille de Chambre hearing there were words between us, and fearing that hoftilities would enfue in courfe, had crept filently out of her clofet, and it being totally dark, had ftolen fo clofe to our beds, that fhe had got herfelf into the narrow paffage which feparated them, and had advanc'd fo far up as to be in a line betwixt her miftrefs and me—

So that when I ftretch'd out my hand, I caught hold of the Fille de Chambre's

END OF VOL. II.

Figure 6   *A Sentimental Journey*, vol. 2, p. 208.

case of the marbled page which is demonstrably not commonplace, there being no other works known making use of this device, there are no expectations being overturned. It is clear that if one considers a fairly random list of major examples of prose fiction in the sixty years prior to *Tristram Shandy*: *New Atalantis* (1709), *Robinson Crusoe* (1719), *Gulliver's Travels* (1726), *Pamela* (1740), *Tom Jones* (1749), and *Peregrine Pickle* (1751), that, apart from being for the most part written in prose and containing (vastly varying) elements of the fictional, there is very little these works have in common.

One might think of *Tristram Shandy* as evidence of an age when anything is acceptable. But whilst there was an audience apparently prepared to read the great variety of works of prose fiction without remark on the fact that each was *sui generis*, at the same time there was developing a strong movement, mainly among critics but also including a few of the readers and writers, which felt that it was necessary to impose order on the chaos. It is, after all, a basic function of criticism to rationalise and therefore simplify the complexities of works of art.

One of the letters prefixed to the first edition of *Pamela* declared, with, one feels, something of an excess of wishful thinking:

> This little Book will infallibly be looked upon as the hitherto much-wanted Standard or Pattern for this Kind of Writing.[10]

J.B.D.F., the writer of the letter, evidently felt that, despite the efforts to define made by such writers as Congreve as much as fifty years before the publication of *Pamela*, there is still no 'Standard or Pattern' by which such a work can be constructed, and against which a work may be judged. That, to a relatively minor extent, Richardson's work was taken as an archetype can be illustrated by a letter of Horace Walpole to Mann of 20 December 1764:

> There is a Madame de Beaumont who has lately written a very pretty novel, called, *Lettres du Marquise de Roselle*. It is imitated too

from an English standard, and in my opinion a most woeful one; I mean the works of Richardson, who wrote those deplorably tedious lamentations, *Clarissa* and *Sir Charles Grandison*, which are pictures of high life as conceived by a bookseller, and romances as they would be spiritualised by a Methodist preacher: but Madame de Beaumont has almost avoided sermons, and almost reconciled sentiments and common sense.[11]

In another letter, written to this same Madame de Beaumont's husband, Walpole managed to put his finger on one of the inevitable problems which any notion of a 'Standard or Pattern' raises:

> To tell you the truth, it was not so much my intention in writing The Castle of Otranto to recall the exploded marvels of ancient romance, as to blend the wonderful of old stories with the natural of modern novels. The world is apt to wear out any plan whatsoever . . . . Madame de Beaumont must forgive me if I add that Richardson had, to me at least, made that kind of writing insupportable.
>
> (*Letters*, vol. 40, pp. 379-80)

Walpole was one of the few readers and critics in the first sixty years of the century who did perceive that there were a small number of recurrent elements in contemporary prose fiction. The general perceptions, conflicting as they all too often were, have been discussed in chapter 1. Here one may consider some of the more specific areas commented upon: structure, style, diction.

Steele in the *Spectator* commented upon the conventional *terminus ad quem* of fiction:

> A Gentleman where I happened to be last Night, fell into a Discourse which I thought shewed a good Discerning in him: He took Notice, that whenever Men have looked in their Heart for the Idea of true Excellency in humane Nature, they have found it to consist in suffering after a right Manner and with a good Grace. Heroes are always drawn bearing Sorrows, struggling with Adversities, undergoing all Kinds of Hardships, and having in the

Service of Mankind a Kind of Appetite to Difficulties and Dangers. The Gentleman went on to observe, that it is from this secret Sense of the high Merit which there is in Patience under Calamities, that the Writers of Romance, when they attempt to furnish out Characters of the highest Excellence, ransack Nature for Things terrible; they raise a new Creation of Monsters, Dragons, and Giants: where the Danger ends, the Hero ceases; when he won an Empire, or gained his Mistress, the rest of his story is not worth relating.[12]

In the final decade of the century Robert Bage made similar noises:

If the careless writer of a novel closes his book without marrying, or putting to death, or somehow disposing, not only of his principal personages, but of all who have acted a part in the drama above the degree of a candle-snuffer, he creates an unsatisfactory want in the minds of his readers, especially his fair ones, and they hardly part friends. As everybody knows I live but to love and oblige these charming critics, I will in this chapter endeavour to give them all the satisfaction I can . . . .

'And pray,' say a thousand of my fair readers all at once, 'pray, Mr. Glen, how can you think of closing your book without giving us complete satisfaction respecting Sir Charles and Miss Campinet? Many things fall out between the cup and the lip. They might marry, or they might not. Are we at liberty to suppose which we please? For what END then did you write your book?'

Pardon me, dear ladies; I knew, or thought I knew, that there must be a total conformity of conclusion in your minds respecting this great event; and my hopes were, that you would have the goodness to marry them, when, and where, and how you pleased, But since otherwise is your pleasure, I, as in duty bound, submit.[13]

A good deal of *Hermsprong* operates on a parodic level and

Bage here is mocking both the pedlars and the eager customers of the convention.

Steele proposed marriage or elevation to a throne as terminal actions: Bage perceived marriage or death similarly. When in *Amelia* Fielding chose to use marriage not as the *terminus ad quem* but as the *terminus a quo*, John Cleland in *The Monthly Review* was quick to point out this divagation from the norm:

> The ingenious author of this piece is already so well known to the public for his talents in novel-writing, and especially that original turn which he gives to all his works in that way, that it would be superfluous to say any thing more of his literary character.
>
> To give a just idea of this his last production, which, from the choice of his subject, appears to be the boldest stroke that has been yet attempted in this species of writing, will be sufficient.
>
> The author takes up his heroine at the very point at which all his predecessors have dropped their capital personages. It has been heretofore a general practice to conduct the lover and his mistress to the door of matrimony, and there leave them, as if after that ceremony the whole interest in them was at an end, and nothing could remain beyond it worthy of exciting or keeping up the curiosity of the reader. Instead of which, Mr. *Fielding*, in defiance of this established custom, has ventured to give the history of two persons already married, but whose adventures, hardships, and distressful situations form a chain of events, in which he has had the art of keeping up the spirit of his narration from falling into that languor and flatness which might be expected from the nature of the subject; for, virtuous and laudable as the tenderness and constancy of a wife to her husband must for ever be considered, these affections are, however, too often esteemed as merely matter of pure duty, and intirely in course; so that he who does not peruse this work, will hardly imagine how the relish of such conjugal endearments, as compose the basis of it, could be

quickened enough to become palatable to the reader. The author, however, has interwoven such natural situations, such scenes of trial, taken also from nature, that the attention is for ever kept on the stretch, and one is led on by the attraction of a curiosity artfully provoked, to pursue the *heroine* through all her adventures, and an impatience to know how the married pair will be extricated out of the successive plunges in which they are represented, and in which the writer often successfully presses vice into the service of virtue.[14]

Sterne's comparable disregard for what was seen by certain readers as a norm in his use of digression was eyed somewhat less favourably by Walpole, who wrote to Dalrymple:

> At present nothing is talked of, nothing admired, but what I cannot help calling a very insipid and tedious performance: it is a kind of novel called, The Life and Opinions of Tristram Shandy; the great humour of which consists in the whole narration always going backwards. I can conceive a man saying that it would be droll to write a book in that manner, but have no notion of his persevering in executing it.
>
> (*Letters*, vol. 15, p. 66)

That this was not a universally accepted view, however – there are no truths universally accepted in these matters – may be evidenced by an extract from Charles Churchill's 'The Ghost':

> Could I, whilst *Humour* held the Quill,
> Could I *digress* with half that skill,
> Could I with half that skill return,
> Which we so much admire in STERNE,
> Where each *Digression*, seeming vain,
> And only fit to entertain,
> Is found, on better recollection,
> To have a just and nice Connection,
> To help the whole with wond'rous Art,
> Whence it seem idly to depart.[15]

Another critical observer, the anonymous author of *An Essay on the New Species of Writing founded by Mr Fielding*, also saw in the works of one of his contemporaries the creation of a form which could set a pattern, and in doing so illustrated the importance of pattern to the critic:

> *The new Sect of Biographers (founded by Mr.* Fielding*) is already grown so very numerous from the Success of the Original, that an Attempt of this Kind is in some Measure necessary, to put a Stop to the unbounded Liberties the Historians of this comic Stamp might otherwise indulge themselves: and, if possible, to prevent any from undertaking the Labours of Mr.* Fielding, *without an adequate Genius. Should the following Sheets be of Force enough to hinder the weak, sickly Birth of a* Joe Thompson, Charlotte Summers, *or* Peregrine Pickle, *in Embrio; the Town would undoubtedly be glad to exchange the heavy Work of a voluminous Scribler for the more easy Burden of a loose Pamphlet.*
>
> *The first Critics drew their Rules from the first Professors of the Art they made their Observations on; which were afterwards the settled Standards by which the Worth of their Successors was to be determin'd. In Imitation of so great an Example are the Rules for the future Historians of this kind drawn from the Works of their Original Mr.* Fielding.[16]

'Standards' reappears: without 'Standards', without 'settled Standards' a critic would be in no position to evaluate a work adequately. The same pamphlet is further notable for providing one of the rare occasions when minor details of the structure of imaginative literary works was discussed. The writer considers Fielding's use of chapter divisions:

> At the same time Mr. *Fielding* ordain'd, that these Histories should be divided into Books, and these subdivided into Chapters; and also that the first Chapter of every Book was not to continue the Narration, but should consist of any Thing the Author chose to entertain his Readers with. These if I don't forget, Mr. *Fielding* himself has nominated, the several Stages of his History, which he metaphorically called a Journey, in which he and his Readers are Fellow-

Travellers. His particular Success in these preliminary
Essays demonstrates (notwithstanding what the Author of
Charlotte Summers hints on that Head) that these are not the
easiest Part of his Task: Which I believe Mr. *Fielding*
somewhere says himself. (pp. 18-19)

What is more revealing of critical intelligence is the same
writer's subsequent discussion of chapter headings in the
course of which there is an interesting comparison of the
relative successes in this area of Fielding, Smollett and the
anonymous author of *Charlotte Summers*. The scope of the
argument is broadened to include the importance of the titles
of works of fiction:

> As I am fallen on the Subject of the Titles to his Chapters,
> it will not be improper to consider them more largely, since
> it will only be mentioning now some Remarks I should be
> obliged to make by-and-by, which, for the Sake of the
> Connection, I rather chuse to insert here. And perhaps I
> may convince the Reader, these little Scraps, if rightly
> manag'd, conduce more to his Entertainment than he is at
> first aware of. 'Tis quite opposite to the Customs of the
> very best Writers in this Way, to give too full an Account
> of the Contents: it should be just hinted to the Reader
> something extraordinary is to happen in the seven or eight
> subsequent Pages, but what that is should be left for them
> to discover. Monsieur *Le Sage*, in his *Gil Blas*, (one of the
> best Books of the Kind extant) has always pursu'd this
> Method: He tells us Gil Blas is going to such or such a
> Place, but does not discover the least of his Adventures
> there; but he is more particularly cautious when any
> unexpected Event is to happen. The Title to one of his
> Chapters of that Kind is – *A Warning not to rely too much upon
> Prosperity*. – To another – *Chapter the fifth, being just as long as
> the preceding:* With many others which it is needless to
> enumerate. Note, 'Tis to be wish'd this Custom had been
> observ'd by the Author of *Roderick Random*, who tells us in
> his Preface, his Book is wrote in Imitation of the *Gil Blas* of

Monsieur *Le Sage*. But with very little Success in my
humble Opinion. As to the Titles of his Chapters, he is
particularly tedious in them. This judicious Method of
detaining the Reader in an agreeable Suspence, though it is
right at all Times, is more particularly necessary when the
History is near ended. No Writer has so strictly kept up to
this as Mr. *Fielding*, in his *Tom Jones*. We are too well
assured of *Gil Blas*'s Prosperity a long Time beforehand, to
be surpriz'd at it. But at the Beginning of the last Book of
Tom Jones, the reader is apt to think it an equal chance
whether he is to be hanged or married; nor does he
undeceive him but by gradual Narration of Facts: And lest
the Reader's Curiosity should pry too far into the Truth,
what admirable Titles has he invented for his Chapters in
order to keep him the longer in the Dark! such as – *In which
the History draws near to a Conclusion: In which the History draws
nearer to a Conclusion*, &c. &c. which every Body will own
conduces greatly to their Entertainment, and a Reader of
the least Discernment will perceive how much more
Consequence the clever Management of these Scraps
prefix'd to each Chapter is of than he at first imagin'd.
With how little Judgment has the Author of *Charlotte
Summers* conducted this Particular! whose great Fault is
Anticipation: that is, forestalling, by too explanatory a
Title, the most remarkable Occurrences in his History.
This appears even in the Title to his Book, which is, *The
History of* Charlotte Summers: *or The FORTUNATE Parish
Girl*. What Mr. *Addison* says of the Tragedies that conclude
happily, may with equal Justice be apply'd here. 'We see
without Concern (says he) illustrious People in Distress,
when we are sure they will at last be deliver'd from their
Misfortunes.' Other Writers content themselves with
entitling their Pieces, *The History of a Foundling, of Joseph
Andrews, of Gil Blas, Roderick Random*, &c. without informing
us as to the Event. As I find myself drawn into an
unforeseen Length, I shall only subjoin one Instance from
his Chapters [i.e. of the author of *Charlotte Summers*], but at
the same Time such an one, as will convince the Reader of

Mr. *Fielding*'s Excellence in this Particular. The Eighth
Chapter of the last Book is perhaps one of the most
interesting in the whole History, and I dare say drew Tears
from many Readers. For my own Part, I am not ashamed
to own I have so much of the 'Milk of human Nature' in
me, that I should have been in the greatest Concerns for
the Misfortunes of the unhappy Miss *Summers*, if unluckily
the Author had not assur'd me before I enter'd on these
distressful Scenes, she would certainly be deliver'd from
her momentary Afflictions before I had read three Leaves
further. To confess the Truth I was vastly angry with him
for depriving me of such entertaining Sadness. We hope
this Instance will convince all future Writers, that the
Pleasure of the Reader is much more exquisite from the
Reserve in the Title. These Thoughts upon the Inscriptions
to the Chapters were thrown together to shew, that Mr.
Fielding had another Intention besides making the World
laugh in the Lines prefix'd to each Portion of his History.
Permit me therefore, gentle Reader, upon the Authority of
a Critic, to banish from all Histories above the Rank of
those printed in *Black-fryars*, and sold at the small Price of
one Penny, to tell us – *As how* Thomas Hickathrift *carried a
Stack of Corn*. Or – Thomas Thumb *was swallow'd by a Cow*,
in a Title longer than the Chapter itself. (pp. 21-7)

But such discussions are rare. There are remarkably few
topics in this area where one can offer more than a handful of
examples of expressed opinion. The most notable of these few
is perhaps the use of the epistolary form in fiction. It is, of
course, Richardson's work that comes in for most comment,
and it is Richardson himself who provides a good deal of it.
In the second edition of *Pamela* he printed an unsigned letter
from a gentleman whom Ioan Williams describes, with
admirable restraint, as his 'fulsome admirer' Aaron Hill.[17] In
one of his less fulsome moments Hill wrote:

One of the best-judg'd Peculiars, of the Plan, is that These
Instructions being convey'd, as in a Kind of Dramatical

Representation, by those beautiful *Scenes*, Her own Letters and Journals, who acts the most moving and suffering *Part*, we feel the Force in a threefold Effect, – from the Motive, the Act, and the Consequence.[18]

When it came to the prefatory material for *Clarissa* it was Richardson himself who provided the comment upon the form, basing, he added, his statement upon the opinions of those favoured readers who had been permitted access to the text prior to publication:

Length will naturally be expected, not only from what has been said, but from the following Considerations:

That the Letters on both Sides are written while the Hearts of the Writers must be supposed to be wholly engaged in their Subjects: The Events at the time generally dubious: – So that they abound, not only with critical Situations; but with what may be called *instantaneous* Descriptions and Reflections; which may be brought home to the Breast of the youthful Reader: – As also, with affecting Conversations; many of them written in the Dialogue or Dramatic Way.

To which may be added, that the Collection contains not only the History of the excellent Person whose Name it bears, but includes The Lives, Characters, and Catastrophes, of several others, either principally or incidentally concerned in the History.

But yet the Editor (to whom it was referred to publish the Whole in such a Way as he should think would be most acceptable to the Public) was so diffident in relation to this Article of *Length*, that he thought proper to submit the Letters to the Perusal of several judicious Friends; whose Opinions he desired of what might be best spared.

One Gentleman, in particular, of whose Knowlege, Judgment, and Experience, as well as Candour, the Editor has the highest Opinion, advised him to give a Narrative Turn to the Letters; and to publish only what concerned the principal Heroine; – striking off the collateral

Incidents, and all that related to the Second Characters; tho' he allowed the Parts which would have been by this means excluded, to be both instructive and entertaining. But being extremely fond of the affecting Story, he was desirous to have everything parted with, which he thought retarded its Progress.

This Advice was not relish'd by other Gentlemen. They insisted, that the Story could not be reduced to a Dramatic Unity, nor thrown into the Narrative Way, without divesting it of its Warmth; and of a great Part of its Efficacy; as very few of the Reflections and Observations, which they looked upon as the most useful Part of the Collection, would, then, find a Place.[19]

He went a step further in his preface to the second edition when he quoted with evident approval the laudatory observations of one of his own creations:

Besides the four principal persons, several others are introduced, whose Letters are characteristic: And it is presumed that there will be found in some of them, but more especially in those of the chief character among the men, and the second character among the women, such strokes of Gaiety, Fancy, and Humour, as will entertain and divert; and at the same time both warn and instruct.

All the Letters are written while the hearts of the writers must be supposed to be wholly engaged in their subjects (The events at the time generally dubious): So that they abound not only with critical Situations; but with what may be called *instantaneous* Descriptions and Reflections (proper to be brought home to the breast of the youthful Reader); as also with affecting Conversations; many of them written in the dialogue of the dramatic way.

'*Much more* lively and affecting, says one of the principal characters (Vol. VII. Let. 22.) must be the Style of those who write in the height of a *present* distress; the mind tortured by the pangs of uncertainty (the Events then hidden in the womb of Fate); *than* the dry, narrative,

unanimated Style of a person relating difficulties and
dangers surmounted, can be; the relater perfectly at ease;
and if himself unmoved by his own Story, not likely greatly
to affect the Reader.'[20]

One is left wondering if this is further evidence of
Richardson's attempts to pass off the letters as genuine and
his own contribution as merely editorial, or whether this is an
example of startlingly self-regarding naivety. If the latter, he
appears to have been encouraged in his view: *The Gentleman's
Magazine* was edited by Edward Cave, a close friend of
Richardson, and in June and August 1749 the magazine
contained a translation of a lengthy review of *Clarissa* by
Albrecht von Haller which had originally appeared in the
Bibliotèque raisonée (vol. 42 [1749]). Much of the review is
highly complimentary and where von Haller had been so
presumptuous as to suggest minor weaknesses he is answered
in extended footnotes by Richardson himself, though as with
Pamela and *Clarissa* the authorship of the material is not
openly acknowledged. In these footnotes Richardson takes
the opportunity to heap praises upon his own head with
remarks of the order of, 'The author of *Clarissa* seems to know
human nature too well, to attempt to draw a character,
however nearly perfect, absolutely so.'[21] For the present
argument what is interesting is von Haller's observations
upon Richardson's use of the epistolary form:

> The method which the author has pursued, in the history
> of *Clarissa*, is the same as in the life of *Pamela*; both are
> related in familiar letters, by the parties themselves, at the
> very time in which the events happened; and this method
> has given the author great advantages, which he could not
> have drawn from any other species of narration. The
> minute particulars of events, the sentiments and
> conversation of the parties, are, upon this plan, exhibited
> with all the warmth and spirit that the passion, supposed
> to be predominant at the very time, could produce, and
> with all the distinguishing characteristicks, which memory

can supply, in a history of recent transactions. Romances in general, and *Marivaux*'s among others, are wholly improbable; because they suppose the history to be written after the series of events is closed by the catastrophe; a circumstance, which implies a strength of memory, beyond all example and probability, in the persons concerned, enabling them, at the distance of several years, to relate all the particulars of a transient conversation: Or rather it implies a yet more improbable confidence and familiarity between all these persons and the author. There is, however, one difficulty attending the epistolary method, for it is necessary that all the characters should have an uncommon taste for this kind of correspondence, and that they should suffer no event, nor even a remarkable conversation to pass without immediately committing it to writing; but, for the preservation of these letters, once written, the author has provided with great judgment, so as to render this circumstance highly probable. (p. 345)

Von Haller noted that there were difficulties inherent in the form, and another of these basic problems was taken up by Mrs Donellan, one of the many female correspondents Richardson acquired as a result of his successes:

The epistolary style is yours, 'tis speaking, 'tis painting; but I think there must be a friend to tell some things that man can't tell of himself, for I am very delicate on the subject of self-praise, and think it should be as much avoided as possible; but when the scenes presented are passionate, they must come from the persons concerned, or they lose their spirit. Fine sentiments, and noble actions consequent to them, form the character to the reader without the persons being obliged to point them out themselves, and those I am persuaded you can point out to me.[22]

That Richardson himself saw yet another factor requiring caution on the part of the writer who chose to employ the epistolary form may be deduced from a letter to Johannes Stinstra in which he discussed the work in progress on *Sir Charles Grandison*:

I will not bespeak your Favour for my new Piece. I am sure you will approve of my *Intention* when you come to peruse it. There are some of my Friends, who speak very highly of what they have seen of it. But the Partiality of Friends must be allowed for. This only will I say, It is entirely new & unborrowed, even of myself; tho' I had written so voluminously before. It is said to abound with delicate Situations. I hope it does; for what indelicate ones can a good Man be involved in? – Yet he must have his Trials, his Perplexities – And to have them from good Women, will require some Management. In Clarissa, my Favourite Clarissa, there is a twofold Correspondence necessary, one between her and Miss Howe; the other between Lovelace and Belford. The Subject of one Letter arose often out of another. It was necessary it should. In the new Work (except one or two Letters of each of the Respondents, as I may call them) the Answers to the Letters of the *Narratist* are only supposed, & really sunk; yet Seven Volumes are, to my Regret, made of it, when I have scratched out the quantity of two, & should have been glad to have comprised the whole in Four – Whence you will judge that the unpublished Work, whether it will be thought equal or not, must have cost me most Pains: As indeed it has. But I designed it as my last Work; & as the completion of my whole Plan – If a Man may be allowed to say *Plan*, who never was regular enough to write by one; & who when he ended one Letter, hardly knew what his next would be.[23]

Long-windedness was recognised by readers as being a problem. Thomas Turner recorded in his diary, '*Clarissa Harlow*, I look upon as a very well-wrote thing, tho' it must be allowed it is too prolix';[24] and during the course of a notice of one of the many Richardsonian imitations *The Critical Review* observed, 'Memoirs written in the epistolary manner, necessarily appear prolix and redundant.'[25]

Not many eighteenth century critics seem to have made the point which to many modern readers looms large: that Richardson's epistolary structure when set against Fielding's narrative format provides a good deal of material for discussion. One of those who did was Richard Cumberland, the dramatist, who, in an extensive comparison of the two writers, extracts from which relating to morality have been considered above in chapter 4, took as one of his premises the notion of form:

Two authors of our nation began the fashion of novel-writing, upon different plans indeed, but each with a degree of success, which perhaps has never yet been equalled: Richardson disposed his fable into letters, and Fielding pursued the more natural mode of a continued narration, with an exception however of certain miscellaneous chapters, one of which he prefixed to each book in the nature of a prologue, in which the author speaks in person: he has executed this so pleasantly, that we are reconciled to the interruption in this instance; but I should doubt if it is a practice in which an imitator would be wise to follow him.

I should have observed, that modern novelists have not confined themselves to comic fables, or such only as have happy endings, but sometimes, as in the instance of 'The Clarissa,' wind up their story with a tragical catastrophe; to subjects of this sort, perhaps, the epistolary mode of writing may be best adapted, at least it seems to give a more natural scope to pathetic descriptions; but there can be no doubt that fables replete with humourous situations, characteristic dialogue, and busy plot, are better suited to the mode which Fielding has pursued in his inimitable novel of 'The Foundling,' universally allowed the most perfect work of its sort in ours, or probably any other language.[26]

Another element frequently given much attention in modern criticism is diction, and in this area it is possible to trace in the eighteenth century a gradual heightening of interest. In the first half the general attitude is neatly summed up by Fielding during the course of his prefatory remarks to the second edition of his sister's *The Adventures of David Simple* (1744):

The Sentiments are in general extremely delicate; those particularly which regard Friendship, are, I think, as noble and elevating as I have any where met with: Nor can I help remarking, that the Author hath been so careful, in justly adapting them to her Characters, that a very indifferent Reader, after he is in the least acquainted with the Character of the Speaker, can seldom fail of applying every Sentiment to the Person who utters it. Of this we have the strongest Instance in Cynthia *and* Camilla, *where the lively Spirit of the former, and the gentle Softness of the latter, breathe through every Sentence which drops from either of them.*

The Diction I shall say no more of, than as it is the last, and lowest Perfection in a Writer, and one which many of great Genius seem to have little regarded: so I must allow my Author to have the least Merit on this Head: Many Errors in Style existing in the first Edition, and some, I am convinced, remaining still uncured in this; but Experience and Habit will most certainly remove this Objection; for a good Style, as well as a good Hand in Writing, is chiefly learn'd by Practice.[27]

Though one seldom finds such an explicitly dismissive attitude to the whole concept of diction being voiced, the general nature of the observations about the idiosyncratic sentiments is entirely typical. Aaron Hill's gratulatory letters prefixed to the second edition of *Pamela* follow the same pattern:

– No Sentiments which I have here, or in my last, express'd, of the sweet *Pamela*, being more than the bare Truth, which every Man must feel, who lends his Ear to the inchanting Prattler, why does the Author's Modesty mislead his Judgment, to suspect the Style wants Polishing? – No, Sir, there is an *Ease*, a *natural Air*, a dignify'd *Simplicity*, and measured Fullness, in it, that, resembling Life, outglows it! He has reconciled the *Pleasing* to the *Proper*. The *Thought* is every-where exactly *cloath'd* by the *Expression:* And becomes its Dress as roundly, and as close, as *Pamela* her Country-habit. Remember, tho' she put it on with humble Prospect, of descending to the Level of her Purpose, it *adorn'd* her, with such unpresum'd *Increase* of Loveliness; sat with such neat Propriety of Elegant Neglect about her, that it threw out All her Charms, with tenfold, and resistless Influence – – – And so, dear Sir, it will be always found. – – – When modest Beauty seeks to hide itself by casting off the *Pride* of *Ornament*, it but displays itself without a *Covering:* And so, becoming more distinguished, by its Want of *Drapery*, grows *stronger*, from its *purpos'd Weakness*.[28]

Hill returned to the notion of the suitability of diction to its
subject, though the idea was still presented in such a manner
as to preclude any direct engagement or disagreement with
his argument. Hill's letter at this point was supposedly
designed to answer some specific objections raised against
Pamela by an unnamed 'Gentleman':

> The Writer of this Letter is for having the Style *rais'd*, after
> *Pamela*'s Advance in her Fortune. But surely, This was hasty Advice;
> because, as the Letters are writ to her Parents, it wou'd have look'd
> like forgetting, and in some sort, insulting, the Lowliness of their
> inferior Condition, to have assum'd a new Air in her Language, in
> Place of retaining a steady Humility. But here, it must not be pass'd
> unobserv'd, that in her Reports of Conversations that follow'd her
> Marriage, she *does*, aptly and beautifully, heighten her Style, and her
> Phrases; still returning however to her decent Simplicity, in her
> Addresses to her Father and Mother. (pp. xxiv-xxv)

Eventually he did attend to detail, though the detail was
limited to one word and one phrase:

> 'But, when he goes on, to object against the Word *naughty*, (as
> apply'd in the Phrase *naughty Master*) I grow mortified, in Fear for
> our human Sufficiency, compar'd with our Aptness to blunder! For,
> here, 'tis plain, this Director of Another's Discernment is quite
> blind, Himself, to an Elegance, one wou'd have thought it *impossible*
> not to be struck by? – – – Faulty, wicked, abominable, scandalous,
> (which are the angry Adjectives, he prefers to that sweet one) wou'd
> have carried Marks of her Rage, not Affliction – – – whereas *naughty*
> contains, in One single significant Petulance, twenty thousand
> inexpressible Delicacies! – – – It insinuates, at once, all the beautiful
> Struggle, between her Contempt of his Purpose, and tender Regard
> for his Person; her Gratitude to Himself and his Family; her
> Recollection of his superior Condition. – – – There is in the elegant
> Choice of this half-kind, half-peevish, *Word*, a never-enough to be
> prais'd speaking Picture of the Conflict betwixt her Disdain, and her
> Reverence! See, Sir, the Reason I had, for apprehending some
> Danger that the refin'd Generosity in many of the most charming
> Sentiments wou'd be *lost*, upon the too coarse Conception of some,
> for whose Use the Author intended them.
> 'It is the same Case again, in *foolish Thing that I am!* which this

nice, un-nice, Gentleman wou'd advise you to change, into *foolish that I am!* He does not seem to have tasted the pretty Contempt of Herself, the submissive *Diminutive*, so distant from Vanity, yet allay'd by the gentle Reluctance in Self-condemnation; – and the other fine Touches of Nature: which wou'd All have been lost, in the grave, sober Sound of his *Dutch emendation.*' (pp. xxvi-xxvii)

Swift's dictum, 'Proper words in proper places, make the true definition of style', seems to have been taken much more to heart by critics towards the end of the century. At times they offered quite precise objections to linguistic details. In December 1790 *The Monthly Review* printed a notice of James Thomson's *The Denial; or, the Happy Retreat*, which observed:

> In regard to the general character of Mr. Thomson's performance, it certainly is not void of merit. The volumes abound with pious and moral reflections, not unworthy the pen of a clergymen: but we should have admired this piety and this morality still more, had the language (especially of the earlier letters), been less verbose, and the style less stiffened with hard words. Terms of the same signification are frequently coupled together: a mode of writing rather suitable to an indenture than a book of entertainment; and peculiarly inconsistent with the natural ease and freedom of the epistolary style.[29]

To this was appended a footnote detailing some of the objections:

> For instance, 'black criminality,' pref. p.7.; 'Wanton lasciviousness,' ib. p.9.; 'mutual reciprocation,' ib. p.16.; 'cautious timidity,' p.32. – Other expressions, which we have remarked, seem much too stiff and pedantic for the characters that use them – as, 'Pray, Madam,' answers Mr. Wilton to a question from his lady mother, 'what prompts the interrogation?' – 'My dear Henry,' says the countess, 'I am afraid the air of your native country, after so long an absence in the warmer climates of France and Italy, is not *congenial* to your health, as you seem to have *acquired* a

slight indisposition this morning,' p.33.; and the Hon. Mr. W. is, in like manner, accosted by his honourable sister, with 'Pray, Henry, if our native air be more *salubrious* than that of the continent' – p.36. With equal solemnity does the young nobleman answer his Right Hon. father's haughty commands to marry the lady not of his choice: 'The will hath a certain prerogative, in the exercise of which it admits of no compulsory methods to corrode its happiness. It thinks, it acts with *spontaneity*; and when opposed, suffers a diminution of its pleasure.' p. 37, &c. &c.

We would just observe, also, that the hero of this piece is said to be the only son of the Earl Wilton, and yet he is merely styled the *Hon. Mr.* Wilton. Every Earl has a secondary title, which by courtesy, is borne by his eldest son; and his daughters are addressed as *Lady Ann, Lady Mary*. &c.

That these details should have been relegated to a footnote rather than being incorporated into the body of the review possibly indicates a continued underlying acceptance of Fielding's view that this is the 'lowest Perfection in a Writer'; though it may be questioned whether the second paragraph in the footnote is primarily concerned with the matter of diction or with those expectations of reality and accuracy which have so frequently been noted in the criticism of the century. Whichever is the true motivation, what is of concern here is that such comments are being made and they are for the most part clearly sensible. This was not always the case. There are times when a surprising imperception is revealed. *The Critical Review* of March 1792, during the course of a notice of William Cowper's blank verse translation of Homer, stated firmly:

A single word may serve as an instance: Hero (Ἥρως) has with us a determinate sense, and is appropriated to military characters; but it is not so in Homer: he prefixes it to many names in the Odyssey, on whom, had he first written in English, he would never have bestowed it. We

184

have the Hero Halitherses, the Hero Egyptus, the Hero
Medon, and the Hero Megapenthes; yet no military exploit
is recorded or alluded to of either. Mr. C. therefore should
not have adopted the same word.[30]

Leaving aside for the moment, if it is possible, the
marvellously manic notion that Homer might have had a
choice of languages – including English – to write in, and
acknowledging that this is from a review of poetry, not prose,
and thus is expected to deal in greater detail with niceties of
diction, one is left with the assertion that the word 'hero' is
only applicable in English in 1792 to military characters.
How unfortunate that Fielding, describing *Tom Jones* in 1749,
and ten years later Sterne describing *Tristram Shandy*, should
have demonstrated such a lack of awareness of the 'rule'.

Rather more valid criticism is to be found in *The
Gentleman's Magazine* of September 1798 in a review of J. Fox's
Santa Maria; or, The Mysterious Pregnancy, though it should be
noted that the general praise of apt diction seen above in the
remarks of Fielding and Hill has been replaced by specific
condemnation of the inept, and in this instance (an unusual
feature) recognition of particular passages meriting an
approving voice:

> The style is often turgid and rough; frequently bombast,
> and sometimes obscure. The following sentences are justly
> reprehensible: Vol. I. p.23, 'If thou has ever seen thy
> dearest bosom friend *topping* headlong into the dreary
> recess of the grave.' '*Topping* into the grave' is an entirely
> new phrase; perhaps it has an allusion to the bathing-
> machines, and the *manner* in which the *visitors* at Brigh*ton*
> are *dipped*. – P.153, 'The Count, on this, proceeded to the
> other chest, and likewise found *all empty* there.' – P.202,
> 'The sounds, so heavenly and attractive, *perched them*
> immediately on the stair, which they were preparing to
> quit.' – P.206, 'Here, however, I arrived at last, covered
> with bruises from head to foot, and, what is more
> extraordinary, *soberer* than ever I was in my life.' We might

point out several similar inaccuracies in the remaining volumes, but we forbear. – We think Mr. F. might have selected a female name more grateful to the ear than *Mopso*, who is occasionally introduced. While we thus honestly give our sentiments on the execution of this romance, we are far from viewing Mr. Fox as incapable of furnishing the publick with a good novel; and, amidst the absurdities that are here noticed, have occasionally met with a passage composed in a masterly manner; such is the description of the storm at Naples, and the eruption of Mount Vesuvius, and of the last moments of Father Conrad.[31]

There is a certain irony that the eighteenth century, so often held up as the age of the excessively rational – an error from which the nation was freed by the white knight of romanticism – should have been the great age of true variety in English prose fiction, and that it should have been the critics and writers of the romantic period who were primarily responsible for restricting this flourishing output into a more regular and, to their eyes, more acceptable uniformity. The motley crew was at long last required to conform to the much wanted standards.

CHAPTER 6

———◆———

'THE MOST
HETEROGENEOUS IDEAS
ARE YOKED BY VIOLENCE
TOGETHER'

B Y the time Jane Austen came to write her celebrated defence of novels in the fifth chapter of *Northanger Abbey* (1816, but probably written by 1803), the notion of the form appears to have achieved a measure of common consent, and that the romance/novel dichotomy continued is evident from the *Morning Chronicle*'s advertisement, 'Northanger Abbey, a Romance; and Persuasion, a Novel. By the Author of Pride and Prejudice, Mansfield Park, &c.'[1]

The standardisation derived its impetus from two sources. Critics tend to the taxonomic – it makes life simpler, and as has been seen from the writings of such as Beattie the final quarter of the eighteenth century saw some intelligent attempts to categorise prose fiction, even though these attempts were at times Procrustean. Simultaneously commercial considerations were at work. Between 1780 and 1788 Harrison and Company issued twenty-three volumes entitled *The Novelist's Magazine*. Of these *Clarissa* occupied two volumes as did *Sir Charles Grandison*, while *Pamela* and its continuation and Smollett's translation of *Don Quixote* filled a volume each. Into the remaining seventeen volumes the publishers managed to cram a further fifty-six titles. The choice was eclectic. Of Fielding's works, there were *Joseph Andrews*, *Amelia*, *Tom Jones*, *Jonathan Wild* and *Journey from this world to the next*; of Sterne's, both *Tristram Shandy* and *A*

Sentimental Journey; of Smollett's, *Roderick Random, Peregrine Pickle, Ferdinand Count Fathom, Sir Launcelot Greaves, Humphry Clinker* and *Adventures of an Atom*, together with his translations of *Don Quixote* and *Gil Blas*. Other notable works included *Gulliver's Travels, Robinson Crusoe, Rasselas, The Vicar of Wakefield* and *Zadig*. These were indiscriminately bound up with such efforts as Mrs Haywood's *Betty Thoughtless* and *Jemmy and Jenny Jessamy*, and Samuel Humphrey's translation from the French of *Peruvian Tales, related in one thousand and one hours, by one of the select Virgins of Cusco, to the Ynca of Peru, to dissuade him from a resolution he had taken to destroy himself by Poison*. These volumes contained no introductory material, no justification or rationale of selection. Some works appear to have been selected by length, in that they conveniently made up a volume to a size compatible with others in the series. But the effect of the random application of the term in a popular series was to start the process of conditioning the reader to a retroactive notion of form.

This was reinforced by a number of highly successful publishing ventures. At the turn of the century C. Cooke of Paternoster Row issued *Cooke's Edition of Select Novels, Or, Novelist's Pocket Library Being a complete collection of universally approved histories, adventures, anecdotes, &c. by the most esteemed authors*. That the series title should equate anecdotes and novels indicates the looseness of application. But the series was seized upon so avidly by the public that it was copied by Henshall of Dublin even down to the use of the same ornament on the title pages.

A sole Canute-like effort to stem the tide of undiscriminating application of 'novel' was made by Mrs Barbauld. In 1810 she produced an edition of *The British Novelists* which ran to fifty volumes, and this series proved so popular that it was reprinted in its entirety in 1821. Unlike *The Novelist's Magazine* where many works were crammed into as few volumes as possible, Mrs Barbauld's selection was considerably easier on the reader's eye: *Clarissa* and *Sir Charles Grandison* occupy the first fifteen volumes, and the total is a relatively manageable twenty-eight works. What sets Mrs Barbauld's apart from

188

any other contemporary publishing venture of this sort is the evident critical concern which has gone into the process of selection. Prefixed to the first example of every author concerned (save one: Francis Coventry) there is a biographical and critical essay judiciously exploring the strengths and weaknesses of the work selected, offering reasons for the selection, and from time to time explaining why other works by the same writer have been omitted.

These prefatory essays consider those major critical views which also concerned the eighteenth century, and they occasionally manifest the same weaknesses. The key terms 'novel' and 'romance' continue to be used with unfortunate elasticity of meaning, though as is proper in a series denominated *The British Novelists* the former predominates. What is far more important is the recognition that there may be limits to the useful application of these terms. Mrs Barbauld's essay on Defoe opens: 'The first publication which appears in this selection has so little air of a common novel, that many will probably be surprised to see it included under that denomination.'[2] This is a refreshing frankness. She proceeds to justify its inclusion, notwithstanding the reader's probable surprise, mainly on the grounds of its realism: 'But the truth is, this favourite of our early years, though it has no pretensions to the graces of style, nor aims at touching the tender passions, yields to few in the truth of its description and its powers of interesting the mind' (vol. 16, p.i). Some indication of the extent of Defoe's efforts to create realism have been explored in chapter 3 and it is clearly an area where Mrs Barbauld is aware of major pitfalls. Defoe's works on the whole she considers 'possessed in a remarkable degree the power of giving such an air of truth and nature to his narrative that they are rather deceptions than imitations' (vol. 16, pp. i-ii), where 'deceptions' has pejorative connotations; and her reservations on this topic are manifested in comments upon *Journal of the Plague Year*:

It is written in the person of a citizen, a shopkeeper, who is supposed to have staid in the metropolis during the whole time of the calamity; and the particulars are so striking, so awful, and so circumstantial, that it deceived most of his readers, and amongst others it is said Dr. Mead, into a belief of its authenticity; – an exercise of ingenuity not to be commended; – though, after all, the particulars were most of them true, though the relater was fictitious. (vol.16, p.iv)

Just as we have noted in contemporary reactions to *Amelia* an apparent belief that the representation of reality has boundaries, so too for Mrs Barbauld realism as a praise-worthy element in fiction has its limits. *Robinson Crusoe* is praised for the 'truth of its description': *Journal of the Plague Year* is decried for its 'authenticity' being a mere 'exercise of ingenuity'. One is reminded of Richardson's dismissal of Fielding's powers on the grounds that his characters were taken from life. In contrast Mrs Barbauld observes of *The Vicar of Wakefield*, 'the character of Burchell, alias Sir William, is too romantic for a representation of real life' (vol.20, p.xi). We crave and praise fictional reality, but the very term isolates its own paradoxical nature.

Throughout the essays there is a recognition very similar to that in the final chapter of *Hermsprong* of the inevitable conflict between our expectations of the real and our equally strong expectations of conventions. The general point is made, 'A novel-writer must violate probability somewhere, and a reader ought to make all handsome and generous allowances for it' (vol.1, p.xxx). Sometimes an author is damned for inclining too far towards the demands of convention, as in the remarks on *Roderick Random*:

Towards the hero of this tale the reader feels little interest; but after he has been led through a variety of adventures, in which he exhibits as little of the amiable qualities as of the more respectable ones, the author, according to the laudable custom of novel-writers, leaves him in possession of a beautiful wife and a good estate. (vol.30, p.vii)

Sometimes an author is damned for failing to incline

sufficiently, as is Richardson in the matter of *Sir Charles Grandison*:

> He had already continued it a whole volume beyond the proper termination – the marriage of his hero; and having done so, he might, without more impropriety, have gone on to the next point of view, and the next, till he had given the history of two or three generations. (vol.1, p.xliii)

Where Richardson had felt it quite proper to pursue the adventures of his hero beyond marriage, that living death, where Sterne had seemingly terminated his major work at a moment chronologically some years prior to his opening chapter, where Bage had been able to mock the foolishness of conventional endings, Mrs Barbauld appears to be serious in her strictures on *Grandison*. A notion which had only evolved towards the end of the eighteenth century is employed to criticise adversely a work written nearly half a century before – further proof, if any were needed, of the false nature of criticism based upon historical misconceptions. And it is presumably to this same misconception that we can attribute Mrs Barbauld's remark on Fanny Burney, 'on the winding up of *Cecilia* and *Camilla* we are somewhat tantalised with imperfect happiness' (vol.28, p.x).

It is a nod to convention of a different nature which leads to the downgrading of the achievement of Mrs Radcliffe. Initially the praise is high:

> Though every production which is good in its kind entitles its author to praise, a greater distinction is due to those which stand at the head of a class; and such are undoubtedly the novels of Mrs. Radcliffe, – which exhibit a genius of no common stamp. She seems to scorn to move those passions which form the interest of common novels. (vol.43, p.i)

But subsequently Mrs Barbauld pinpoints the basic weakness of this author:

In novels of this kind, where the strong charm of suspense
and mystery is employed, we hurry through with
suspended breath, and in a kind of agony of expectation;
but when we are come to the end of the story, the charm is
dissolved, we have no wish to read it again; we do not
recur to it as we do to the characters of Western in *Tom
Jones*, or the Harrels in *Cecilia*; the interest is painfully
strong while we read, and once we have read it, it is
nothing; we are ashamed of our feelings, and do not wish to
recall them. (vol.43, p.vii)

It is fairly easy to point out inconsistency here: the critic who
praises Defoe's 'truth to nature' condemns Mrs Radcliffe's
failure to maintain the fiction. But Mrs Barbauld's remarks
are introduced as being applicable to 'novels of this kind', by
which one must assume she intends the reader to think of
'romance' – yet again the right term is essential to our proper
understanding.

Plot, which like the notion of convention had not been a
major feature of earlier eighteenth century writings on fiction,
assumes a far greater importance in critical assessment.
Roderick Random is briefly dismissed; '*Roderick Random*, like *Gil
Blas*, has little or nothing of regular plot, and no interest is
excited for the hero, whose name serves to string together a
number of adventures' (vol.30, p.v). *Clarissa* on the other
hand is praised for reasons dangerously close to those used to
damn Smollett: 'The plot, as we have seen, is simple, and no
under-plots interfere with the main design. No digressions, no
episodes. It is wonderful that without these helps of common
writers he could support a work of such length. With Clarissa
it begins – with Clarissa it ends' (vol.1, p.xvi). That there is
still a hangover however from the apparent eighteenth
century notion of the relative unimportance of plot is to be
seen in her remark on *Tom Jones*, 'But intricacy of plot,
admirable as this is, is still of secondary merit compared with
the exhibition of character, of which there is in this work a
rich variety' (vol.18, p.xxi). Praise of *Tom Jones* is tempered:
'Upon the whole, *Tom Jones* is certainly for humour, wit,

character, and plot, one of the most entertaining and perfect novels we possess. With regard to its moral tendency we must content ourselves with more qualified praise' (vol.18, p.xxvii). And it is clear that morality, though not as all-consuming as it appears to have been to some critics of the previous century, to Mrs Barbauld writing in 1810 remains a consideration of some weight. Thus in her reasons for excluding *Pamela*, after indicating its historical value, 'the fame of this once favourite work is now somewhat tarnished by time, as well as eclipsed by the author's subsequent publications; but the enthusiasm with which it was received, shows incontrovertibly, that a novel written on the side of virtue was considered as a new experiment' (vol.1, p.xi), the turning down of the thumb is on moral grounds: 'The indelicate scenes in this novel have been justly found fault with, and are, indeed, totally indefensible' (vol.1, p.xiv). Even *Clarissa*, which receives the seal of approval, is not accepted uncritically in this matter, 'the too high colouring of some of the scenes has been objected to, as tending to inflame passions which it was the author's professed aim to regulate' (vol.1, p.xxviii).

These wide-ranging essays are valuable not only as perceptive and informative discussions of specific major British writers; they are also of interest to the history of criticism in that they appear to be the last bastions against the belief that fiction and novel are synonymous. To reinforce her case Mrs Barbauld prefixed to the series as a whole an essay 'On the Origins and Progress of Novel-writing'. This essay assesses the importance of the form, attempts to trace its history, considers how the reader's expectations are aroused and how they are satisfied, discusses the importance of reality and morality, and, possibly most importantly, and certainly at the time uniquely, explains what the criteria of selection have been and why certain named works have been rejected.

As editor of a fifty-volume collection entitled *The British Novelists*, Mrs Barbauld's claims for the importance and tradition of the form might be viewed as special pleading similar to that engaged in by Fanny Burney in her justificatory preface to *Evelina*. Mrs Barbauld writes:

> When the range of this kind of writing is so great, it seems evident that it ought to hold a respectable place among the productions of genius; nor is it easy to say, why the poet, who deals in one kind of fiction, should have so high a place allotted to him in the temple of fame; and the romance-writer so low a one as in the general estimation he is confined to. To measure the dignity of a writer by the pleasure he affords is not perhaps using an accurate criterion; but the invention of a story, the choice of proper incidents, the ordonnance of the plan, occasional beauties of description, and above all, the power exercised over the reader's heart by filling it with the successive emotions of love, pity, joy, anguish, transport, or indignation, together with the grave impressive moral resulting from the whole, imply talents of the highest order, and ought to be appreciated accordingly. A good novel is an epic in prose, with more of character and less (indeed in modern novels nothing) of the supernatural machinery. (vol.1, pp.2-3)

Her key term here is taken from Fielding and her elements of successful novel writing would be equally applicable to successful literary works of many genres. However this is her opening ranging shot and the precise fire is to follow. The essay traces what its author sees as the origins of the novel form: she accepts Heliodorus' *Theagenes and Chariclea* (c.220-50) as 'a genuine novel' (vol.1, pp.4-5) and is also prepared to admit Apuleius' *Golden Ass* (c.180); on the other hand, 'the *Pantagruel* of Rabelais is rather a piece of licentious satire than a romance' (vol.1, p.12). Unlike Beattie who had attempted to marshal all prose fiction into fixed categories, Mrs Barbauld recognises that there are mavericks which cannot be so neatly disposed of. Her wide reading is revealed by her exploration of the development of fiction in France, Spain and Germany, and there is even, she says, an acceptable Chinese novel, *The pleasing history, or the adventures of Hau Kiou Chan*. Though these various foreign examples spanning many centuries are considered properly termed novels, when it comes to the novel in English she is much more ready to be exclusive. One of the most revealing observations comes at the end of a lengthy discussion of the stature of such early prose works as More's *Utopia* (1516), Barclay's *Argenis* (1621), and Harington's *Oceana* (1656):

> All these, though works of fiction, would greatly disappoint those who should look into them for amusement. Of the lighter species of this kind of writing, *the Novel*, till within half a century we had scarcely any. (vol.1, p.34)

'Fiction' and 'novel' are not interchangeable terms in Mrs Barbauld's eyes. Writing as she was in 1810, the period 'within half a century' would require the novel form to be the production of the second half of the eighteenth century. But the selection that follows includes works by Defoe, Richardson and Fielding, all of whose output appeared prior to 1760. That she had some reservations about Defoe has been seen above, as has also the erroneously based nature of her criticism of *Grandison* which anachronistically demanded conformity with a convention not existing at the time of Richardson's writing. I believe that Mrs Barbauld recognised that the novel, as she understood the term, flourished in the second half of the century, and that she felt it necessary to include in her series two or three earlier examples of great prose fiction which, though failing to conform to expectations, nevertheless had sufficient in common, and were sufficiently highly regarded, as to be acceptably offered as establishing a tradition. As with Fanny Burney in *Evelina*, and Wordsworth and Coleridge in their preface to *Lyrical Ballads*, at the turn of the eighteenth century it was felt important to be able to trace one's forebears even when, particularly with *Lyrical Ballads*, the product on offer bore very little resemblance to the exhumed ancestors.

What is vital in the passage above is the introduction of the notion of the importance of amusement. Amusement had not been a dominant feature of eighteenth century criticism and reader response. Thomas Turner, who I have suggested to be a possibly representative common reader, was constantly to be found confiding to his diary how impressed and improved he had been by the morality of the works he had been reading.[3] He does not appear to have regarded amusement as an appropriate response to literature. But to Mrs Barbauld this is virtually the *sine qua non*:

> If the end and object of this species of writing be asked, many no doubt will be ready to tell us that its object is, – to call in fancy to the aid of reason, to deceive the mind into embracing truth under the guise of fiction . . . with such-like reasons equally grave and dignified. For my own part, I scruple not to confess that, when I take up a novel, my end and object is entertainment; and as I suspect that to be the case with most readers, I hesitate not to say that entertainment is their legitimate end and object. To read the productions of wit and genius is a very high pleasure to all persons of taste, and the avidity with which they are read by all such shows sufficiently that they are calculated to answer this end. (vol.1, pp.43-4)

The point is repeated with some vigour:

> We cut down the tree that bears no fruit, but we ask nothing of a flower beyond its scent and colour. The unpardonable sin of a novel is dullness: however grave or wise it may be, if its author possesses no powers of amusing, he has no business to write novels; he should employ his pen in some more serious part of literature. (vol. 1, p.45)

This is a major shift in the writer-reader relationship. Defoe's prefaces suggest very strongly that he expects his readers to be constantly aware of the moral or ethical usefulness of his works; Richardson's obsessive concern with his readers' correct moral interpretation of his writings is even more overpowering. The correspondence generated by *Pamela*, *Clarissa* and *Sir Charles Grandison* shows that his readers to a large degree satisfied their author's expectation. When we come to Mrs Barbauld the position has been reversed: the reader now has expectations of the author:

> It may be added with regard to the knowledge of the world, which, it is allowed, these writings are calculated in some degree to give, that, let them be as well written and with as much attention to real life and manners as they can possibly be, they will in some respects give false ideas, from the very nature of fictitious writing. Every such work is a *whole*, in which the fates and fortunes of the personages are brought to a conclusion, agreeably to the author's own preconceived idea. Every incident in a well written composition is introduced for a certain purpose, and made to forward a certain plan. A sagacious reader is never disappointed in his forebodings. If a prominent circumstance is presented to him, he lays hold on it, and may be very sure it will introduce some striking event; and if a character has strongly engaged his affections, he need not fear being obliged to withdraw them; the personages never turn out differently from what their first appearance gave him a right to expect; they gradually open, indeed; they may surprise, but they never disappoint him. Even from the elegance of a name he may give a guess at the amenity of the character. But real life is a kind of chance-medley, consisting of many unconnected scenes. The great author of the drama of life has not finished his piece; but the author must finish his; and vice must be punished and virtue rewarded in the compass of a few volumes; and it is a fault in *his* composition if every circumstance does not answer the reasonable expectation of the reader. (vol.1, pp.52-3)

This is a major reversal, and is connected very closely with perceptions of truth and reality. Where an author is attempting to pass his work off as truth, then clearly convention is a destructive alien presence. At no point in *Journal of the Plague Year* can the reader have any precise notion of what is to come. That we expect *Robinson Crusoe* to be rescued from his isolation is based upon the fact that we have his account in our hands, and that somehow the manuscript must have returned to England; Crusoe's activities after being taken off the island are sufficiently surprising to be evidence of the absence of conventional structure to the work. Richardson carries on Grandison's story for an entire volume beyond his marriage; Sterne offers to tear out the next page if the reader can guess what is to happen. These writers do not recognise that there are demands the reader is entitled to make. But the opening of the final chapter of *Mansfield Park* shows unequivocally that by the turn of the century convention has become firmly rooted, so firmly that it can be mocked:

> Let other pens dwell on guilt and misery. I quit such
> odious objects as soon as I can, impatient to restore every
> body, not greatly in fault themselves, to tolerable comfort,
> and to have done with all the rest.[4]

In order to demonstrate the importance of reader expectation, and show the extent to which it departs from any idea of reality, Mrs Barbauld offers a lengthy discussion of *Tom Jones*. Her choice is revealing, for of the great writers of the first half of the eighteenth century Fielding stands out by virtue of his not attempting to pass his works off as truth, and though Mrs Barbauld's argument here is perceptive and convincing it must be recognised that its premises could not be applied to, say, *Roxana* or *Clarissa*:

> In short, the reader of a novel forms his expectations from
> what he supposes passes in the mind of the author, and
> guesses rightly at his intentions, but would often guess
> wrong if he were considering the real course of nature. It
> was very probable, at some periods of his history, that *Gil
> Blas*, if a real character, would come to be hanged; but the
> practised novel-writer knows well that no such event can
> await the hero of the tale. Let us suppose a person
> speculating on the character of *Tom Jones* as the production

of an author, whose business it is pleasingly to interest his readers. He has no doubt but that, in spite of his irregularities and distresses, his history will come to an agreeable termination. He has no doubt but that his parents will be discovered in due time; he has no doubt but that his love for *Sophia* will be rewarded sooner or later with her hand; he has no doubt of the constancy of that young lady, or of their entire happiness after marriage. And why does he foresee all this? Not from the real tendencies of things, but from what he has discovered of the author's intentions. But what would have been the probability in real life? Why, that the parents would either never have been found, or have proved to be persons of no consequence – that *Jones* would pass from one vicious indulgence to another, till his natural good disposition was quite smothered under his irregularities – that *Sophia* would either have married her lover clandestinely, and have been poor and unhappy, or she would have conquered her passion and married some country gentleman with whom she would have lived in moderate happiness, according to the usual routine of married life. But the author would have done very ill so to have constructed his story. If *Booth* had been a real character, it is probable his *Amelia* and her family would not only have been brought to poverty, but left in it; but to the reader it is much more probable that by some measure or other they will be rescued from it, and left in possession of all the comforts of life. (vol.1, pp.53-5)

We know this argument is inapplicable to *Clarissa* for Mrs Barbauld's own edition of Richardson's correspondence shows that many readers expected or desired that Clarissa would follow the conventions of society and marry Lovelace. But Richardson was as unprepared to accept conventions of society of which he disapproved as he was unaware of any convention of literary form to be employed.

For Mrs Barbauld amusement may be the touchstone of the novel, but it is not her sole criterion. In an argument similar to that expressed by Johnson when writing of Cowley,

'Whatever professes to benefit by pleasing must please at once',[5] she puts entertainment first, but accepts that there may be other motives of importance, though they are subordinate:

> But it is not necessary to rest the credit of these works on amusement alone, since it is certain they have had a very strong effect in infusing principles and moral feelings. It is impossible to deny that the most glowing and impressive sentiments of virtue are to be found in many of these compositions, and have been deeply imbibed by their youthful readers. (vol.1, p.45)

Proper concern for moral issues is something for which an author should be rightly praised: 'It is one of the merits of Sterne that he has awakened the attention of his readers to the wrongs of the poor negroes, and certainly a great spirit of tenderness and humanity breathes throughout the work' (vol.1, p.39), but that a novel can be life-enhancing or improving is a view regarded with a certain jaundice: 'Least of all will a course of novels prepare a young lady for the neglect and tedium of life which she is perhaps doomed to encounter' (vol.1, p.51).

This air of common sense is to be found in her concluding remarks on her principles of choice:

> With regard to this particular selection, it presents a series of some of the most approved novels, from the first regular productions of the kind to the present time: they are of very different degrees of merit; but none, it is hoped, so destitute of it as not to afford entertainment. Variety in manner has been attended to. As to the rest, no two people probably would make the same choice, nor indeed the same person at any distance of time. (vol.1, p.58)

What has been discussed so far would be enough to mark out Mrs Barbauld as a singularly perceptive critic in her age. But there is one other aspect of her introductory survey which is of particular relevance to the argument of this book. There are works, in Mrs Barbauld's opinion, which some of her readers may expect to find in a series entitled *The British Novelists*, but which are not included. Several are proposed and rejected. To a twentieth century reader two or three are unsurprising exclusions.

Thomas Amory's *Life of John Buncle*, the most extensively reviewed work of fiction of the century, is paired with the same author's *Memoirs of Several Ladies* and described as 'singular', not apparently a word of praise in Mrs Barbauld's vocabulary, and as 'very whimsical' (vol.1, p.37). Charles Johnstone's *Chrysal* (1760-65), which will be looked at in more detail below, is unceremoniously thrown out because of its highly dubious morality:

> Certainly if a knowledge of the vicious part of the world be a desirable acquisition, *Chrysal* will amply supply it; but many of the scenes are too coarse not to offend a delicate mind, and the generation it describes is past away. (vol.1, p.38)

Henry Brook's *The Fool of Quality* (1765-70) does not measure up to the test for rather different reasons:

> Many beautiful and pathetical episodical stories might be selected from it, but the story runs out into a strain romantic and improbable beyond the common allowed measure of this kind of writing, so that as a whole it cannot be greatly recommended (vol.1, p.40)

Mrs Barbauld's reasons for excluding works are straightforward and sensible; 'coarse', 'romantic', 'improbable', and 'singular'. This last word is worth noting, for it implies that the work concerned is so far from any norm that categorisation, and thus valid criticism, is not available to the reader or critic. And 'singular' is used to describe the works of one author whose absence might raise an eyebrow on the twentieth century reader who has been conditioned to see all fiction as examples of novels.

The omission which is remarkable is Sterne. The reason offered is straightforward:

201

> About fifty years ago a very singular work appeared,
> somewhat in the guise of a novel, which gave a new
> impulse to writings of this stamp; namely, *The Life and
> Opinions of Tristram Shandy*, followed by *The Sentimental
> Journey*, by the Rev. Mr. Sterne, a clergyman of York. They
> exhibit much originality, wit, and beautiful strokes of
> pathos, but a total want of plan or adventure, being made
> up of conversations and detached incidents. (vol.1, p.38)

Originality, wit and pathos may contribute to a novel, but a
'total want of plan or adventure' means that the qualities of
expression are misleading, and the result is not a novel, it is
'somewhat in the guise of a novel'. *Tristram Shandy* is even
acknowledged to have been influential on the writings of
those who came later, writings which are 'of this stamp', but
those who imitated elements of Sterne's work could not
retroactively bestow upon his work the denomination applicable to their own.

It is unfortunate for the history of prose fiction that in the
year in which the second edition of Mrs Barbauld's collection
appeared the public were also offered the first volumes of
what was essentially a hack project; but the hack was of the
highest class – Walter Scott. Scott was a partner of John
Ballantyne, an Edinburgh bookseller, and it was for *Ballantyne's Novelist's Library* that he produced a series of biographical and critical sketches by way of prefaces. Between 1821
and 1824 there appeared ten volumes containing the writings
of fourteen authors. Ballantyne died in June 1821, and it is
generally accepted that Scott was solely responsible for the
selection of these exemplars of his conception of the novel.
The list is very illuminating: Fielding, Smollett, Le Sage,
Charles Johnstone, Sterne, Goldsmith, Samuel Johnson,
Mackenzie, Walpole, Clara Reeve, Richardson, Bage, Cumberland, and Mrs Radcliffe. Omissions from this list may be
rapidly dispensed with. The rights to the works of such recent
writers as Jane Austen were still held by other publishing
houses and such absences are not to be taken as denial of
novelist status; and that the series appears to have been

aborted after ten volumes is sufficient explanation for the
absence of such possible contenders as Charlotte Lennox and
Fanny Burney. What is important for the history of the idea
of the novel is the range of those included and Scott's
justification of their inclusion.

The first volume, containing the works of Fielding, was
prefixed with a 'Life' opening with the bald statement, 'Of all
the works of imagination to which the English genius has
given origin the novels of the celebrated Henry Fielding are,
perhaps, most decidedly and exclusively her own.'[6] At no
point in the fourteen biographical sketches did Scott deem it
necessary to provide any definition of the key word or provide
a general essay upon the topic. There is at times a looseness
of expression reminiscent of earlier critics: *Roderick Random* is
described as 'the second example of the minor romance or
English novel' (p.36); *The Vicar of Wakefield* as 'one of the most
delicious morsels of fictitious composition on which the
human mind was ever employed' (p.152); *The Castle of Otranto*
is termed a 'romance' while Clara Reeve's *Old English Baron* is
always a 'novel', and Mrs Radcliffe is described as a novelist
(e.g. p.304) but her individual productions are 'romances'
(same page). Richard Cumberland, alternatively, is 'a writer
of fictitious history', an expression close to oxymoron which
recalls so much of the confusion of vocabulary seen
throughout the previous century.

Scott was on thinnest ice with his inclusion of Charles
Johnstone and Samuel Johnson. Charles Johnstone's *Chrysal,
or the adventures of a guinea* (1760-65) was a *roman à clef* very
similar to Mrs Manley's *New Atalantis*. Johnstone's was a
loosely constructed work based upon a simple but effective
idea. Chrysal is a guinea which constantly changes hands and
records the activities of the persons in whose possession it
finds itself. The anecdotes meander through a variety of
different countries and social settings and many of the owners
of the guinea are readily identifiable historical personages – a
good deal of attention is devoted to the activities of the
members of the Hell-fire Club. Apart from the framework
there is little of fiction. And as of Johnstone's other works

Scott merely observed, 'these publications we perused long since, but remember nothing of them so accurately as to hazard an opinion on their merits' (p.103), the sole justification for including this writer as an exemplar of the novelist is *Chrysal*. Yet in the discussion of the work, the words 'novel' and 'novelist' are conspicuously absent. We are given 'secret history' (p.103), 'Scandalous Chronicle' (p.104), 'satire' (p.105), 'prose Juvenal' (p.105), 'the caustic pages of *Chrysal*' (p.107), and 'this singular work' (p.111).

Mrs Barbauld specifically excluded this work; why did Scott include it? Johnstone is praised for being 'an unsparing and compromising censor' (p.105); it is suggested that he was an accurate historian of his age, 'the infamous and horrid scenes described in *Chrysal* were not in the slightest exaggerated' (p.106), and there is the resounding claim:

> But, feeling and writing under the popular impression of
> the moment, Johnstone has never failed to feel and write
> like a true Briton, with a sincere admiration of his
> country's laws, an ardent desire for her prosperity, and a
> sympathy with her interests, which more than atone for
> every error and prejudice. (p.111)

There is nothing here about characterisation, narrative form or technique, or development of plot. Ardent patriotism is sufficient to make a novelist.

Samuel Johnson's tenuous right to be included is at least more openly acknowledged: 'such has been the reputation which it [*The Dictionary*] has enjoyed that it renders useless even the form of an abridgment, which is the less necessary as the great Lexicographer only stands connected with the department of fictitious narrative by the brief tale of *Rasselas*' (p.156). *Rasselas* is subsequently described as 'this beautiful tale' (p.158), and Scott even goes so far as to admit 'the work can scarce be termed a narrative' (p.161).

Nevertheless, despite the acknowledgment that *Rasselas* cannot really be regarded as a novel, and thus Johnson cannot be a novelist, despite the recognition that *Chrysal* is

204

'singular' and thus not a work which lends itself to categorisation, which suggests that Johnstone is no novelist either, both these writers are included in the series.

It is hard to overestimate Scott's influence on subsequent critical thought and the reading public's perception. Though seldom read today, in the nineteenth century he was regarded as a colossus. And though he did not sign the prefaces, the fact that the first was dated 'Abbotsford, 25th October 1820' made quite clear who the writer was. That these sketches were Scott's work gave them a cachet; they were *ex cathedra* judgments handed down to be accepted. If Sir Walter Scott said these fourteen writers were novelists, novelists they were. And as they were novelists there was little reason not to accept that virtually every other writer of prose fiction was a novelist too.

Once this happened, criticism tended to the mechanical. No longer was there concern for accurate perception of form so that right judgment could be made. The form was taken as read, and other areas were explored by critics. Works such as *The Rise of the Novel, The English Novel: Chaucer to Galsworthy, The English Novel in the Time of Shakespeare*, even *The Novel in Antiquity*[7] all work on an assumption that the books discussed were of a kind, and seldom was there a pause to consider if indeed this was true. Criticism had created a taxonomic division so vast as to be meaningless.

But between the works of the major prose writers of the eighteenth century and the novels of, say, Jane Austen, there are some fairly obvious differences. For a start there has developed an air of confidence in the reader's abilities. Jane Austen does not employ prefaces, footnotes or postscripts to ensure the reader is aware of the nature of and intention of the work. She is not producing a work of a kind professedly new or different; there is no need for a signpost. Together with this apparent shift in the writer's perception of the reader, there is also a shift in intention. In *Northanger Abbey*, Jane Austen's defence of the novel and its writers includes material which permits the reader to form an idea of her view of the nature of the species:

Alas! if the heroine of one novel be not patronized by the
heroine of another, from whom can she expect protection
and regard? I cannot approve of it. Let us leave it to the
Reviewers to abuse such effusions of fancy at their leisure,
and over every new novel to talk in threadbare strains of
the trash with which the press now groans. Let us not
desert one another; we are an injured body. Although our
productions have afforded more extensive and unaffected
pleasure than those of any other literary corporation in the
world, no species of composition has been so much
decried . . . there seems almost a general wish of decrying
the capacity and undervaluing the labour of the novelist,
and of slighting the performances which have only genius,
wit, and taste to recommend them. 'I am no novel reader –
I seldom look into novels – Do not imagine that *I* often
read novels – It is really very well for a novel.' – Such is
the common cant. – 'And what are you reading, Miss – ?'
'Oh! it is only a novel!' replies the young lady; while she
lays down her book with affected indifference, or
momentary shame. – 'It is only Cecilia, or Camilla, or
Belinda;' or, in short, only some work in which the greatest
powers of the mind are displayed, in which the most
thorough knowledge of human nature, the happiest
delineation of its varieties, the liveliest effusions of wit and
humour are conveyed to the world in the best chosen
language.[8]

The works cited, *Cecilia*, *Camilla* and *Belinda* are by writers,
Fanny Burney and Maria Edgeworth, who, I suggest, are the
true founders of the novel in English. Genius, wit and taste,
knowledge of human nature, best chosen language – these are
the salient points of Jane Austen's view. There is no
suggestion, as found in the prefaces of Defoe and Richardson,
that such works should be passed off as authentic records;
there is none of Richardson's insistence upon the essential
moral didacticism of his writings; Jane Austen's concern for
'best chosen language' is in direct contrast to Fielding's
dismissal of the importance of diction in his preface to *David*

Simple. It would not be difficult to add considerably to this list of differences.

Perception of the differences is vital to a proper appreciation of the achievements of these eighteenth century authors. The first half of the century was a period of fecundity. Writers of fiction were engaged in experimenting with forms and presentation. Defoe frequently bases his narrative upon genuine experiences – of such people as Alexander Selkirk – and the result is sold to the readership as truth. Contemporaneously Mrs Manley, also basing her works on identifiable historical personages, openly, though ironically, insists it all to be fiction. Richardson follows the lead of Defoe in presentation, but adopts a different form, the epistolary: Fielding includes the problem word 'History' in his titles, and in *Tom Jones* offers a work of patently artificially symmetrical construction. Smollett tells a more or less chronological story: Sterne throws chronology out of the window. Thereafter critical and commercial pressures start to create notions of conventions, conventions which become so rapidly accepted that before the century is out writers like Bage are in a position to mock quite openly the very conventions inside which they operate. This acceptance of convention is paralleled by the rise of the word *novel* to describe certain works of fiction. The early writers, Defoe, Richardson and Fielding, employed it as a term of abuse; Smollett tentatively adopted it; Fanny Burney and the late century periodical critics gave the word the cachet of literary respectability, though the moral acceptability of works so described was not so generally acknowledged. But the word carries with it connotations, and arouses expectations. It is manifestly unreasonable to condemn a work for failing to live up to expectations to the satisfaction of which its author did not aspire.

Faced with a work of fiction, and naturally wishing to engage in the exercise of right judgment as to the form of the work so that his subsequent criticism is not based upon false premises, the reader should bear in mind the advice offered in one of the key works[9] in the period of the shift from fiction to the novel:

This last word may stagger the faith of the world – but remember, 'La Vraisemblance (as *Baylet* says in the affair of *Liceti*) n'est pas toujours du Cotè de la Verité.'

NOTES

---◆---

Chapter 1 'A small tale, generally of love'

1 William Congreve, *Incognita: or, Love and Duty Reconcil'd*, London, 1692, A5b-A6a.

2 Horace Walpole, *The Castle of Otranto*, ed. W. S. Lewis, Oxford, Oxford University Press, 1982, p.7.

3 W. S. Lewis (ed.), *Horace Walpole's Correspondence*, New Haven, Conn., Yale University Press, 48 vols, 1937-84, vol. 40, p. 337. Hereafter cited in text as *Letters*.

4 Clara Reeve, *The Old English Baron*, ed. James Trainer, Oxford, Oxford University Press, 1977, pp.3-4. This work, without the preface, originally appeared in 1777 under the title *The Champion of Virtue*.

5 Gregory Griffin (pseud.), *The Microcosm*, Windsor, 1787, pp.295-300.

6 *The British Critic*, vol. 8, 1796, p.527.

7 Donald F. Bond (ed.), *The Spectator*, Oxford, Clarendon Press, 5 vols, 1965, vol. 2, pp. 280, 526. Hereafter cited in text as Bond.

8 Laurence Sterne, *The Life and Opinions of Tristram Shandy, Gentleman*, ed. Melvyn and Joan New, Gainesville, University Presses of Florida, 2 vols, 1978, vol. 1, p.120.

9 Daniel Defoe, *Moll Flanders*, ed. G. A. Starr, London, Oxford University Press, 1972. p.1.

10 Hugh Blair, 'Lecture 37', in *Lectures on Rhetoric and Belles Lettres*, London, 2 vols, 1783, vol. 2, p.303.

11 Cited in Ioan Williams, *Novel and Romance 1700-1800: A Documentary Record*, London, Routledge & Kegan Paul, 1970, p.270.

12 From the second edition of 1751, cited in Williams, op. cit., p.167.

13 Mrs. Eugenia Stanhope (ed.), *Letters written by the Late Right Honourable Philip Dormer Stanhope, Earl of Chesterfield, to his Son*, London, 2 vols, 1774, vol. 1, letter LII, p.130.

14 Fanny Burney, *Camilla*, ed. Edward A. and Lillian D. Bloom, Oxford, Oxford University Press, 1983, p.5.

15 Alexander Campbell, *Lexiphanes*, 2nd edn, London, 1768 (facsimile reprint, Farnborough, Gregg International, 1972), pp.2-3.

16   Samuel Johnson, *The Rambler*, ed. W. J. Bate and Albrecht B. Strauss, New Haven, Conn., Yale University Press, 3 vols, 1969, vol. 1, p.19.

17   *The Monthly Review*, vol. 15, 1756, pp.497-512, 585-604. *John Buncle*, which contains *inter alia* verse, religious controversy and detailed discussion of mathematical formulas, is of all eighteenth century works possibly the one least conducive to classification.

18   *Caveat lector*. This interesting view is cited in Williams, op. cit., p.304. I have been unable to find this passage, or the essay Williams prints. It is not in *Essays Moral and Literary*, London, Edward and Charles Dilly, 1778.

19   Cited in Williams, op. cit., p.358.

20   Cited in Williams, op. cit., p.437.

21   Henry Fielding, *The History of Tom Jones, A Foundling*, ed. Martin C. Battestin and Fredson Bowers, Oxford, Clarendon Press, 2 vols, 1974.

22   *An Essay on the New Species of Writing founded by Mr Fielding*, ed. A. D. McKillop, Los Angeles, William Andrews Clark Memorial Library, 1962, Augustan Reprint Society, no. 95.

23   Cited in Williams, op. cit., p.128.

24   Henry Fielding, *Joseph Andrews*, ed. Martin C. Battestin, Oxford, Clarendon Press, 1967, p.3.

25   Cited in Ronald Paulson and Thomas Lockwood (eds), *Henry Fielding: The Critical Heritage*, London, Routledge & Kegan Paul, 1969, p.148.

26   Arthur Murphy (ed.), *The Works of Henry Fielding, Esq.*, London, 4 vols, 1762, vol. 1, pp.39-40.

27   James Beattie, *Essays*, Edinburgh, 1776, pp.110-11n (written 1762).

28   Henry Pye, *A Commentary illustrating the Poetic of Aristotle*, London, 1792, p.182.

29   James Burnet, Lord Monboddo, *Of the Origin and Progress of Language*, Edinburgh, 6 vols, 1776, vol. 3, pp.134-5.

30   London, 1720, p.101.

31   William K. Wimsatt and Frederick A. Pottle (eds), *Boswell for the Defence*, New York, McGraw Hill, n.d., p.96.

32   Sarah Fielding, *David Simple*, ed. Malcolm Kelsall, London, Oxford University Press, 1969, p.6.

33   Tobias Smollett, *Ferdinand Count Fathom*, ed. Damian Grant, London, Oxford University Press, 1971, pp.2-3.

34   Tobias Smollett, *Roderick Random*, New York, Signet, 1964, pp.xvi-xvii.

35   Alexander Pope, *The Dunciad*, ed. James Sutherland, London, Methuen, 1943, pp.52 and 119 n.149.

36   Francis Coventry, *Pompey the Little*, ed. Robert Adams Day, London, Oxford University Press, 1974, pp.xli-xliii.

37   Fanny Burney, *Evelina*, ed. Edward A. Bloom, Oxford, Oxford University Press, 1982, pp.7-9.

38   The interpretation of the word *nature* is so complex during the eighteenth century as to defy analysis in the space available here. The distinction Richardson is making appears to depend upon the contrasting notions of generality and specificity.

39   *Mary, and, The Wrongs of Women*, ed. Gary Kelly, Oxford, Oxford University Press, 1983.

40   David McCracken (ed.), Oxford, Oxford University Press, 1977.

41   Peter Faulkner (ed.), Oxford, Oxford University Press, 1985.

42   Seamus Deane (ed.), London, Oxford University Press, 1973.

43   Arthur Friedman, (ed.), Oxford, Oxford University Press, 1981, p.3.

Chapter 2 'On Fable and Romance'

1   London, 1783, pp.503-74. The extracts cited are taken from pp. 505-18, 522, 550-1, 557, and 562-74.

2   Michael Seigneur de Montaigne, *Essays*, trans. Charles Cotton, London, 3 vols, 1685-6, vol. 3, p.101.

Chapter 3   Amelia's nose: perceptions of reality

1   R. W. Chapman (ed.), *Jane Austen's Letters*, Oxford, Oxford University Press, 1979, p.394.

2   *The Secret History of Queen Zarah*, Albigion [i.e. London], 1705, (facsimile edn Patricia Koster, Gainesville, Scholars Facsimiles and Reprints, 1971), A4a-b.

3   Henry Fielding, *Amelia*, ed. Martin C. Battestin and Fredson Bowers, Oxford, Clarendon Press, 1983.

4   Cited in Ronald Paulson and Thomas Lockwood (eds), *Henry Fielding: The Critical Heritage*, London, Routledge & Kegan Paul, 1969, p.303.

5   Hester Lynch Piozzi, *Anecdotes of the Late Samuel Johnson, LL.D.*, ed. Arthur Sherbo, London, Oxford University Press, 1974, p.134.

6   'Three Notes on Fielding,' *Papers of the Bibliographical Society of America*, vol. 47, 1953, pp.72-5.

7   Cited in F. T. Blanchard, *Fielding the Novelist*, New Haven, Conn., Yale University Press, 1926, p.90.

8   Cited in Paulson and Lockwood, op. cit., pp.32-3.

9   See 'Historical Collation' in the edition of Battestin and Bowers, op. cit., pp.565-82.

10 J. and A. L. Aikin, *Miscellaneous Pieces*, London, 1773, pp.202-3.

11 Jean Donnison, *Midwives and Medical Men*, New York, Schocken Books.

12 Henry Fielding, *Tom Jones*, ed. Martin C. Battestin and Fredson Bowers, Oxford, Clarendon Press, 2 vols, 1974, vol. 1, p.503.

13 Edmund Burke, *A Philosophical Enquiry into the Origins of our Ideas of the Sublime and Beautiful*, 2nd edn, London, 1759, pp.76-7.

14 W. S. Lewis (ed.), *Horace Walpole's Correspondence*, New Haven, Conn., Yale University Press, 48 vols, 1937-84, vol. 33, pp. 356-7. Hereafter cited in text as *Letters*.

15 For another example of conflicting notions of poetic justice and reality see George Birkbeck Hill and L. F. Powell (eds), *Boswell's Life of Johnson*, Oxford, Clarendon Press, 6 vols, 1979, vol. 1, p.389, n.2.

16 J. and A. L. Aikin, op. cit., pp.203-6.

17 James Trainer (ed.), Oxford, Oxford University Press, 1977, pp.4-5.

18 *An Essay on the New Species of Writing founded by Mr Fielding*, ed. A. D. McKillop, Los Angeles, William Andrews Clark Memorial Library, 1962, Augustan Reprint Society, no. 95, pp.15-16.

19 Vol. 8, 1796, pp.527-8.

20 Cited in Williams, op. cit., p.435.

21 James T. Boulton (ed.), Oxford, Oxford University Press, 1972.

22 Leeds, James Lister, c.1750, pp.iii-v.

23 London, 1722.

24 G. A. Starr (ed.), London, Oxford University Press, 1976, p.1.

25 J. Donald Crowley (ed.), Oxford, Oxford University Press, 1981, p.1.

26 Hugh Blair, 'Lecture 37', in *Lectures on Rhetoric and Belles Lettres*, London, 2 vols, 1783, vol. 2, p.309.

27 Jane Jack (ed.), London, Oxford University Press, 1964, pp.1-2.

28 London, 1720.

29 London, 1728, pp.i-ii.

30   George Birkbeck Hill and L. F. Powell (eds) *Boswell's Life of Johnson*, Oxford, Clarendon Press, 6 vols, 1979, vol. 4, pp.333-4.

31   Shelf-mark: Williams 540.

32   G. H. Healey (ed.), *The Letters of Daniel Defoe*, Oxford, Clarendon Press, 1955, *passim*.

33   *The Second Part, or, a Continuation of the Secret History of Queen Zarah, and the Zarazians*, Albigion [i.e. London], 1705, A2a-A3a.

34   *The Mercenary Lover: or, the Unfortunate Heiress*, 3rd edn, London, 1728, A2a.

35   Reprinted in *Pamela*, 2nd edn, London, 2 vols, 1741, vol. 1, pp. iii-vi.

36   Ibid., p.xvii.

37   John Carroll (ed.), *Selected Letters of Samuel Richardson*, Oxford, Clarendon Press, 1964, pp.39-41.

38   A. C. Guthkelch and D. Nichol Smith (eds), Oxford, Clarendon Press, 1920, *passim*.

39   Though the recent Penguin edition by Angus Ross (Harmondsworth, 1985) is textually accurate, it does not reproduce the material discussed here.

40   See Stanley Morison, *Ichabod Dawks and His News-Letter*, Cambridge, Cambridge University Press, 1931.

41   See William Merritt Sale, Jr, *Samuel Richardson: A Bibliographical Record*, New Haven, Conn., Yale University Press, 1936, pp.63-4.

42   Laurence Sterne, *The Life and Opinions of Tristram Shandy, Gentleman*, ed. Melvyn and Joan New, Gainesville, University Presses of Florida, 1978, pp.341-2.

43   Cited by James L. Clifford in his edition of *Peregrine Pickle*, London, Oxford University Press, 1969, p.xvi.

44   See Clifford, op. cit., p.xviii.

45   Paul-Gabriel Boucé, *The Novels of Tobias Smollett*, London, Longman, 1976, p.137.

46   Clifford, op. cit, p.xxvi.

47   Ibid., p.xvii.

48   Sale, Jr, op. cit., p.52.

49   W. S. Lewis (ed.), Oxford, Oxford University Press, 1982, pp.3-4.

Chapter 4 'Romances, Chocolate, Novels, and the like Inflamers'

1 Samuel Holt Monk (ed.), London, Oxford University Press, 1970, pp.1-2.

2 John Robert Moore, *A Checklist of the Writings of Daniel Defoe*, Connecticut, Archon Books, 1971.

3 4th ed, London, 1738, p.vii.

4 G. A. Starr (ed.), London, Oxford University Press, 1976, p.1.

5 Jane Jack (ed.), London, Oxford University Press, 1964, pp.2-3.

6 Edward Niles Hooker (ed.), *The Critical Works of John Dennis*, Baltimore, Johns Hopkins Press, 2 vols, 1967, vol. 2, pp.5-6.

7 Albigion [i.e. London], 1705, A6a-b.

8 2nd edn, London, 1723, pp.1-2.

9 London, 1748, pp.1-3.

10 Katharine C. Balderstone (ed.), *The Collected Letters of Oliver Goldsmith*, Cambridge, Cambridge University Press, 1928, p.60.

11 Cited in Ioan Williams, *Novel and Romance 1700-1800: A Documentary Record*, London, Routledge & Kegan Paul, 1970, pp. 196-7.

12 Temple Scott (ed.), *The Prose Works of Jonathan Swift*, London, G. Bell and Sons, 1910, vol. 4, pp.214-15.

13 T. Row, letter to *The Gentleman's Magazine*, 1767, cited in Williams, op. cit., p.272.

14 Richard Brinsley Sheridan, *The Rivals*, Act I, scene ii.

15 Henry Pye, *A Commentary illustrating the Poetic of Aristotle*, London, 1792, pp.145-6.

16 Vol. 58, 1788, cited in Williams, op. cit., p.367.

17 When Elizabeth Carter published her translation of Epictetus in 1758 the reviewers expressed considerable surprise that a woman should know any Greek at all, let alone to the standard displayed in this translation.

18 Cited in *Fifty Penguin Years*, Harmondsworth, Penguin, 1985, p.65.

19 Ioan Williams (ed.), *The Criticism of Henry Fielding*, London, Routledge & Kegan Paul, 1970, p.189.

20 George Birkbeck Hill and L. F. Powell (eds), *Boswell's Life of Johnson*, Oxford, Clarendon Press, 6 vols, 1979, vol. 2, p.49.

21 Cited in Williams, *Novel and Romance*, pp. 274-5.

22 See note 18 to chapter 1 above.

23 John Carroll (ed.), *Selected Letters of Samuel Richardson*, Oxford, Clarendon Press, 1964, pp.46-7.

24 Ibid., pp. 54-5.

25 Donald F. Bond (ed.), *The Spectator*, Oxford, Clarendon Press, 5 vols, 1965, vol. 3, p.374.

26 Helge Rubinstein, *The Chocolate Book*, Harmondsworth, Penguin, 1982, p.261. One might also note the importance of this substance in *Cosi fan tutte*.

27 John Carroll, op. cit., pp. 236-7.

28 See, e.g., T. C. Duncan Eaves and Ben D. Kimpel, 'Richardson's revisions of *Pamela*', *SB*, vol. 20, 1967, and 'The composition of *Clarissa*', *PMLA*, vol. 83, 1968.

29 John Carroll, op. cit., pp.196-7.

30 Ronald Paulson and Thomas Lockwood (eds), *Henry Fielding: The Critical Heritage*, London, Routledge & Kegan Paul, 1969, pp. 318-19.

31 Ibid., p.351.

32 Ibid., pp.305-6.

33 It would be possible to write a monograph on the eighteenth century use of the term *low*. As with so many other key words, one needs to know something of the speaker and his circumstances in order to appreciate the semantic niceties.

34 Cited in Williams, *Novel and Romance*, pp. 333-5.

35 Anna Seward, *Variety: a Collection of Essays, written in the Year 1787*, cited in Williams, *Novel and Romance*, pp.363-5.

36 William Merritt Sale, Jr, *Samuel Richardson: A Bibliographical Record*, New Haven, Conn., Yale University Press, 1936, p.49.

37 A. D. McKillop (ed.), Los Angeles, William Andrews Clark Memorial Library, 1962, Augustan Reprint Society, no. 95, pp.40-2.

38 W. S. Lewis (ed.), *Horace Walpole's Correspondence*, New Haven, Conn., Yale University Press, 48 vols. 1937-84, vol. 5, p.383.

39 Cited in Williams, *Novel and Romance*, p.368.

40 Vol. 34, 1766, cited in G. S. Rousseau (ed.), *Goldsmith: The Critical Heritage*, London, Routledge & Kegan Paul, 1974, p.44.

41 Vol. 1, 1760, cited in Alan B. Howes (ed.), *Sterne: The Critical Heritage*, London, Routledge & Kegan Paul, 1974, p.53. Hereafter cited as Howes.

42 Howes, p.61.

43 Howes, p.61.

44 Howes, p.90.

45 Howes, p.77.

46 London, 1760, Facsimile reprint, New York, Garland Publishing, 1975.

47 Thomas Turner, *The Diary of a Georgian Shopkeeper*, ed. G. H. Jennings, Oxford, Oxford University Press, 1979, p.5. Cf. also p.47: 'in the even I read Gibson *On Lukewarmness in Religion*, and a sermon of his, *Trust in God the best Remedy against Fears of all kinds*: both of which I look upon as extreme good things.'

48 Samuel Johnson, *Lives of the English Poets*, London, Dent, 2 vols, 1961, vol. 2, p.36.

49 Ibid., p.273.

Chapter 5   *Motley emblems and much wanted standards*

1 Laurence Sterne, *The Life and Opinions of Tristram Shandy, Gentleman*, ed. Melvyn and Joan New, Gainesville, University Presses of Florida, 1978, p.89.

2 Ibid., p.93.

3 L. P. Curtis (ed.), *Letters of Laurence Sterne*, Oxford, Clarendon Press, 1967, p.99.

4 There had been works of fiction prior to *Tristram Shandy* which had been illustrated, but the illustrations had always been made after the book had been out for some time. Thus *Tale of a Tub* was first ornamented in its fifth edition, and *Pamela* in its sixth.

5 Somewhere in the region of 4000 copies were printed of the first edition of volume 3 of *Tristram Shandy*. One of the resulting 8000 marble pages is reproduced on the cover of the present work. For a detailed description of the process of marbling, see W. G. Day, '*Tristram Shandy*: the marbled leaf,' *Library*, 5th series, vol. 27, 1972, pp.143-5.

6 Vol. 3, 1760, cited Alan B. Howes (ed.), *Sterne: The Critical Heritage*, London, Routledge & Kegan Paul, 1974, p.96.

7 Gardner D. Stout (ed.), *A Sentimental Journey through France and Italy by Mr Yorick*, Berkeley, University of California Press, 1967, p.65.

8 George Watson, letter to *The Times Literary Supplement*, 4 March 1977, p.74.

9 See Allardyce Nicoll, *The Garrick Stage*, Manchester, Manchester University Press, 1980, pp.29, 97-8, 110.

10   Reprinted in *Pamela*, 2nd edn, London, 2 vols, 1741, vol. 1, p.vii.

11   W. S. Lewis (ed.), *Horace Walpole's Correspondence*, New Haven, Conn., Yale University Press, 48 vols, 1937-84, vol. 22, p.271. Hereafter cited as *Letters*.

12   Donald F. Bond (ed.), *The Spectator*, Oxford, Clarendon Press, 5 vols, 1965, vol. 3, p.129.

13   Robert Bage, *Hermsprong*, ed. Peter Faulkner, Oxford, Oxford University Press, 1984, pp. 246, 248.

14   Vol. 5, 1751, cited in Ronald Paulson and Thomas Lockwood (eds), *Henry Fielding: The Critical Heritage*, London, Routledge & Kegan Paul, 1969, pp.304-5.

15   D. Grant (ed.), *Poetical Works of Charles Churchill*, Oxford, Clarendon Press, 1956, 'The Ghost,' Book 3, lines 967-76, p.131.

16   A. D. McKillop (ed.), Los Angeles, William Andrews Clark Memorial Library, 1962, Augustan Reprint Society, no. 95, pp.i-ii.

17   Ioan Williams, *Novel and Romance 1700-1800: A Documentary Record*, London, Routledge & Kegan Paul, 1970, p.102.

18   London, 2 vols, 1741, vol. 1, p.xviii.

19   London, 7 vols, 1748, vol. 1, pp.iv-vi.

20   Cited in Williams, op. cit, p.166.

21   *The Gentleman's Magazine*, vol. 19, 1749, p.347.

22   Cited in Williams, op. cit., p.148.

23   John Carroll (ed.), *Selected Letters of Samuel Richardson*, Oxford, Clarendon Press, 1964, pp.234-5.

24   Thomas Turner, *The Diary of a Georgian Shopkeeper*, ed. G. H. Jennings, Oxford, Oxford University Press, 1979, p.2.

25   Cited in Williams, op. cit., p.234.

26   Cited in Williams, op. cit., pp.332-3.

27   Sarah Fielding, *The Adventures of David Simple*, ed. Malcolm Kelsall, London, Oxford University Press, 1969, pp.7-8.

28   *Pamela*, London, 2 vols, 1741, pp.xx-xxi.

29   Cited in Williams, op. cit., pp.371-2.

30   *The Critical Review*, new series, vol. 4, 1792, p.244.

31   Cited in Williams, op. cit., p.447.

Chapter 6 'The most heterogeneous ideas are yoked by violence together'

1 R. W. Chapman (ed.), *Northanger Abbey and Persuasion*, Oxford, Clarendon Press, 1944, p.xiii.

2 Anna Laetitia Barbauld (ed.), *The British Novelists*, London, 50 vols, 2nd ed., 1821, vol. 16, p.i.

3 Thomas Turner, *The Diary of a Georgian Shopkeeper*, ed. G. H. Jennings, Oxford, Oxford University Press, 1979. For example: 'My wife read to me that moving scene of the funeral of Miss Clarissa Harlowe. Oh, may the Supreme Being give me grace to lead my life in such a manner as my exit may in some measure be like that divine creature's' (p.2).

4 R. W. Chapman (ed.), *Mansfield Park*, London, Oxford University Press, 1970, p.461.

5 Samuel Johnson, *Lives of the English Poets*, London, Dent, 2 vols, vol. 1, p.40.

6 *Lives of the Novelists*, London, 1906, p.1.

7 Ian Watt, *The Rise of the Novel*, London, Chatto & Windus, 1957; R. H. Bloor, *The English Novel: Chaucer to Galsworthy*, Folcroft, Folcroft Library Editions, 1935; J. J. Jusserand, *The English Novel in the Time of Shakespeare*, new edn., London, Ernest Benn, 1966; Thomas Hägg, *The Novel in Antiquity*, Oxford, Basil Blackwell, 1983 (originally published as *Den Antika Romanen*, Uppsala, Bokförlaget Carmina, 1980).

8 *Northanger Abbey*, pp.37-8.

9 *Laurence Sterne, The Life and Opinions of Tristram Shandy, Gentleman*, ed. Melvyn and Joan New, Gainesville, University Presses of Florida, 1978, p.347.

INDEX

◆

Titles are entered under author. The notes are not indexed except where additional material is offered.